A NEW ENVIRONMENTAL ETHICS

No one looking ahead at the middle of the last century could have foreseen the extent and the importance of the ensuing environmental crises. Now, more than a decade into the next century, no one can ignore it.

A New Environmental Ethics: the Next Millennium for Life on Earth offers clear, powerful, and oftentimes moving thoughts from one of the first and most respected philosophers to write on the environment. Rolston, an early and leading pioneer in studying the moral relationship between humans and the earth, surveys the full spectrum of approaches in the field of environmental ethics. This book, however, is not simply a judicious overview. Instead, it offers critical assessments of contemporary academic accounts and draws on a lifetime of research and experience to suggest an outlook for the future. As a result, this focused, forward-looking analysis will be a necessary complement to any balanced textbook or anthology in environmental ethics, and will teach its readers to be responsible global citizens, and residents of their landscape, helping ensure that the future we have will be the one we wish for.

Holmes Rolston III is University Distinguished Professor of Philosophy at Colorado State University in Fort Collins.

A NEW ENVIRONMENTAL ETHICS

The Next Millennium
for Life on Earth

Holmes Rolston III

Routledge
Taylor & Francis Group

NEW YORK AND LONDON

First published 2012
by Routledge
711 Third Avenue, New York, NY 10017

Simultaneously published in the UK
by Routledge
2 Park Square, Milton Park, Abingdon, Oxon OX14 4RN

Routledge is an imprint of the Taylor & Francis Group, an informa business

© 2012 Taylor & Francis

Library of Congress Cataloging in Publication Data
Rolston, Holmes, 1932-
    A new environmental ethics : the next millennium for life on earth / Holmes Rolston III.
    p. cm.
    Includes bibliographical references and index.
    1. Environmental ethics. I. Title.
    GE42.R65 2011
    179'.1—dc22
    2011009978

ISBN: 978-0-415-88483-9 (hbk)
ISBN: 978-0-415-88484-6 (pbk)
ISBN: 978-0-203-80433-9 (ebk)

Typeset in Bembo and Stone Sans
by EvS Communication Networx, Inc.

CONTENTS

PREFACE

I am seeking, in the book you have in hand, to put you in your place. You will be finding out who you are, where you are, and what you ought to do. You will be seeking to learn what you most need to know about nature: how to value it. That's quite a promise, so this is, you should know, an introduction, but only an introduction. Read it, and you will be well introduced to environmental ethics—I guarantee that.

I also expect that you will be frustrated because many issues here are briefly and inconclusively treated. Readers of introductions have to live with that. I experienced that frustration before you did. The citations provide not only documentation but also suggestions for further reading, whether just to pursue your interests or because you need to write a research paper for class. The citations prove that books can be, and often have been, written about what is here covered in just a single section (or paragraph).

There are more such citations than is typical in texts of this kind, and they are gathered at the end of each chapter (rather than at the end of the book), where they may be considered a bibliography for further reading--relieving some of your frustrations. Don't just skip those pages, but look over the titles and see what catches your interest. You should be impressed how much activity there is addressing environmental concerns. Also I rather anticipate that you will be using this single-authored text alongside one of the many excellent anthologies in the field, where you are confronting the consensus and divergence of multiple authors.

You will not find any list of "study questions" at the end of the chapters; but, quite frequently as you read along, you will find sentences that end in a question mark. Consider those your study questions. Consider those assignments for group sections, bringing back a report to class. If you finish this book having thought about how to answer half those questions, you will be educated—at least half-way.

Notice also the bibliographic websites of the International Society for Environmental Ethics. Environmental ethics is about a natural world out there, an offline web of life, independent of, if also related to, human beings. But students today live online and surf their web-world forming their worldview. Students need to be simultaneously computer literate and environmentally literate, on the ground and in the air—so to speak. Another thing that can keep you on the ground are the case studies, some indicated in the text, many others in more detail in the referenced book and website resources. If you think there are more than enough references here, you will be overwhelmed with the ten thousand and more references you can pull in off these sites.

Another frustration is likely to be how environmental ethics spills over into almost everything that goes on in the world. You start out thinking environmental ethics is about the bears and birds, about wildlands, which it is. But you are soon asking about industry, agriculture, Acts of Congress, driving your automobile, recycling, eating organic food, global capitalism, rich and poor. It sometimes seems as though we cannot fix anything until we fix everything. A risk of reading this book is a certain sense of hopelessness. We are, of course, in an environmental crisis. Do remember that environmental ethics is trying to save the world—and do not expect that to be easy or simple.

I make an effort to introduce you to both sides of a controversial issue, often several sides. That goes with the complexity just mentioned. Many sentences in the text have a "perhaps" or a "maybe" in them. That's a cue that I am, for a bit, considering an alternative view, which also likely contains a further reference. You will get more alternative views if you are also using an anthology text.

But I am not a neutral author (textbook authors seldom are). In the first place, authors must think the field is important, else they would not be writing the text. They have to select what they think is important, on the cutting edge of the field. In the second place, they want students to explore with them this important field, and to gain some excitement about its importance. In the third place, authors do want to lead, to educate students to be, in their turn new leaders in an oncoming generation.

The human genius involves ideas transmitted from mind to mind. We will conclude (in Chapter 2) that this sets us apart from any other animals in the natural world. You are seeking an education, which is mostly about passing ideas from one generation to another, critically evaluating them in the passing. That launches an ongoing search for increased knowledge and wisdom. Were that to fail, the cultural achievements of thousands of years would go extinct in a few decades. In today's educational environment, you have access to more ideas than any generation that has previously lived on Earth. You stand on the shoulders of giants (Newton). Turn the page. Explore your world—and your place in it.

Holmes Rolston, III

ACKNOWLEDGMENTS

Thanks to Philip Cafaro and Peter Wenz for critically evaluating these ideas, testing them out before I offer them to you. Thanks also to several decades of Colorado State University students, undergraduate and graduate, in environmental ethics classes and seminars, who also helped me think through these ideas.

1

THE ENVIRONMENTAL TURN

We are now twelve years into a unique century, the first century in the 35 million centuries (3.5 billion years) of life on Earth in which one species can jeopardize the planet's future. There has been a crescendo of concern in recent decades: an environmental crisis. The environment has become a signature issue, of both timely and timeless, relevant and perennial interest. Philosophers and religious scholars have thought about nature for millennia, in ancient Greece, India, or China. Although there is an ethic implicit in many of these worldviews, this was never developed as an environmental ethics.

In the West, following the Enlightenment and the scientific revolution, nature came to be regarded as a value-less realm, governed by mechanistic causal forces. Values arose only with the interests and preferences of humans, for whom nature was natural resources. For four centuries, Western philosophy and theology were both dominantly human-centered, anthropocentric. People were all that counted in ethics. In the second half of the last century, somewhat ironically, just when humans, with their increasing industry and technology, seemed further and further from nature, having more knowledge about natural processes and more power to manage them and rebuild their environments, the natural world emerged as a focus of ethical concern.

No one attempting to foresee the future of philosophy at the middle of the last century predicted the environmental turn in philosophy. Nevertheless, with an environmental crisis on the world agenda, philosophers awakened—and awakened rapidly. They had to wake up after Earth Day was established in 1970 by U.S. Senator Gaylord Nelson. Twenty million people participated in that first Earth Day; today, over half a billion participate in over 170 countries. Environmental concern, according to Paul Hawken, is the "the largest movement in the world," considering the number and force of environmental organizations around the globe (Hawken, 2007).

The plan in this chapter is first to look at what's staring us in the face, and then to look backward over our shoulders. Setting off on a drive, one looks ahead at what is immediately in front of and surrounding the car, but one needs also to look in the rear view mirror before one takes off in forward drive. We will highlight this environmental turn, looking at a dozen or so movements on the contemporary landscape. These have demanded and launched an environmental ethics: theory and practice about appropriate concern for, values in, and duties to the natural world.

1. BP Oil Spill Disaster

Deepwater Horizon was an oil platform near the Mississippi Delta, about forty miles offshore, under the control of British Petroleum (BP). On April 15, 2010, methane gas from their well reached the rig and an explosion set fire to it. A number of ships tried to extinguish the fire and failed. The platform burned a day and a half; most workers escaped in lifeboats, but eleven were never found, presumed dead. Safety equipment above surface failed; some of it had not been properly maintained. Below surface a blowout preventer failed. Soon an oil slick revealed deep trouble. Nobody knew how much oil was pouring forth into the Gulf of Mexico, the meters at the wellhead had failed. Different groups made different estimates, and it took weeks to find out, with estimates steadily growing dramatically worse—1,000 barrels a day to 100,000 barrels a day. Final figures were in the 50,000 to 60,000 barrels a day range (Zeller, 2010).

By April 30, the oil spill covered 3,850 square miles. The spill was now threatening the Delta National Wildlife Refuge and Breton National Wildlife Refuge. Oil was washing up on the beaches of Gulf Islands National Seashore, along 125 miles of Louisiana beaches, and also found in Alabama and Florida. Gulf Coast communities were in near panic about impending damage. Nobody knew what it would be, only that it would be enormous. Nor, in view of conflicting reports, did anybody know what the oil was doing below the surface.

Nor was it clear how to stop it. Operating remote machinery a mile undersea is complex, and this challenge unprecedented. Repeated efforts failed to stop the flow; some of the gushing oil was captured on ships, but much continued to leak, with conflicting reports about how much. Storms interrupted these efforts, also the drilling of a relief well. The gushing wellhead was not contained until July 15, 2010, when it was capped. For three months media daily featured social and environmental chaos. The spill released an estimated 4.4 million barrels into the Gulf, the largest spill in the history of the petroleum industry, ten times that of the Exxon *Valdez* spill and the worst environmental disaster in U.S. history (Crone and Tolstoy, 2010).

The spill caused extensive economic damage to the Gulf's fishing and tourism industries as well as to marine and wildlife habitats. Skimmer ships, containment booms, sandfilled barricades along shorelines, and dispersants were used trying to protect hundreds of miles of beaches, wetlands and estuaries from the spreading oil. There were also immense underwater plumes of dissolved oil causing damage that proved difficult to appraise. Over 170 ships of various kinds, large and small, and over seven thousand people took part in cleanup of the waters, tens of thousands were cleaning up on land, some paid, but many of them volunteers. There was a six-month moratorium on offshore drilling, with resulting loss of jobs.

There was confusion about responsibility, about the causes, about how to cap the gushing well, about the cleanup, both on sea surface and in the water column, about cleanup on shores and wetlands, about the costs, about levels of responsibility—federal (U.S. Coast Guard, Environmental Protection Agency, U.S. Geological Survey, Army Corps of Engineers), about state, county, local responsibilities (Urbina, 2010). The U.S. government named BP as the responsible party, and BP officials committed to holding the company accountable for all cleanup costs and other damage. The Deepwater Horizon platform was actually operated by another company on behalf of BP, and that complicated responsibility. BP admitted that it made mistakes which led to the spill.

The president of the United States, the most powerful man on Earth, commanded neither the know-how nor the power at hand to fix a big leak a mile undersea. Even the BP technicians were groping. In the public sphere, people need someone to hold responsible. Decision makers need to blame somebody else to protect their image and get re-elected. President Obama demanded and got from BP executives a commitment to create a $20 billion response fund to cover natural resource damages, state and local response costs, and personal losses, with the further stipulation that damages might be far higher (Weisman and Chazan, 2010).

There was threat to wildlife, as much as to people. More than four hundred species that live in the Gulf islands and marshlands were judged at risk, including the endangered Kemp's Ridley turtle, the Green Turtle, the Logger-head Turtle, the Hawksbill Turtle, and the Leatherback Turtle. Birds affected included gulls, pelicans, roseate spoonbills, egrets, terns, and blue herons. The area of the oil spill includes over eight thousand species, more than twelve hundred fish, two hundred birds, fourteen hundred mollusks, fifteen hundred crustaceans, the four sea turtles, and twenty-nine marine mammals. Nearly seven thousand dead animals were collected. Nearly eighty-seven thousand square miles, or about 36% of Gulf of Mexico federal waters, were at one time closed to fishing (Biello, 2010).

The BP oil spill disaster forced a summer-long soul searching, with the disaster daily in the public face in the media. Americans were awakened to deep water petroleum technology; they were surprised by its power, and admired the technological achievements, first to drill the well, then to cap it. They were simultaneously dismayed at technological arrogance, at risk taking, at technocrats who did not know what was going on. They appreciated BP's repeated willingness to pay damages, but feared that cost cutting and corporate profit making had produced the tragedy. They damned the oil company, then reminded themselves that Americans, addicted to oil, had both demanded and permitted the drilling.

There was outrage at the damage caused, anxiety about future deep water drilling to quench American thirst for oil, blame at causing the event, at greed for money and oil, wondering about the tradeoffs between need for oil and environmental integrity. There was fear that the Gulf oil spill might be a har-binger of forthcoming similar disasters. Amidst all this wake-up, confusion, and disaster, Americans seemed to be gaining consensus that environmental conservation must be high on the national agenda. The big spill left no doubt about that.

At least it did not across summer 2010. But a year later environmentalists found themselves wondering if Americans had really learned what was still staring them in the face. They were still drilling for oil, had not yet put in place more stringent drilling standards, still demanding oil as much as before—all this in the wake of the largest oil spill in history. Americans seemed ready and willing to fault others (BP executives, government regulators), but neither ready nor willing to examine their own lifestyles.

2. Global Warming

There is another environmental threat of first magnitude that still stares us in the face, orders of magnitude more serious than the BP oil spill: global climate change. The Intergovernmental Panel on Climate Change, sponsored by the United Nations, meeting in Paris in 2007, released a bleak and powerful assessment of the future of the planet. The report affirmed that Earth is warming, that humans primarily are causing that warming through greenhouse gas emissions and deforestation, and that this warming threatens the well-being of billions of people today and in the future (Intergovernmental Panel on Climate Change, 2007).

That was followed by the Copenhagen Climate Summit in 2009, attended by delegations from 193 countries, of which 123 gave some account of domestic policies within their nations to address climate change. The Climate Summit was the largest gathering ever for the cause of the environment, exceeding UNCED 1992. There were 40,000 delegates, including a huge number of journalists. There was a "People's Climate Summit (the Klimaforum), a parallel event to the official negotiations with tens of thousands of participants.

The negotiations and discussions were in the media for weeks, even if there was widespread disappointment that the Summit failed to produce effective results, due largely to the unwillingness of the United States and China to make meaningful commitments. In the closing days of the conference, there was a new media article published or aired every second. The developing countries contended they needed help from the developed countries, who had been and were continuing to cause the problem. The developed nations were themselves contentious, but U.S. President Barack Obama managed to achieve a modest break-through with a joint statement by key nations that they would take steps to prevent global warming exceeding 2 degrees Celsius. By the time of the follow-up Cancun Conference in 2011, it was clear that little of real importance followed Copenhagen.

Climate change is of unprecedented importance on the world agenda. If anyone is in doubt, the unprecedented dispute about it establishes that point (Hulme, 2009). The intense dispute is provoked attempting to overcome a strong consensus among scientists that global surface temperatures have increased in recent decades and that the trend is caused mainly by human-induced emissions of greenhouse gases. No scientific body of national or international standing disagrees with this view (Oreskes, 2007). There is more dispute in public debates; media debates have included debates over how much attention to give each side, especially in the United States. (We return to this in Chapter 7, thinking about climate change on global scales.)

Still, a 2009 survey found that Europeans rate climate change as the second most serious problem facing the world today, the first being either poverty or the current economic downturn (European Commission, Eurobarometer, 2009). Albert Gore, who once was almost president of the United States, was recognized with the 2007 Nobel Peace prize, along with the Intergovernmental Panel on Climate Change, for his media presentation An Inconvenient Truth.

But there remains public disagreement, and now there may be the additional argument that those with vested interests in oil are funding the dispute. The Union of Concerned Scientists produced a report entitled *Smoke, Mirrors & Hot Air* blasting ExxonMobil:

In an effort to deceive the public about the reality of global warming ExxonMobil has underwritten the most sophisticated and most success-ful disinformation campaign since the tobacco industry misled the public about the scientific evidence linking smoking to lung cancer and heart disease.... ExxonMobil has funneled about $16 million between 1998 and 2005 to a network of ideological and advocacy organizations that manufacture uncertainty on the issue.

(Union of Concerned Scientists, 2007, p. 1)

Afterward, Exxon claimed that it was no longer going to fund these groups. Gregg Easterbrook, a vocal and longtime critic of global warming, concluded: "I have a long record of opposing alarmism But based on the data I'm now switching sides regarding global warming, from skeptic to convert" (Easter-brook, 2006).

John T. Houghton is one of the principal figures in the Intergovernmental Panel on Climate Change, also longtime a professor of atmospheric physics at Oxford. He was once Director General of the UK Meteorological Office (often called the MET). Houghton jarred political leaders with the claim that global warming already threatens British national security more than global terrorists, and that politicians were neglecting this "one duty above all others … to protect the security of their people" (Houghton, 2003). The heat is first climatological, but secondly economic and political, and, in the end, moral.

3. Sustainability

The United Nations Conference on Environment and Development (UNCED) in 1992 brought together the largest number of world leaders that had ever assembled to address any one issue (surpassed only in 2010, by the Copen-hagen Climate Summit). The UNCED Summit drew 118 heads of state and government, delegations from 178 nations, virtually every nation in the world, 7,000 diplomatic bureaucrats, 30,000 advocates of environmental causes, and 7,000 journalists. That Conference entwined its twin concerns into "sustain-able development."

"Sustainable development is development that meets the needs of the pres-ent without compromising the ability of future generations to meet their own needs" (United Nations World Commission on Environment and Develop-ment, 1987, p. 43). "Sustainable" coupled with "development" expects contin-ued growth but not such as degrades opportunities for the future. So defined, sustainability could apply to social institutions (colleges, banks, population, culture) as well as environments. But UNCED intended it to apply to agricul-ture, forestry, water use, pollution levels, industry, resource extraction, urban-ization, national environmental policies and strategies.

Sustainable development has for the two decades since Rio remained the favored model. Over 150 nations have endorsed sustainable development. The World Business Council on Sustainable Development includes 130 of the world's largest corporations. The duty seems unanimous, plain, and urgent. Only so can this good life continue. No one wants unsustainable development. "Sustaining" is about like "surviving," and nobody can be against it.

Nobody can be against it, but if you are for it, what are you for? You are for an economy "in equilibrium with basic ecological support systems," Robert Stivers had said over a decade before (Stivers, 1976, p. 187). Ecologists had long been talking about "carrying capacity," and some had been warning that there are "limits to growth" (Meadows, 1972). A few prophetic economists were advocating "steady-state economics" (Daly, 1973). But neither in the First or Third Worlds did developers wish to hear about limits or steady-states, so they immediately and enthusiastically accepted "sustainable development."

The idea has become a mantra in ongoing consultations, a phrase heard around the world. The United Nations *2005 World Summit Outcome Document* refers to the "three components of sustainable development—economic development, social development, and environmental protection—as interdependent and mutually reinforcing pillars" (United Nations World Summit, 2005, p. 12). Another UNCED document, *Agenda 21* insists that broad public participation in decision making is necessary for achieving sustainable development. A frequent worry has been that the developed countries can welcome long-term planning for sustainability, but the developing countries have to face more immediate needs, whether or not they can see beyond the next harvest. Indeed, third world nations may argue that, far from developing, the rich need to shrink so that the poor can grow. Meanwhile, the general orienting vision seems to be one of ongoing prosperity that is widely shared and long-term.

One contribution of the sustainable development debate has been forcing societies to consider how they need to manage three types of resources (economists may call them forms of "capital"): economic, social, and natural. Planners have to ask which of their resources have substitutes and which do not. We might find that we can replace coal-fired energy plants with wind and solar energy, but it is quite unlikely we can find substitutes to essential ecosystem services, such as the water in rivers and groundwater, or the oxygen provided by forests. Many natural resources produce multiple benefits. Forests provide paper, and perhaps we can go paperless; but forests maintain biodiversity, provide water downstream, and absorb carbon dioxide. Can we do without forests? Perhaps no amount of money in the bank (economic capital) is worth more than air, water, soil (natural capital).

Such discussions have also alerted many to what economists call "market failure," that is to goods—often quite vital ones—that markets cannot effectively price: the air we breathe, for example, or the climate that sustains us. Markets may also fail to ration effectively, or fairly, resources that are running low—such as petroleum or copper. Markets may not deal with spillover, that is, degrading systems that are not priced on the books of the sellers or buyers—as with the pollutants coming out of smokestacks and sewer lines. We will consider below alarms of this kind with toxics and their regulators.

The World Business Council for Sustainable Development (WBCSD) argues that business has to think in terms of eco-efficiency. "Ecoefficiency is reached by the delivery of competitively priced goods and services that satisfy human needs and bring quality of life, while progressively reducing environmental impacts and resource intensity throughout the life cycle to a level at least in line with the earth's carrying capacity" (DeSimone and Popoff, 1997, p. 47). All this has challenged the "business as usual" mentality with alarms about sustainability. Those who do business, or run a university, or run for political office will—at least for public relations—endorse sustainability in some form or other.

4. Environmental Justice

Environmental justice demands an equitable distribution of burdens and benefits to racial minorities, the poor, and those in developing nations.

This movement arose in the United States, especially in the South, in the early 1980s. Environmentalism in the 1970s had been advocating saving nature, wildlife and wildlands (as we see below in John Muir and Aldo Leopold. Or it had been championing sustainable development. But with environmental justice the focus is on LULUS (locally unwanted land uses) and NIMBYS (not in my backyard). Like Rachel Carson's alarm about pesticides (as we also see below), the movement started grassroots, and was soon and forcefully demanding legislation to redress inequitable distributions of environmental burdens.

Advocates wish to change attitudes, but realize that this may require changing laws (Schlosberg, 2007; Rhodes, 2003; Shrader-Frechette, 2002; Cutter, 1995; Bullard, 1994). Although an environmental justice act has never been passed by Congress, the Environmental Protection Agency created the Office of Environmental Justice in 1992. President Bill Clinton signed an executive order for federal action to address environmental justice in minority populations and lowincome populations into law in 1994.

The EPA Office says:

> Environmental Justice is the fair treatment and meaningful involvement of all people regardless of race, color, national origin, or income with respect to the development, implementation, and enforcement of environmental laws, regulations, and policies. EPA has this goal for all communities and persons across this Nation. It will be achieved when everyone enjoys the same degree of protection from environmental and health hazards and equal access to the decisionmaking process to have a healthy environment in which to live, learn, and work.
>
> (U.S. Environmental Protection Agency, 1992, 2010)

Often the burdens of development fall unfairly on the poor, or on non-Caucasian races. Communities with greater minority populations are more likely to contain hazardous waste sites. A notorious case is "Cancer Alley," an 85-mile stretch of the Mississippi River between Baton Rouge and New Orleans which is home to 125 companies that produce one quarter of the petrochemical products manufactured in the United States. In a hard-hitting report, the United States Commission on Civil Rights concluded that the African American community had been disproportionately harmed by Cancer Alley as a result of Louisiana's current state and local permit system for hazardous facilities, as well as their low socioeconomic status and limited political influence (U.S. Commission on Civil Rights, 1993; Shrader-Frechette, 2002).

Another wake-up call was in 1982 in Warren County, North Carolina. The state selected the Shocco Township to host a hazardous waste landfill containing 30,000 cubic yards of polychlorinated biphenyl (PCB)contaminated soil. Over two thirds of the population there is nonwhite, and the township has the third lowest per capita income in the state. Protests broke out and police and soldiers from nearby Fort Bragg quelled the protests, arresting a local congressman and some church leaders, but the event drew national media attention (LaBalme, 1988). Two studies, one by the U.S. General Accounting Office (USGAO) (1983) and the other by the United Church of Christ's Commission for Racial Justice (1987) documented this environmental racism.

In Hinckly, California, a Pacific Gas and Electric Company plant knowingly let Chromium 6 leak into the groundwater for three decades, causing health problems. Environmental justice advocates filed a lawsuit. The giant utility paid the largest toxic tort injury settlement in U.S. history: $333 million in damages to more than 600 Hinkley residents (California Environmental Protection Agency, 2010). In 1986, Congress passed The Emergency Planning and Community Right-to-Know Act requiring business to disclose to the public what chemicals they store, use, and release in the area.

Dumping may be overseas, in developing nations, or under sea, in open water (Park, 1998). The city of Philadelphia had ash from the incineration of toxic waste which they did not want to put in local waste dumps. They contracted with a private company to take it overseas. The Khian Sea, the ship on which the ash was put, found that no country would accept it. The ship owners finally dumped the waste on a beach in Haiti in the middle of the night, with the label Fertilizer. The infuriated (though weak) government of Haiti demanded that the waste be removed, but the company would not do it. Fighting over who was responsible for the waste went on for many years. Philadelphians felt some responsibility and, eventually, the waste was taken back to a site just outside Philadelphia and disposed of there (Pellow, 2007, pp. 107–123).

A related movement is that for ecojustice. Ecojustice blends justice in the social order and integrity in the natural order. Ecojustice may claim to be a more inclusive and comprehensive ethic than environmental justice, which is mostly about people (Gibson, 2004). Caring for humanity requires caring for the Earth; these are complements—not opposites as so often argued. One does not need to sacrifice nature to benefit people, rather people benefit from a nature that is protected and conserved. All living things ought to be sustained, equally people and nature, and these two go together. "Sustainable development," Ronald Engel tells us, with emphasis, "may be defined as *the kind of human activity that nourishes and perpetuates the historical fulfillment of the whole community of life on Earth*" (1990, pp. 10–11). That puts human and biotic communities together comprehensively. Everybody counts, plants, animals, and people. We seek sustaining communities in which people are fulfilled; beyond that, what is sustained is the entire community of life. Although this caring for people-justice which complements the integrity of creation sounds vaguely reasonable so long as it is kept reasonably vague, on closer analysis, one wonders whether the fulfillment of the human community is historically possible with the simultaneous fulfillment of the whole biotic community.

When Iowa is plowed to plant corn, it can hardly be said that the grasslands of Iowa reach their historical fulfillment. The bison are displaced, and there will be fewer bobolinks (grassland birds with distinctive markings)—sacrificed that Europeans may build their culture on the American continent. The most we can say is that Iowans can and ought to sustain their agriculture within the hydrology, soil chemistries, nutrient recycling processes, and so on, that operate on the Iowa landscape. But justice for the bobolinks and bison? There is no human inhabiting of Iowa that leaves the natural history of Iowa unblemished. Legitimate human demands cannot be satisfied without some sacrifice of nature. We will return to such value tradeoffs, wondering if environmental ethics can always be "win–win" in the next chapter, also in Chapter 5.

5. Toxics, Pollutants, Invasives

People get excited about their environment quite quickly when someone screams: "Poison!" That scream has led to over 1,200 Superfund sites, and fears that there are twice that many more that ought to be designated. Love Canal, a neighborhood in Niagara Falls, New York, became the subject of national controversy and environmental notoriety following the discovery of 21,000 tons of toxic waste that had been buried beneath the neighborhood by a chemical company. The company sold the site to the Niagara Falls School Board, reluctantly, explicitly detailing the danger contained within the site and including a liability limitation clause. During subsequent construction, heavy rainstorms released the chemical waste, leading to a public health emergency and an urban planning scandal (Levine, 1982).

In northeast Ohio, the Cuyahoga River caught fire on June 26, 1969, burning an oily film and debris on the surface. Ohioans became aware that their river was one of the most polluted in America, with no visible signs of life in it at all. Smaller fires had previously broken out thirteen times. Featured in newspapers across the country, this led to demands that produced the Clean Water Act and further increased pressures on the Environmental Protection Agency to enforce water pollution laws.

In Grand Junction, Colorado, uranium was mined by the Climax Uranium Company (now AMAX) from 1951 through 1970 on the south edge of town. The tailings, containing 85% of the original radioactivity but thought harmless, were widely used as construction materials in thousands of homes, in schools, and in sidewalks. Not until 1970 did physicians notice a marked increase in leukemia, cleft lip and palate, and Down's syndrome. Federal and state governments took emergency action, though uncertain about just what remedial action to take. They needed the latest report of the National Research Council's Advisory Committee on the Biological Effects of Ionizing Radiations (BEIR III). But this had not been published, because of the inability of members of the committee to reach a consensus.

At the federal Hanford Nuclear Weapons Site in Washington state, very large releases of radioiodine were made secretly starting the 1940s, especially during 1944–1947, and continuing until 1957. The U.S. government justified the secrecy as part of the war effort. Radioiodines are produced in high abundance in the course of nuclear fission and easily become airborne, if released during high temperatures and other malfunctions. Exposure causes hypo-thyroidism, a deficiency of thyroid hormones in bodily organs, including brain damage in children. Persons living nearby were not warned. The "Hanford Downwinders" began to realize what had happened and there has been a tortured effort, involving the Nuclear Regulatory Commission, to find out the facts and assign responsibility.

Kudzu is a Japanese plant introduced to the southeastern United States for erosion control and as a cattle food, especially following the Great Depression of the 1930s. Hundreds of young men in the Civilian Conservation Corps were given work planting it, and farmers were paid as much as $8 an acre to plant it. Today, it covers over eight million acres in the deep South. The vines can grow a foot a day, covering trees, fields, telephone poles, houses, and anything else in its path. Conservationists are calling it "the vine that ate the South." Cheatgrass, or Japanese brome grass (*Bromus tectorum*) is an invasive weed across much of western North America from British Columbia to California. Other species of *Bromus* may also become noxious weeds.

Starlings (the common or European starling, *Sternus vulgaris*) were introduced to the United States from Europe in Central Park in New York, in an effort to have all the birds mentioned in Shakespeare present in the United States. The original sixty birds have proliferated in enormous numbers, and today over 200 million of them frequent urban and rural habitats, displacing native birds, such as the purple martin. A roost may contain 1.5 million birds, and their droppings can kill trees. In 2008 the U. S. government managed to kill 1.8 million starlings, more than any other nuisance species. Starlings have also become a major problem in other nations, especially Australia. Similarly English sparrows are a nuisance and a persistent adversary of bluebirds, wrens, phoebes, chickadees, tree sparrows, tanagers, and robins. There is increasing evidence that invasive species endanger native species.

6. Living Locally: Green and Grassroots

"Think globally, act locally." That adage has become a contemporary proverb, urging people to take the global view and let that inspire home-town and home-country concern, a sense of belonging on a landscape (Heise, 2008). People may start voting for open space, and shop for organic food, preferably grown locally. They may press for more re-cycling, or "going green" in local schools, churches, businesses. "Please recycle," or "Recyclable" is on most of our mail. They want environmental education in their grade schools. They want to know what pollutants are killing fish in the river, or what is coming out of the smokestacks at the power plant. They may volunteer to keep the trash picked up alongside a couple miles of highway. They may pass a state referendum mandating power companies to go 25% wind or solar in the next decade.

This activity pushes for quality of life in a quality environment. It has deeper philosophical and emotional convictions. We bring the sense of residence into focus at native range. What is the logic of residence in a our home territory? Goose pimples sometimes rise when persons sing, *America, the Beautiful* (lyrics written by Katharine Lee Bates). The physiological reaction is to a national heritage, but also before purple mountains' majesties and the fruited plains stretched from sea to shining sea.

That becomes a more bioregional sense in particular places. Daniel Kemmis, formerly speaker of the Montana House of Representatives and mayor of Missoula, explains how the capacity for public life is entwined with a sense of place, evidenced in Montana community, even in the name of the state (Kemmis, 1990). There nature governs, as well as the legislature. We will recall below how Aldo Leopold's land ethic was planted in the sand counties of Wisconsin, how John Muir was heart-broken at the loss of Hetch Hetchy.

We need roots in locality. We cherish our hills of home, our rivers, our bays, our country drives. Most of us identify so with some countryside that we get a lump in the throat when we must leave it, or when we return after an absence. We must live in what psychologists call "built environments," urban and rural, but the environmental turn has thrown into new relief how such culture is subtended by the earthen life-support systems that also enter into our well-being. One needs time to rejoice in the sunshine and the rain, in seedtime and harvest, in peaks and prairies, in the orchard in bloom, in the smell of the new-mown hay.

But this is threatened by smog and acid rain. Remember the Cuyahoga

River on fire, Love Canal, and the Hanford Downwinders. The Environmental Protection Agency, a new force in *national* politics, came out of *local* alarms. Rachel Carson's "silent spring" found its first audience in women's garden clubs; the women were not silent, but so outspoken that Congress found that it had to listen.

Too often we are disappointed when we return to some natural area that we formerly enjoyed—where we could find warblers migrating in the spring—to find that it has been blitzed for development. We wonder if we ought not to consider what we are undoing as well as what we are doing. That may provoke renewing one's membership in the Audubon Society, national and local. We had thought we wanted to be cosmopolitan; now we realize that sometimes we want to be provincial. Grassroots environmentalism is a key to success at home and abroad (Cable and Cable, 1995; Ghai and Vivian, 1992).

7. Biodiversity

Earth, conservation biologists are shouting, is facing catastrophic extinction. *Time* magazine ran a special Earth Day issue on saving the Earth. Edward O. Wilson, Harvard biologist, puts the consensus: "Researchers of biodiversity agree that we are in the midst of the seventh mass extinction" (Wilson, 2000, p. 30; also see Carpenter and Bishop, 2009. This quenching of life's exuberant diversity seems wrong, dreadfully wrong. There is a rising alarm and concern for saving endangered species, or, more comprehensively, biodiversity. These biologists may be quite forceful. One of the surprising developments in biology in the last half century (one that few biologists predicted) has been the development of the Society for Conservation Biology, with over 10,000 members, one of the largest professional associations in biology and "a discipline with a deadline."

Edward O. Wilson exclaims: "The biospheric membrane that covers the Earth, and you and me,… is the miracle we have been given." If we do not shift our present development course, "at least a fifth of the species of plants would be gone or committed to early extinction by 2030, and half by the end of the century" (Wilson, 2002, p. 21, p. 102). The International Union for Conservation of Nature calculated in 2010 that 33–39% of all species that have been evaluated are endangered (IUCN, 2010).

The U. S. Congress, deploring the lack of "adequate concern (for) and conservation (of)" species, passed the Endangered Species Act (U.S. Congress, 1973). That Act, as first passed, was tougher than was realized by many of those who passed it. In a celebrated case, involving a small fish, the snail darter, blocking a TVA dam, the U.S. Supreme Court, interpreting the law, said that species are to be conserved with "no exception" at "whatever the cost," even overriding the "primary missions" of federal agencies (*TVA v. Hill*, 437 U.S. 153 (1978) at 173, 184, 185).

Also, in the Act, "economic" (value in the marketplace) is not among the listed criteria of value. But, since economic costs must sometimes be considered, Congress, in 1978 amendments, authorized a high-level, interagency committee to evaluate difficult cases. Should this committee deem fit, it can permit human development at cost of extinction of species that impede development. This committee is identified by the rather nondescript name, "The Endangered Species Committee," in the legislation, but almost at once it was nicknamed "the God committee." The name mixes jest with ultimate concern. Any who destroy species in the name of development take, fearfully, the prerogative of God.

A quite effective international convention from the same year, 1973, is the Convention on International Trade in Endangered Species of Wild Fauna and Flora (CITES, 1973). The United Nations Conference on Environment and Development (UNCED, the Earth Summit), meeting in Rio de Janeiro, passed the Convention on Biological Diversity in 1992. This grew out of the Earth Summit in Rio de Janeiro and, when enough nations had ratified it, came into force the following year. Conserving biodiversity is called "a common concern of human kind" (United Nations, 1992, Preamble). The Convention has now been ratified by most nations on Earth, for whom it is legally binding, but was never ratified by the United States Congress. There is a series of ongoing meetings to expand and increase enforcement. We return to biodiversity concerns in detail in Chapter 5.

8. Lynn White: Dominion of Man

In an attack published in *Science* (White, 1967), historian Lynn White famously laid much of the blame for the ecological crisis on the Christian belief that humans had dominion over nature. In the first chapter of the Bible, at creation, God says to the first couple: "Be fruitful and multiply, and fill the earth and subdue it; and have dominion..." (Genesis 1.27-28). White claimed that God's command for humans to "have dominion" flowered in medieval Europe, licensed the exploitation of nature, and produced science and technology to satisfy human cares, and this has resulted in an ecological crisis. So, the Bible launches an arrogantly misplaced exploitation of Earth. White's claim, made as it was in a prominent scientific journal, was widely echoed.

Theologians replied that appropriate dominion requires stewardship and care (Birch, Eakin, and McDaniel, 1990; Northcott, 1996; Fern, 2002; Cobb, 1972; Nash, 1991; Brown, 2010). True, there is a sense of dominion that means "Earth-tyrant," humans subduing nature in a repressive sense, as a conqueror does his enemy. But there are more positive senses of dominion. Even within the military metaphor, a general has command over his own soldiers, about whom presumably he cares. Such an "Earth-commander" finds the interests of the commander and the commanded inseparably entwined. Jeremy Cohen, from a Jewish perspective, concludes: "Rarely, if ever, did premodern Jews and Christians construe this verse (in Genesis) as a license for the selfish exploitation of the environment" (Cohen, 1989, p. 5).

To the contrary, loving the land is a central theme of the Hebrew Bible. Biblical faith was from the start a landed faith. Israel is given their "promised land—"a good and broad land, a land flowing with milk and honey" (Exodus 3.8; Deuteronomy 27.3). The land is watched over by God's care (Deuteronomy 11.11-12). Yearning for a sense of place is a perennial human longing, and Israel's sense of living on a land given by God, of human placement on the earth, can yet speak to the landlessness, and lostness, of modern persons. All peoples need a sense of "my country," of their social communities in place on a sustaining landscape they possess in care and in love.

In the landscape surrounding him, Jesus found ample evidence of the presence of God. The birds of the air neither sow nor reap yet are fed by the heavenly Father, who notices the sparrows that fall. Not even Solomon is arrayed with the glory of the lilies, though the grass of the field, today alive, perishes tomorrow (see Matthew 6.25-33). There is in every seed and root a promise. Sowers sow, the seed grows secretly, and sowers return to reap their harvests. God sends rain on the just and unjust. Jesus teaches that the power organically manifest in the wild flowers of the field is continuous with the power spiritually manifest in the kingdom he announces. There is an ontological bond between nature and spirit. This also seems to be connecting the good land, the rural landscape, with deeper natural powers, present also in wild nature. Nevertheless White's criticism launched much soul-searching within Christianity and Judaism about caring for creation, and how religious faith could and ought to enter environmental policy (Rolston, 2010).

9. Ecofeminism: The Woman's Touch

Ecofeminists argue that a strong connection is found between the oppression of women and the degradation of nature. They dislike what they call binary opposites that justify power: higher ranking categories that are privileged over lower ranking categories: dominants over subordinates, men over women ("the weaker sex"), culture over nature, white over black, developed nations over non-developed nations, civilized over primitive, humans over animals, predators over prey, animals over plants. For centuries, societies have been patriarchal—not only the Western ones, but typically also those of Asian and aboriginal peoples. Women could not vote, had limited capacities to own land, receive inheritances, or to work in public life. For decades, economics has been capitalist, with the rich exploiting the poor. Ecofeminists protest against all kinds of inequalities that produce "victims."

Vandana Shiva (1988), an Indian woman, wants to reconsider how societies look at the activities of both women and nature. A river in a forest is not fully productive if it only provides drinking water for villagers, habitat for animals, and fish for locals to eat. The river—say the powerful men—needs to be damned also to get hydropower. Nature needs to be tamed, exploited, subdued—so the developers claim. "There is domination inherent in the view created by western man over the last three centuries through which he could subjugate,... domination of the South by the North, of women by men, of nature" (p. 30). Nature is thought of as feminine, mother nature, to be mastered by ruling men skilled in know-how—agriculture and technology. This permeates science, politics, economics, and religion. But this overlooks how women may have more profound connections than do men with the rhythms of nature.

> Women in subsistence economies, producing and reproducing wealth in partnership with nature, have been experts in their own right of holistic and ecological knowledge of nature's processes. But these alternative modes of knowing, which are oriented to social benefits and sustenance needs, are not recognised by the capitalist reductionist paradigm, because it fails to perceive the interconnectedness of nature, or the connection of women's lives, work, and knowledge with the creation of wealth.
>
> (Shiva, 1988, p. 24)

Women (and sometimes men) philosophers and theologians have been quite outspoken about this, joining with those concerned for ecojustice. Among philosophers, Karen Warren wrote an early and classic article contesting "the logic of domination" and hierarchical "up-down thinking" (greater than/less than) with its "value-dualism" placing reason above emotion, mind over body, men over women, men over nature. "What *all* ecofeminists agree about, then, is the way in which *the logic of domination* has functioned historically within patriarchy to sustain and justify the twin dominations of women and nature" (Warren, 1990, p. 131; see also Warren, 2000; Ruether, 1992). The dominant have this creed: Make it to the top.

The ecofeminists: Be a friend of the Earth.

Ecofeminists may argue that to think of nature as natural resources is pervaded with this logic of domination. Humans have the right to use nature, that seems inevitable; but this quickly transforms into a right to exploit nature. A dominant method in natural resource policy is cost-benefit analysis, but that presumes that humans can manage animals, plants, ecosystems, conserving what brings more benefits than costs to humans. Those who make such decisions are, unsurprisingly, typically wealthy males, usually white males of European origins. Even if one shifts from economic benefit/cost analysis to the more recently popular concern for "ecosystem services" (see Chapter 6, sec. 3), or to "sustainable development" (see above, also Chapter 2, sec. 2). the logic of domination remains.

In Australia, Val Plumwood (1939–2008) made similar arguments, with particular attention to the Australian aboriginals. She critiques what she describes as "the standpoint of mastery," a set of views of the self and its relationship to the other associated with sexism, racism, capitalism, colonialism, and the domination of nature. This hierarchical standpoint involves seeing the other as radically separate and inferior, the background to the self as foreground, as one whose existence is secondary, derivative or peripheral to that of the self or center, and whose agency is denied or minimized.

The human/nature dualism is part of a series of problematic, gendered dualisms, including human/animal, mind/body, male/female, reason/emotion, and civilized/primitive. For instance, women are said to be less rational than men, rather than men being seen to be less emotional than women. This is exacerbated through a "hyperseparation" between the entities, in which qualities which they might share are ignored or minimized and qualities which differentiate them are exaggerated and overemphasized. This underpins the ecological crisis (Plumwood, 1993).

Plumwood is celebrated for a near-death experience, recounted in "Being Prey" (2000). She was in a canoe alone in rugged Australian territory and failed to recognize a floating log as a crocodile. During her attempt to get ashore, she was seized in the leg by the crocodile. The crocodile tried to drown her with "death rolls" but she escaped and managed to crawl two miles to a rescue point.

The men who rescued her went back to kill the crocodile, claiming that once it had tasted human blood, it would be more dangerous than ever. Plumwood went on Australian national television pleading that the crocodile not be killed, contrary to the masculine man-over-beast mentality. But she was forced to incorporate the event into her worldview, thinking how most creatures are prey.

> As my own narrative and the larger story in which it was embedded were ripped apart, I glimpsed beyond my own realm a shockingly indifferent world of necessity in which I had no more significance than any other edible being.... Although I had been a vegetarian for some ten years before the encounter and remain one today, this knowledge makes me wary.... Ethical eating may not always preclude the taking of life, and predation may take forms that are understood in ethical terms.... I am a vegetarian primarily because ethical and ecological forms of predation are only exceptionally available in contemporary Western society, with its factory farming and commodified relationships to food.
>
> (Plumwood, 2000, pp. 142–144)

If Plumwood's plea for the crocodile seems outlandish, many do regret colonialism, and now judge the British attitude to the aboriginals as quite arrogant. The Western settlers claimed that Australia was *terra nullius,* no man's land, an uninhabited or barbarous country, and theirs for the taking, even though there were (an estimated) three quarters of a million people who had been living on the coastal and outback lands for centuries. Ecofeminists have been forceful advocates, calling those who profited from empire to repentance from the colonial past, both from what it did to native peoples and to their lands. The Australian High Court overturned terra nullius in 1992, resulting in the restoration of some lands to the aboriginals. Americans will find uncomfortable parallels with treatment of native Americans or with Gifford Pinchot seeking civilized prosperity by leading the U.S. Forest Service in "an attack on what nature has given us" (recounted below).

10. Animal Welfare: Peter Singer, Tom Reagan

There has emerged over recent decades much concern for the way that humans treat animals. Advocates approach the issue from diverse perspectives, but they share the conviction that animals, especially mammals, ought to be considered members of the moral community and treated compassionately. This typically limits, if not prohibits, their use for food (two million pigs killed each week in the United States; 70 billion chickens annually in the world), for research (some 12–20 million annually in the U.S), entertainment (zoos, circuses, dolphin shows). Two philosophers prominent in this movement are Peter Singer and Tom Regan, among dozens of others, such as Richard Ryder, Andrew Linzey, Bernard Rollin, Mary Midgley. Internationally known celebrity figures, for example, Jane Goodall, have enlarged this concern.

Millions who shop in supermarkets ask about "factory farming," wanting information about the conditions under which the animals they eat were reared. Many persons have become vegetarian; most university food services provide vegetarian alternatives, which would not have been the case thirty years ago. Invasive research on primates has essentially been stopped; universities may decline to house such facilities. Every university has an animal use and care committee; experiments must be justified. Many women refuse to wear fur coats.

Peter Singer's *Animal Liberation* (1975) proved a linchpin in the movement, originating from an article "Animal Liberation," published in *The New York Review of Books* and attracting national attention. It has since been translated into seventeen languages. Singer is an Australian philosopher who has for a number of years been at Princeton University. He is a utilitarian and advocates the idea that what makes animals due moral consideration is the fact that they suffer. Perhaps they cannot reason or speak, or themselves act morally, but they are nevertheless to be considered because of their interests in their own well-being. Animals can be graded on their differing capacities for sentience (chimpanzees versus rats), but toleration for the mistreatment of animals is a prejudice that, like sexism and racism, does not have a rational basis. Failure to take into account animal suffering is to be guilty of "speciesism," unjustified preference for one's own kind (Jamieson, 1999).

Tom Regan was long a philosopher at North Carolina State University. His key book is *The Case for Animal Rights* (1983/2004), which has made him a public intellectual. Animals have inherent worth, or value, because they have feelings, desires, beliefs, preferences, memories, expectations, and purposeful behavior. What happens to them matters to them. This gives them rights. "Being kind" and "avoiding cruelty" is not enough; the answer to factory farming is not "bigger cages" but "empty cages." Animals ought to have legally enforceable rights to respectful treatment (Regan, 2005).

In philosophical circles, these two philosophers set off a chain reaction with exploding concern about animal welfare. The U.S. Congress has enacted a number of laws dealing with animal care, such as the Animal Welfare Act (1966) and the Marine Mammal Protection Act (1972). Animal law is now taught in well over half of the law schools in the United States (Miller, 2011). We return to consider these issues at more length in Chapter 3.

11. Environmental Ethics: Philosophers Wake Up

Environmental ethics was unknown in Western philosophy until the mid-1970s. That was to change rapidly. Across the next three decades, over three dozen anthologies and another three dozen systematic works were published (see lists under, Anthologies and Systematic Works, ISEE Bibliography website). There are four journals. The bibliographies of the International Society of Environmental Ethics, found on its websites, list over fifteen thousand relevant articles and books, not only by philosophers but by policy makers, lawyers, environmental professionals, foresters, economists, developers, business persons, and citizens, with an ethical concern about the environment and human uses of it (see ISEE websites in references). There are encyclopedias and large anthology collections (Callicott and Frodeman, 2009; Callicott and Palmer, 2005). There are case study books and websites (Newton and Dillingham, 2002; Derr and McNamara, 2003; Gudorf and Huchingson, 2003; Keller, 2011).

Among the earliest philosophers to ask about an environmental ethics were two Australians. First, Richard Routley (later Richard Sylvan) wondered about the need for a new environmental ethics in a lecture given at a World Congress of Philosophy in Varna, Bulgaria in 1973 and rather obscurely published in those proceedings (Routley, 1973). A second Australian was John Passmore, who answered, in effect, no, but we do need to re-apply traditional ethics to what humans have at stake in their environment (Passmore, 1974). Australians have continued actively in the field (Elliot and Gare, 1983; Sylvan and Bennett, 1994; Mathews, 2003). Arne Naess, Norwegian philosopher, was by then claiming that was too shallow; we need a "deep ecology" (Naess, 1973). Holmes Rolston III's "Is There an Ecological Ethic?", published in the leading philosophical journal *Ethics,* received widespread attention (Rolston, 1975; Palmer, 2003).

J. Baird Callicott taught the first academic class in environmental ethics in 1971 at the University of Wisconsin, Stevens Point. Holmes Rolston was teaching a similar class at Colorado State University in 1973 (Preston, 2009). In the four decades since, over a thousand schools have followed, either with environmental ethics courses, or as subunits within more inclusive ethics classes. Eugene Hargrove launched the journal *Environmental Ethics* in 1979. The first philosophical conference on environmental ethics was held at the University of Georgia in 1971 (Blackstone, 1974). The Institute for Philosophy and Public Policy, based at the University of Maryland, has kept a sustained interest in environmental issues.

The Royal Institute of Philosophy held its annual conference on the theme "Philosophy and the Natural Environment" in 1993 (Attfield and Belsey, 1994), and British philosophers have continued active (Attfield, 2003; Curry, 2006; Fox, 2006). European philosophers have been outspoken, particularly Dutch and German philosophers (Achterberg, 1994; Drenthen, 1996; Zweers, 2000; Birnbacher, 1980; Meyer-Abich, 1993; Ott, 1993).

On the political scene, and with philosophical and ethical concerns, The German Green Party, founded in 1980, sat in the German federal government from 1995–2005, and remains active in German politics. The United Nations Educational, Scientific and Cultural Organization (UNESCO) commissioned a study in environmental ethics, translated into several languages, and widely distributed to its personnel (ten Have, 2006). UNESCO also sponsored symposia in Russia for several years, in which about three dozen Russian academics teaching environmental ethics, led by Western experts, exchanged further ideas in the field. Mikhail Gorbachev had used his authority and experience to found Green Cross International in the wake of the UNCED conference in 1992. There is a quite active Chinese Society for Environmental Ethics, also groups active in Taiwan and Korea.

Ethics for two thousand years worried about civilizing humans, helping persons relate to persons in ways that were loving, fair, just, equitable, reasonable, caring, and forgiving. Ethics sought to humanize us. Much progress has been made, establishing democracies, for instance, or abolishing slavery, or insuring human rights, or women's equality. Much remains to be done. But what is quite unprecedented in ethical history is this environmental turn. Nowhere in our past has there been anything called an environmental ethics. Today, a vigorous new interest in nature and human responsibilities toward it represents one of the more interesting changes of perspective in philosophy in recent centuries. The chapters that follow will look in sustained detail at the leading concerns of these environmental philosophers.

12. Aldo Leopold, Rachel Carson, John Muir

Three prophetic figures launching this environmental turn have been Aldo Leopold, Rachel Carson, and John Muir. There were others which we could as well consider: David Brower, Henry David Thoreau, Wallace Stegner, Wendell Berry, but these three are forceful enough to recall early and seminal roots. We cannot expect that these three prophets could address, or even envision, the extent of the coming environmental crisis—its global dimensions or climate change, for example. Nevertheless we can appreciate how their concerns were pivotal in waking us up to an environmental crisis. This will complete our look in the rear view mirror, and we can take off in search of environmental ethics in the new millennium.

Aldo Leopold (1887–1948) was a forester and ecologist, in early life with the U.S. Forest Service, long at the University of Wisconsin at Madison. In his later life, toward mid-century, Leopold lamented, "There is as yet no ethic dealing with man's relation to land and to the animals and plants which grow upon it.... The proof that conservation has not yet touched these foundations of conduct lies in the fact that philosophy and religion have not yet heard of it" (1949/1968, pp.203, 210). We ought to love "the land," he insisted, "the natural processes by which the land and the living things upon it have achieved their characteristic form (evolution) and by which they maintain their existence (ecology)." "That land is a community is the basic concept of ecology, but that land is to be loved and respected is an extension of ethics" (pp. 173, 224–225, viii–ix).

People still count, in Leopold's view, but the ecosystems in which people and all other organisms are embedded also count morally. Humans coinhabit Earth with five or ten million other species, and we and they depend on these surrounding biotic communities of life. A decade into this new millennium, there is no philosopher or theologian in the Western world who has not heard of environmental ethics. Leopold's *A Sand County Almanac* (1949/1968), rejoicing in the sand counties of Wisconsin, proved one of the landmark books of the last century (over a million copies sold). Leopold was a principal founder of the Wilderness Society, a principal force in persuading the U.S. Congress to pass the Wilderness Act (1964), which has resulted in hundreds of designated wilderness areas, covering an area larger than the state of California. Leopold anticipates sustainability and biodiversity conservation, living locally and grassroots environmentalism. The land ethic has even gone global, as we shall see. All this would have both surprised and pleased Leopold—who died of a heart attack fighting a woodland fire on a neighbor's homestead shortly before his landmark book appeared in print (Knight and Reidel, 2002; Meine, 1988; Callicott, 1987; Aldo Leopold Foundation, 2011).

Rachel Carson (1907–1964) began her career as a marine fisheries biologist with the U.S. Bureau of Fisheries (predecessor to the U. S. Fish and Wildlife Service), only the second woman so hired, and gained recognition for her insight into marine life in *The Sea Around Us* (Carson, 1951). She turned to the damage that she had discovered DDT and other chemicals were doing to the natural environment in her *Silent Spring* (1962), tracing the build-up of that pesticide in eggshells. DDT was "silencing the birds" by thinning the eggshells and poisoning many native birds. The vanished warblers led up the food chains to include the American national symbol, the bald eagle. *Silent Spring* was first published as a serial in *The New Yorker*, then as a Book-of-the Month selection, giving it wide publicity and national attention, including a CBS television special, viewed by 10 to 15 million persons, and praised by Supreme Court Justice William O. Douglas. The birth defects caused by the drug thalidomide were discovered about this time. Overuse of pesticides ("biocides" Carson called the life-killers) became a major public issue (Lear, 1997; Sideris and Moore, 2008).

Carson's publishers had been threatened with a lawsuit by chemical companies manufacturing pesticides if they published the book, but risked publication because they took her seriously. Her scientific credibility and her personal character were attacked. An American Cyanamid chemist, Robert White-Stevens, labeled Carson "a fanatic defender of the cult of the balance of nature" (quoted in Lear, 1997, p. 434). A former Secretary of Agriculture, Ezra Taft Benson, wrote to President Dwight D. Eisenhower, that she was "probably a communist" (Lear, 1997, pp. 429–430). Vociferous critics argued that, by discouraging the use of DDT against malaria abroad as well as at home, she was killing millions of people, especially children. Nevertheless, her book was endorsed by prominent scientists and spurred a reversal in national pesticide policy—including a nationwide ban on DDT and similar pesticides.

The environmental concern Rachel Carson inspired, often among women's garden clubs and other groups, led to the creation of the Environmental Protection Agency. She anticipates the crisis with toxics, pollutants, invasives, with sustainability, biodiversity. Carson herself became ill with cancer, and, anemic from her treatments, struggled to vindicate herself and her case in national disputes, before her early death. She was posthumously awarded the Presidential Medal of Freedom by Jimmy Carter, the highest civilian honor in the United States. She was honored on a postage stamp in a great Americans series.

John Muir (1838–1914), Scottish-born American naturalist, wrote enthusiastic accounts of his adventures in nature, especially the California Sierra Nevadas, read by millions. His urging was critical in saving Yosemite National Park, Sequoia National Park, and many other areas. He founded the Sierra Club to promote conservation (Worster, 2008; Miller, 1993). He too anticipates the biodiversity crisis, saving of wildlands, ecosystems, living simply, locally, and sustainably; and his Sierra Club continues as one of the most forceful conservation organizations.

When John Muir finished (or at least abandoned) his formal education and turned to live in the Sierra Nevadas, he wrote, "I was only leaving one university for another, the Wisconsin University for the University of the Wilderness" (Muir, 1912/1965, p. 228). He first undertook a walk of 1,000 miles from Indiana to Florida, choosing to go by the "wildest, leafiest, and least trodden way I could find, promising the greatest extent of virgin forest" (Muir, 1916, p. 2). He decided he could best find that in California and booked passage there.

Arriving in California, he went immediately to the Yosemite area. He lived and worked in the Sierra mountains for much of his life. He lived simply, enthusiastically enjoying the mountains (including, famously, windstorms and an earthquake), often entertaining scientists, artists, celebrities, who sought him out. He made scientific studies in geology, advocating the glacial formation of the Sierra topography.

Muir was at first a friend of Gifford Pinchot. Pinchot became the first head of the United States Forest Service and a leading spokesman for the sustainable use of natural resources for human benefit. The two could agree about sustaining forests, about not clear-cutting, and avoiding reckless exploitation of natural resources. But Muir and Pinchot soon clashed, and the clash highlighted two diverging views of the use of the nation's nature. Pinchot was a utilitarian who saw conservation as a means of managing the nation's natural resources for long-term sustainable commercial use.

Pinchot could put this bluntly, with pride in the manifest destiny of Americans to tame the continent: "The first duty of the human race is to control the earth it lives upon.... Out of this attack on what nature has given us we have won a kind of prosperity and a kind of civilization and a kind of man that are new in the world" (Pinchot, 1973, p. 86, 90). Muir thought this arrogant and insensitive. To see the American forests, which Muir called "a great delight to God" and "the best he ever planted" (Muir, 1901, p. 331) as nothing but timber to harvest was "tree farming," in contrast with valuing nature for its deeper spiritual and philosophical qualities. Muir exclaimed: "The clearest way into the Universe is through a forest wilderness" (Wolfe, 1938, p. 313).

Their friendship ended in the summer of 1897 when Pinchot released a statement to a Seattle newspaper supporting sheep grazing in forest reserves. Muir thought sheep were little more that "hooved locusts" and confronted Pinchot. Pinchot insisted on sheep grazing in the national forests, whereupon Muir told him: "I don't want anything more to do with you." This divided environmentalists into two camps: the preservationists, led by Muir, and Pinchot's camp, who claimed the term "conservationists." That tension continues and will figure frequently in the pages to follow.

With population growth continuing in San Francisco, pressures increased to dam the Tuolumne River and create a water reservoir in Hetch Hetchy Valley. Muir passionately opposed the dam. "Dam Hetch Hetchy! As well dam for water-tanks the people's cathedrals and churches, for no holier temple has ever been consecrated by the hearts of man" (Muir, 1912/1965, p. 202) Muir and his Sierra Club fought inundating the valley. Muir wrote to President Teddy Roosevelt (with whom he had gone camping in back country Yosemite) pleading for him to scuttle the project. Roosevelt's successor, William Howard Taft, suspended the Interior Department's approval for the Hetch Hetchy right-of-way. After years of national debate, Taft's successor Woodrow Wilson signed the bill authorizing the dam into law in December 1913. Muir felt a great loss from the destruction of the valley, his last major battle. He died soon after, with—if not of—a broken heart.

Californians have recently inducted Muir into the California Hall of Fame. Muir has been on two postage stamps, and in 2005 Californians chose to place him on the California state quarter (each state has been featured on a special issue quarter coin). California celebrates John Muir day on April 21 each year; he was the first such person to be honored with a commemorative day.

————

So, the environmental turn is forcing us to challenge many of the lifestyle categories in which we have been thinking. By classical philosophical accounts, ethics is people relating to people in justice and love. People are benefitted or harmed by the condition of their environment. So, when the environment is jeopardized, classical ethics becomes concerned. Those concerned for environmental ethics will agree that we must consider helping and harming people, but they will go further to ask about respect for life on Earth, for the animals, the plants, the species, ecosystems, even for the Earth itself. A recent trend in ethics is to be more inclusive. Be comprehensive.

Asking philosophically about goodness leads to the questions: what are the components of a good life? What sorts of activities and things are good in themselves? Right action concerns the principles of right and wrong that govern our choices and pursuits. Understood collectively, such principles constitute a moral code that defines the responsibilities of people who live together. Applied ethics extends these arguments about principle to particular areas of concern. When applied to medicine, this form of applied ethics is called "medical ethics" (sometimes expanded to include biotechnology and called "bioethics"). When applied to commerce, this becomes "business ethics"; when applied to the press, "journalism ethics"; when applied to engineering, "engineering ethics"; when applied to agriculture, "agricultural ethics," and so on. When applied to issues of environmental policy and regulation, we formulate an "environmental ethics."

One thing is different about the last, however. Unlike these other applied fields, those in environmental ethics envision that their scope moves outside the human sphere. All forms of applied ethics can raise some issues of principle (such as whether "death" has occurred with brain death in medical ethics); but environmental ethics raises deep questions about who and what counts morally and why. Should we count animals, plants, endangered species, old growth forests, wilderness areas, Earth? This requires reexamining the human–nature relationship. Many of the debates about the kind of value that nature has (such as whether it is directly or indirectly morally considerable) are debates in what philosophers typically call metaethics. In that sense environmental ethics can be as theoretical as it is applied.

Moral psychology is the study of desire, emotion, and personality in relation to moral questions. We are concerned with whether arguments about what is right in a moral sense do or do not motivate people to change their behavior. Perhaps love (of whales, for instance) moves persons more effectively than argument (about their roles in marine ecosystems) in order to get their support for a ban on commercial whaling. Or, perhaps love (of "killer whales") is misplaced without argument whether the love is appropriate. Perhaps "nature" shapes our ethics more than we like to admit; we act selfishly because we are "born that way." Maybe we have to offset our genetic tendencies with moral education, which frees us to do better than we otherwise would do. Then again, maybe what we "naturally" do, what we are (perhaps instinctively) moved to do can be a good thing—as when a mother cares for her children, or we take compassion on a suffering animal.

Be warned, though, that all this strains the brain. Philosophers think they are good at arguments. Aren't they the faculty who teach logic? Yes, you hear about premise and conclusion. But in considering these diverse movements cumulating into an environmental turn, we have already seen how logic gets mangled in the rough and tumble of the lived world. Often in the real world argument is not so much like the links of a chain as like the legs of a table, where support comes from multiple considerations. Much of this more comprehensive sense of logic involves an interpretive seeing, realizing that observations are heavily theory-laden, that understanding uses background assumptions and models that have been called paradigms (Kuhn, 1970).

Paradigms are governing models that, in some fairly broad range of experience, set the context of explanation and intelligibility. They come to pervade our worldviews as the assumptions that make our activities and outlooks possible. Such models organize reality. They tell us what to look for, what to discount, and what to make of what we find. We catch these patterns with a frame of mind. One sees what is going on only when particulars can be set in a larger gestalt. The answers come to an ethicist gauging morality similarly to the way they do to a judge appraising justice, to a scientist appraising a challenging theory, to a theologian testing a religious creed—by a mingling of argument, of weighting of facts, of notions of plausibility, and even by intuitions that yield an informed judgment.

The holographic character of judgments about values, about justice, right and wrong, requires more crossplay and interweaving, a logical network sometimes said to be more characteristic of the right than of the left cerebral hemisphere, more characteristic of the brain in general than of a computer. In detecting more sophisticated patterns, as when, despite her aging, we recognize the face of a friend whom we have not seen for decades, there is a subtle interplay of textural features by which the whole is constituted. This sort of logic is present in science when a geologist recognizes the facies of rock strata, or when a dendrologist notices the differences between the bark of spruce and that of fir. But it looms much larger as one approaches the perception of plot in a novel, such as *Gone with the Wind,* or in a historical career, as of Abraham

Lincoln. In evaluating natural and world history, and our part in it, one must join earlier and later significances in ways more qualitative than quantitative, more dramatic than linear. One needs a sense of scenic scope.

Meaning judgments are always self-implicating. Values are by definition those things that make a difference. This might be thought to bias a person's capacities for logic. One cannot think clearly about what one is wrapped up in. But the other side of this is that one will not think at all about that for which one does not care, or rightly think about that for which one does not rightly care. One needs cares refocused to get the self off-centered enough to reason aright. The self must be reformed in order to eliminate its tendency toward rationalizing.

An insight from this way of thinking is that we sometimes reach critical paradigm-shifts. What you will be facing in this book is the question whether a new paradigm for life on Earth is needed, or possible, and, if so, what it is. In the pages that follow, you will be challenged whether the environmental turn demands a gestalt-switch.

When you go home and say that you are taking a class in environmental ethics, mom and dad may be doubtful. "Isn't that an ethic for the chipmunks and daisies? Shouldn't you study something more serious? College costs a lot of money!" But, if you study hard, you will have an answer: "I have been searching for a land ethic" (Aldo Leopold). Tell mom and dad that an education these days requires becoming environmentally literate, just as much as it does becoming computer literate.

Environmental ethics is vital because the survival of life on Earth depends on it. The main concerns on the world agenda for the new millennium are: war and peace, escalating populations, escalating consumption, degrading environments. They are all inter-related. For the first time in the history of the planet, one species jeopardizes the welfare of the community of life on Earth.

Becoming educated is becoming civilized. Philosophers often claim that they are vital to an enlightened education. Socrates claimed famously: "The unexamined life is not worth living" (*Apology*, 38). He urged: "Know thyself." The classic search in philosophy has been to figure out what it means to be human. Now, you are about to become wiser than Socrates: "Life in an unexamined world is not worthy living either." Humans are the only species capable of enjoying the promise of culture; humans are also the only species capable of enjoying the splendid panorama of life that vitalizes this planet. You should learn environmental ethics to become a three-dimensional person (as we argue further in the next chapter). The totally urban (urbane!) life is one-dimensional. Life with nothing but artifacts is artificial. One needs experience of the urban, and the rural, and the wild. Otherwise you will be under-privileged.

Be a good citizen, and more. Be a resident on your landscape. True, you must become civilized. But equally: You don't want to live a de-natured life. Humans neither can nor ought to de-nature their planet. Without environmental ethics, we may not have a future—certainly not the one we wish, or ought to have in the next millennium. The destiny of Earth will be set within the lifetime of students taking environmental ethics today. Your future on Earth awaits.

References

Achterberg, Wouter. 1994. *Samenleving, Natuur en Duurzaamheid: Een Inleiding in de Milieufilosofie* [Society, Nature and Sustainability: An Introduction to Environmental Philosophy]. Assen, Netherlands: Van Gorcum.

Aldo Leopold Foundation. 2011. *Green Fire: Aldo Leopold and a Land Ethic for our Time.* Documentary video (www.GreenFireMovie.com). Baraboo, WI: Aldo Leopold Foundation.

Attfield, Robin. 2003. *Environmental Ethics: An Overview for the Twenty-First Century.* Cambridge, UK: Policy Press.

Attfield, Robin, and Andrew Belsey, eds. 1994. *Philosophy and the Natural Environment.* Cambridge, UK: Cambridge University Press.

Biello, David. 2010. "Lasting Menace: Gulf OilSpill Disaster Likely to Exert Environmental Harm for Decades," *Scientific American* 303(no. 1, July), pages 16, 18. Online at: http://www.scientificamerican.com/article.cfm?id=lastingmenace

Birch, C., W. Eakin, J. McDaniel, eds. 1990. *Liberating Life: Contemporary Approaches to Ecological Theology.* Maryknoll, NY: Orbis Books.

Birnbacher, Dieter. 1980. *Ökologie und Ethik.* [Ecology and Ethics]. Stuttgart, Germany: Reclam.

Blackstone, William. 1974. *Philosophy and Environmental Crisis.* Athens: University of Georgia Press.

Brown, William P. 2010. *The Seven Pillars of Creation: The Bible, Science, and the Ecology of Wonder.* New York: Oxford University Press.

Bullard, Robert D. 1994. "Environmental Justice for All: It's the Right Thing to Do," *Journal of Environmental Law and Litigation* 9:281–308.

Cable, Sherry, and Charles Cable. 1995. *Environmental Problems: Grassroots Solutions: The Politics of Grassroots Environmental Conflict.* New York: St. Martins.

California Environmental Protection Agency. 2010. "PG&E Hinkley Chromium Cleanup." Online at: http://www.swrcb.ca.gov/rwqcb6/water_issues/projects/pge/index.shtml.

Callicott, J. Baird. 1987. *Companion to A Sand County Almanac: Interpretive and Critical Essays.* Madison: University of Wisconsin Press.

Callicott, J. Baird, and Robert Frodeman, eds. 2009. *Encyclopedia of Environmental Ethics and Philosophy.* 2 volumes. Detroit, MI: Macmillan Reference, Gale, Cengage Learning.

Callicott, J. Baird, and Clare Palmer, eds. 2005. *Environmental Philosophy: Critical Concepts in the Environment.* 5 volumes. London: Routledge.

Carpenter, Philip A., and Peter C. Bishop. 2009. "The Seventh Mass Extinction: Human-caused Events Contribute to a Fatal Consequence," *Futures* 41:715–722.

Carson, Rachel. 1951. *The Sea around Us.* New York: Oxford University Press.

———. 1962. *Silent Spring.* Boston: Houghton Mifflin.

CITES, Convention on International Trade in Endangered Species of Wild Fauna and Flora. 1973. Prepared and adopted by the Plenipotentiary Conference to Conclude an International Convention on Trade in Certain Species of Wildlife, Washington, D.C., February 12–March 2, 1973, 27 U.S.T, 1088, T.I.A.S 8249.

Cobb, Jr., John B. 1972. *Is It Too Late: A Theology of Ecology.* Beverly Hills, CA: Bruce.

Cohen, Jeremy. 1989. "Be Fertile and Increase, Fill the Earth and Master It." *The Ancient and Medieval Career of a Biblical Text.* Ithaca, NY: Cornell University Press.

Crone, Timothy J., and Maya Tolstoy. 2010. "Magnitude of the 2010 of Mexico Gulf Oil Leak," *Science* 330:634.

Curry, Patrick. 2006. *Ecological Ethics: An Introduction.* Cambridge, UK: Polity Press.

Cutter, Susan L. 1995. "Race, Class and Environmental Justice," *Progress in Human Geography* 19:111–122.

Daly, Herman E., ed. 1973. *Toward a Steady State Economy.* San Francisco: W. H. Freeman.

Derr, Patrick G., and Edward M. McNamara. 2003. *Case Studies in Environmental Ethics.* Lanham, MD: Rowman and Littlefield.

DeSimone, Livio D., and Frank Popoff. 1997. *Ecoefficiency: The Business Link to Sustainable Development.* Cambridge. MA: The MIT Press.

Drenthen, Martin. 1996. "Het zwijgen van de natuur" [The silence of nature], *Filosofie & Praktijk* 17/4: 187–199.

Easterbrook, Gregg. 2006. "Finally Feeling the Heat," *New York Times,* May 24, Sec. A, p. 27. Online at: http://www.nytimes.com/2006/05/24/opinion/24easterbrook. html

Elliot, Robert, and Aaran Gare. 1983. *Environmental Philosophy St. Lucia,* Australia: University of Queensland Press.

Engel, J. Ronald. 1990. "Introduction: The Ethics of Sustainable Development." Pages 1–23 in J. Ronald Engel and Joan Gibb Engel, eds., *Ethics of Environment and Development.* London: Belhaven Press.

European Commission, Brussels, Eurobarometer. 2009. "Europeans' Attitudes Towards Global Climate Change." Online at: http://ec.europa.eu/public_opinion/archives/ebs/ebs_322_en.pdf

Fern, Richard L. 2002. *Nature, God and Humanity.* Cambridge, UK: Cambridge University Press.

Fox, Warwick. 2006. *A Theory of General Ethics: Human Relationships, Nature, and the Built Environment.* Cambridge, MA: The MIT Press.

Ghai, Dharam P., and Jessica M. Vivian. 1992. *Grassroots Environmental Action: People's Participation in Sustainable Development.* London: Routledge.

Gibson, William, ed. 2004. *Ecojustice: The Unfinished Journey.* Albany: State University of New York Press.

Gudorf, Christine E., and James E. Huchingson, 2003. *Boundaries: A Casebook in Environmental Ethics.* Washington, D.C.: Georgetown University Press.

Hawken, Paul. 2007. *Blessed Unrest: How the Largest Movement in the World Came into Being and Why No One Saw It Coming.* New York: Viking.

Heise, Ursula K. 2008. *Sense of Place and Sense of Planet.* New York: Oxford University Press.

Houghton, John. 2003. "Global Warming is Now a Weapon of Mass Destruction," *The Guardian,* 28 July, p. 14.

Hulme, Mike. 2009. *Why We Disagree about Climate Change: Understanding Controversy, Inaction and Opportunity.* Cambridge, UK: Cambridge University Press.

Intergovernmental Panel on Climate Change. 2007. *Climate Change 2007: The Physical Science Basis.* Online at http://www.ipcc.ch

International Society for Environmental Ethics (ISEE). Bibliography websites: http://iseethics. org/, http://www.cep.unt.edu/bib/; http://obet.webexone.com/

International Union for the Conservation of Nature (IUCN). 2010. *Summary Statistics, Red List of Endangered Species.* Online at: http://www.iucnredlist.org/about/summarystatistics#How_many_threatened

Jamieson, Dale, ed., 1999. *Singer and His Critics.* Oxford, UK: Blackwell.

Keller, David, Center for the Study of Ethics at Utah Valley State University. 2011. *Environmental Ethics Case Studies.* Online at: http://environmentalethics.info

Kemmis, Daniel. 1990. *Community and the Politics of Place.* Norman: University of Oklahoma Press.

Knight, Richard L., and Suzanne Riedel, eds. 2002. *Aldo Leopold and the Ecological Conscience.* Oxford , UK: Oxford University Press.

Kuhn, Thomas S. 1970. *The Structure of Scientific Revolutions,* 2nd ed. Chicago: University of Chicago Press.

LaBalme, Jenny. 1988. "Dumping on Warren County." Pages 23–30 in Bob Hall, ed., *Environmental Politics: Lessons from the Grassroots.* Durham, NC: Institute for Southern Studies.

Lear, Linda J. 1997. *Rachel Carson: Witness for Nature*. New York: Henry Holt.

Leopold, A. 1949/1968. *A Sand County Almanac*. New York: Oxford University Press.

Levine, Aldine Gordon. 1982. *Love Canal: Science, Politics, and People*. Lexington, MS: Lexington Books, D.C. Heath and Company.

Mathews, Freya. 2003. *For Love of Matter: A Contemporary Panpsychism*. Albany: State University of New York Press.

Meadows, Donella H. 1972. *The Limits to Growth: A Report for the Club of Rome's Project on the Predicament of Mankind*. New York: Universe Books.

Meine, Curt. 1988. *Aldo Leopold: His Life and Work*. Madison: University of Wisconsin Press.

MeyerAbich, Klaus Michael. 1993. *Revolution for Nature: From the Environment to the Connatural World*. Cambridge, UK: The White Horse Press. Originally in German, 1990.

Miller, Greg, 2011. "The Rise of Animal Law," *Science* 332 (1 April):28–31.

Miller, Sally M., ed. 1993. *John Muir: Life and Work*. Albuquerque: University of New Mexico Press.

Muir, John, 1901. *Our National Parks*. Boston: Houghton Mifflin.

———. 1912/1965. *The Yosemite*. Garden City, NY: Doubleday.

———. 1916. *A Thousand-Mile Walk to the Gulf*. New York: Houghton Mifflin

———. 1965. *The Story of My Boyhood and Youth*. Madison: University of Wisconsin Press.

Naess, Arne. 1973. "The Shallow and the Deep, Long-Range Ecology Movements: A Summary," *Inquiry* 16:95–100.

Nash, James A. 1991. *Loving Nature: Ecological Integrity and Christian Responsibility*. Nashville, TN: Abingdon Cokesbury.

Newton, Lisa, and Catherine K. Dillingham. 2002. *Watersheds 3: Ten Cases in Environmental Ethics*. Belmont, CA: Wadsworth/Thomson Learning.

Northcott, Michael S. 1996. *The Environment and Christian Ethics*. Cambridge, UK: Cambridge University Press.

Oreskes, Naomi. 2007. "The Scientific Consensus on Climate Change: How Do We Know We're Not Wrong?" Pages 65–99 in Joseph F. C. DiMento and Pamela Doughman, eds., 2007, *Climate Change: What It Means for Us, Our Children, and Our Grandchildren*. Cambridge, MA: The MIT Press.

Ott, Konrad. 1993. *Ökologie und Ethik: Ein Versuch praktischer Philosophie* [Ecology and Ethics: An Attempt at Practical Philosophy]. Tübingen, Germany: Attempto Verlag.

Palmer, Clare. 2003. "An Overview of Environmental Ethics." Pages 15–37 in Andrew Light and Holmes Rolston III, eds., *Environmental Ethics: An Anthology*. Malden, MA: Blackwell.

Park, Rozelia S. 1998. "An Examination of International Environmental Racism through the Lens of Transboundary Movement of Hazardous Waste," *Indiana Journal of Global Legal Studies* 5:659–709.

Passmore, John. 1974. *Man's Responsibility for Nature*. New York: Scribner.

Pellow, David Naguib. 2007. *Resisting Global Toxics: Transnational Movements for Environmental Justice*. Cambridge, MA: The MIT Press.

Pinchot, Gifford. 1973. "The Fight for Conservation." Pages 84–95 in Donald Worster, ed., *American Environmentalism: The Formative Period, 1860–1915*. New York: Wiley.

Plumwood, Val. 1993. *Feminism and the Mastery of Nature*. London: Routledge.

———. 2000. "Being Prey." Pages 128–146 in James O'Reilly, Sean O'Reilly, and Richard Sterling, eds., *The Ultimate Journey: Inspiring Stories of Living and Dying*. San Francisco: Travelers' Tales.

Preston, Christopher J. 2009. *Saving Creation: Nature and Faith in the Life of Holmes Rolston, III*. San Antonio, TX: Trinity University Press.

Regan, Tom. 1983/2004. *The Case for Animal Rights*. Berkeley: University of California Press.

———. 2005. *Empty Cages: Facing the Challenge of Animal Rights*. Lanham, MD: Rowman and Littlefield.

Rhodes, Edwardo Lao. 2003. *Environmental Justice in America*. Bloomington, IN: Indiana University Press.

Rolston, Holmes, III. 1975. "Is There an Ecological Ethic?", *Ethics: An International Journal of Social and Political Philosophy* 85:93–109.

———. 2010. "Saving Creation: Faith Shaping Environmental Policy," *Harvard Law and Policy Review* 4:121–148.

Routley, Richard..1973. "Is There a Need for a New, An Environmental Ethic?" Pages 205–210 in *Proceedings of the XVth World Congress of Philosophy*, 1. Varna, Bulgaria: Sofia.

Ruether, Rosemary R. 1992. *Gaia and God: An Ecofeminist Theology of Earth Healing*. San Francisco: HarperSanFrancisco.

Schlosberg, David, 2007. *Defining Environmental Justice: Theories, Movements, and Nature*. Oxford, UK: Oxford University Press.

Shiva, Vandana. 1988. *Staying Alive: Women, Ecology, and Development*. London: Zed Books.

Shrader-Frechette, Kristin. 2002. *Environmental Justice Creating Equality, Reclaiming Democracy*. New York: Oxford University Press.

Sideris, Lisa H., and Kathleen Dean Moore. 2008. *Rachel Carson: Legacy and Challenge*. Albany: State University of New York Press.

Singer, Peter. 1975. *Animal Liberation*. New York: Avon Books. 2nd ed., 1990. New York: New York Review Book.

Stivers, Robert L. 1976. *The Sustainable Society: Ethics and Economic Growth*. Philadelphia: Westminster.

Sylvan, Richard, and David Bennett. 1994. *The Greening of Ethics: From Human Chauvinism to Deep Green Theory*. Tucson: University of Arizona Press.

ten Have, Henk A.M.J., ed. 2006. *Environmental Ethics and International Policy*. Paris: United Nations Educational, Scientific and Cultural Organization (UNESCO).

Union of Concerned Scientists. 2007. *Smoke, Mirrors and Hot Air — How ExxonMobil Uses Big Tobacco's Tactics to Manufacture Uncertainty on Climate Science*. Online at: http://www.ucsusa.org/assets/documents/global_warming/exxon_report.pdf

United Church of Christ, 1987. *Toxic Waste and Race in the United States*. New York: United Church of Christ.

United Nations Conference on Environment and Development. 1992. Convention on Biological Diversity. Online at: http://www.cbd.int/convention/convention.shtml

United Nations World Summit. 2005. World Summit Outcome Document. Online at: http://www.who.int/hiv/universalaccess2010/worldsummit.pdf

Urbina, Ian. 2010. "At Issue in Gulf: Who Was in Charge?" *New York Times*, June 6, sec. A, p. 1.

U.S. Commission on Civil Rights, Louisiana Advisory Committee, 1993. *The Battle for Environmental Justice in Louisiana: Government, Industry, and the People*. Washington: U.S. Commission on Civil Rights.

U.S. Congress. 1972. Clean Water Act. Public Law 92-500. 86 Stat. 816.

———. 1972. Marine Mammal Protection Act. Public Law 92-522. 86 Stat. 1027.

———. 1973. Endangered Species Act of 1973. Public Law 93205. 87 Stat. 884.

———. 1964. Wilderness Act. Public Law 88-577. 78 Stat. 891.

———. 1986. Emergency Planning and Community Right-to-Know Act. Public Law 99-499. 100 Stat. 1733.

U.S. Environmental Protection Agency. 1992. *Environmental Equity: Reducing Risk for All Communities*. 2 vols. Washington, D.C.: Environmental Protection Agency.

———. 2010. "Environmental Justice." Online at: http://www.epa.gov/environmentaljustice/

U.S. General Accounting Office (USGASO). 1983. *Siting of Hazardous Waste Landfills and Their Correlation with Racial and Economic Status of Surrounding Communities*. Washington, D.C.: General Accounting Office.

Warren, Karen J. 1990. "The Power and Promise of Ecological Feminism," *Environmental Ethics* 12:125–146.

———. 2000. *Ecofeminist Philosophy: A Western Perspective on What It Is and Why It Matters*. Lanham. MD: Rowman and Littlefield.

Weisman, Jonathan, and Guy Chazan. 2010. "BP Agrees to $20 Billion Fund," *Wall Street Journal*, June 17, p. A10.

White, Jr., Lynn. 1967. "The Historical Roots of Our Ecological Crisis," *Science,* 155:1203–1207.

Wilson, Edward O. 2000. "Vanishing Before Our Eyes," *Time,* vol. 255, April 26, pages 28–31, 34.

———. 2002. *The Future of Life.* New York: Alfred A. Knopf

Wolfe, Linnie Marsh, ed. 1938. *John of the Mountains: The Unpublished Journals of John Muir.* Boston: Houghton-Mifflin.

Worster, Donald. 2008. *A Passion for Nature: The Life of John Muir.* New York: Oxford University Press.

Zeller, Jr., Tom, 2010. "Federal Officials Say They Vastly Underestimated Rate of Oil Flow into Gulf." *New York Times,* May 28, sec. A, p. 15.

Zweers, Wim, 2000. *Participating with Nature: Outline for an Ecologization of our World View.* Utrecht, The Netherlands: International Books. English edition of a work first published in Dutch in 1995.

2

HUMANS

People on their Landscapes

Environmental ethics starts with human concerns for a decent, safe, supporting environment, and some think this shapes the ethics from start to finish. Environmental quality is necessary for quality of human life. Humans dramatically rebuild their environments; still, their lives, even when filled with artifacts, are lived in a natural ecology where resources—soil, air, water, photosynthesis, climate—are matters of life and death. Culture and nature have entwined destinies, similar to the way minds are inseparable from bodies. So, ethics needs to be applied to the environment.

As philosophers frequently model this, people arrange a society where they and the others with whom they live do not (or ought not) lie, steal, or kill. This is right, and one reason it is right is that people must cooperate to survive; and the more they reliably cooperate the more they flourish. One way of envisioning this is the so called "original position," where one imagines setting up the political, economic, and social order in which one lives. One has to figure out what is best for any person on average, oblivious to the specific circumstances of one's time and place. One ought to support such a society; this may be called a "social contract." This is where a sense of universality, or at least pancultural-ism, in morality has a plausible rational basis.

A great deal of the work of environmental ethics can be done from within such a best-for-society account. A sustainable, or healthy, or quality environment is desired by all for the benefits this brings to the human cultures residing on landscapes. Most environmental policy is of this kind. Humans are helped or hurt by the condition of their environment, and that there ought to be some ethic concerning the environment can be doubted only by those who believe in no ethics at all. Ethics will have a concern for what humans have at stake there—benefits, costs, and their just distribution, risks, pollution levels, rights and torts, environmental sustainability and quality, the interests of future generations.

1. Environmental Health: Skin In, Skin Out

Environmental ethics will prove much more comprehensive than the simple maxim: Don't foul your nest. But probably the easiest kind of environmental concern to motivate persons is environmental health. Humans desire to be healthy; we have a moral obligation to promote health. Further, health is something we can be scientific about—how many parts per million in the drinking water is dangerous. So, if we suspect that business—industry, agribusiness, commerce, medicine—is releasing something toxic into the environment, we shout a warning and that gets the attention of everybody—consumers, legislators, corporate executives. Recall Love Canal, Hanford, or Cancer Alley from Chapter 1. Health is not simply a matter of biology from the skin-in, but also from the skin-out—because what is outside gets inside. Environmental health is equally as important as bodily health. It is hard to live healthy lives in a sick environment.

Here some will notice that ecology is strikingly like medical science. Both are therapeutic sciences. Ecologists are responsible for environmental health, which is really another form of public health. In 2006 more than 34 million metric tons of chemical substances were produced in, or imported into, the United States every day. These substances ultimately enter Earth's environment; hundreds of these chemicals are routinely detected in people and ecosystems worldwide (Schwartzman and Wilson, 2009). In the next quarter century such production is projected to double.

Many hazardous chemicals have long lifetimes; they migrate from the sites where they are deposited as waste; they build up in food chains. We realized this with discoveries about the unintended consequences of the pesticide DDT—killing songbirds by thinning egg shells, and found everywhere, even in polar icecaps—Rachel Carson's "silent spring." In places, human breast milk has become contaminated at levels that exceed the levels permitted in dairy milk sold in stores. Pregnant women are regularly warned not to eat fish caught in lakes and rivers. Pollution that leaks into groundwater is often impossible to remove. Pollution released into the air moves around the globe. One problem here is that, since these chemicals come from many sources, move around, and long persist, it is hard to pinpoint who is responsible, especially with the so-called non-point sources of pollution.

Typically, in decades past a chemical was presumed innocent until proved guilty. But increasingly now it seems that especially the new more exotic (more unnatural) chemicals ought to be presumed guilty until proven innocent. Longstanding public policies governing chemical design, production, and use need deep restructuring in the light of new science on the health and environmental effects of anthropogenic chemicals. Such reforms are essential to safeguard ecosystem integrity, human health, and economic sustainability. The U.S. Congress has passed numerous laws to address these issues—notably the 1976 Toxic Substances Control Act, the 1977 Clean Water Act, the 1977 Clean Air Act, the 1980 Comprehensive Environmental Response, Compensation, and Liability Act (CERCLA, with its Superfund).

Those laws from several decades back accomplished much, but left many questions unaddressed. Also, once business became aware of increasing legislation enforcing compliance, they became more effective in lobbying against further legislation. Where the legislation might provide for compensation by a business to those harmed, companies have been especially effective with their counter-arguments: that such awards by courts are arbitrary, oblivious to the multiple sources of pollution, do nothing to remove or limit further pollution, or would bankrupt the industry. Unless there are low limits to liability, and a high burden of proof laid on the allegedly harmed, the threat of compensation will result in cancellation of their insurance, and so on. Dumping pollutants into the air, water, and soil meanwhile still continues, more or less of it depending on how much one can get past current regulations.

The ethical issues here are multiple, typically involving who gets the benefits and who bears the costs—equity and consent issues. There is spillover from rich to poor. The risks may be voluntary or involuntary. Workers may be advised of their higher risks—but if they are financially strapped do they assume these risks voluntarily? The victims who live downwater or downwind never gave any free, informed consent and usually have no means of proving their damages or asserting their rights. The wealthy (some of whom are producing the toxics, all of whom are enjoying benefits) can afford to protect themselves. The poor cannot. Such concerns are those of "environmental justice," and we recall the power of that movement in Chapter 1. Nevertheless, typically the rich can say NIMBY (not in my backyard); the poor cannot.

The ill-health effects of pollution often show up first in women, especially pregnant women, and in children. The ill effects may never show up in most of the population, only in a segment of the population that is more susceptible. With the long-lived pollutants the benefits may be enjoyed at present, the suffering borne by future generations. In fact, the toxic effects of many of these pollutants are much longer-lived than the human institutions set up to deal with them. Some nuclear wastes remain hazardous for longer than the history of known civilization, but the government agency that regulates the storage of nuclear wastes may shift policies after the next election.

We said above that often the rich can protect themselves, while the poor cannot. But, as usual, things get more complex. While the developed countries can sometimes insulate themselves from unhealthy conditions in developing countries, this is not always the case. Developed countries, which may have thought themselves protected with their high technologies and advanced medical systems, discover they are still linked with health, human and animal, in the developing world, even in wild nature, and vulnerable to disruptions there, to which they may also be contributing.

Humans do catch some diseases from wild animals. Viruses that originated in animals and spread to humans have caused several of the most significant recently emerging diseases (HIV/AIDS, SARS, and Influenza AH1N1, or Swine Flu). Here one might first say that nature is at fault. Certainly the disease organisms originated in wild nature. When we humans move such organisms into our global capitalist economies, radically altering their habitats from anything resembling an ecosystem, we might first suppose that they will soon wither and die. Many do. But, surprisingly, we are now finding that we can also invite an unprecedented explosion, a pandemic. Humans now provide transportation by jet plane or ocean freighter halfway around the globe in a few hours or days. Often the spread of a pandemic can be traced from airline hub to airline hub. Since we create the context in which the pandemic appears, one can as well say that we humans create the disease as that the disease originates in wild nature.

HIV/AIDS, before jumping to humans, existed in primate populations in Africa, with which it had co-evolved. It might never have emerged as pandemic if it were not for the social disruptions in post-colonial and sub-Saharan Africa, with the bush-meat trade, the movement of rural populations to large and crowded cities, with disrupted family structures promoting promiscuity and prostitution, all of which facilitate HIV transmission (Morens, Folkers, and Fauci, 2004).

The 1998–1999 Malaysian Nipah virus epidemic emerged when pigs (raised for international trade) were crammed together in pens located in or near orchards. The orchards attracted fruit bats whose normal habitats had been disrupted by deforestation; their droppings contained the as yet unknown paramyxovirus and infected the pigs. The overcrowding led to explosive transmission rates and to infections in pig handlers. So, a virus that was once not disruptively epidemic became so because of human disruptions of natural habitats of bats and overcrowding of pigs, driven by global commercial interests. The Malaysian government culled over one million pigs (Morens et al., 2004; Dobson, 2005).

The 1918 flu epidemic that killed forty million people is known to have originated in birds (Abbott and Pearson, 2004). Such contagions escalate with crowding, both of animals and of people. Pathenogenic microbes can evolve rapidly and are quite versatile. In their former ecologies, there had been time for co-evolution between parasite and host, often producing non-pathological co-existence and not infrequently symbiotic relations (Wilson, 2005). Even in humans, most internal microfauna is harmless; indeed, most of it seems to be useful. The body's internal microbes, by recent accounts, should be thought of as much as partners as parasites (Pennisi, 2010). But exposure to novel pathogens can prove quite hazardous. Globalism sets up atypical ecological conditions favorable for invasives and pathogens. The result is human disease but the inclusive framework is social upset of natural ecologies.

One of the classical proverbs of ecologists is that everything is connected to everything else. Though something of an overstatement, this proverb is true often enough to bear recalling. Increasingly, for better or for worse, it is proving true with links between ecological and human health, links that tie local to global events, in both nature and culture. The larger framework, suggest two veterinarians at the Wildlife Conservation Society, requires thinking holistically "based on the understanding that there is only one world—and only one health" (Karesh and Cook, 2005, p. 50; see also Rolston, 2005). That links conservation concerns and medical concerns, in what is now called "conservation medicine" (Aguire et al., 2002). "Health effects ripple throughout the web of life. Health connects all species" (Tabor, 2002, p. 9). Human health requires thinking in ecological contexts, increasingly in more global ones. This further suggests more inclusive ethical concerns: global, international, and interspecific, beyond the immediate protection of human individuals from disease. That thought, "one world, one health," moves us toward thinking of healthy sustainable development, which, we again find, mixes human well being with the health of ecosystems.

2. Sustainable Development

One of the powerful movements in the environmental turn, we said in Chapter 1, has been the turn to sustainable development, growing out of the United Nations Conference on Environment and Development (UNCED, 1992). Advocates will now argue that the basic principle of people living on landscapes is sustainability. Proponents argue that sustainable development is useful just because it is a wide angle lens. Yes, you must seek "development that meets the needs of the present without compromising the ability of future generations to meet their own needs," as we already heard the United Nations Commission say. But the specifics are unspecified, giving peoples and nations the freedom and responsibility of self-development (although the UN has further suggested some indicators of sustainable development; United Nations DESA, 2007). This is an orienting concept that is at once directed and encompassing, a coalition-level policy that sets aspirations, thresholds, and allows pluralist strategies for their accomplishment. Work your development out however you wish—provided only that it is sustainable now and in the future.

Critics reply that sustainable development is proving to be an umbrella concept so diffuse that it requires little but superficial agreement, bringing a constant illusion of consensus, glossing over deeper problems with a rhetorically engaging word. The French philosopher Luc Ferry complains: "I know that this term is obligatory, but I find it also absurd, or rather so vague that it says nothing." The term is trivial by a proof of contradiction: "who would like to be a proponent of an 'unsustainable development'! Of course no one!... The term is more charming than meaningful" (2007, p. 76). Sustainable development can be twisted to fit any ongoing worldview; the term risks being co-opted by individuals and institutions that really wish to perpetuate the expansionist model, only now pretending that they are doing what they and their successors can do forever.

Seen at more depth, there are two ways of thinking about sustainability, complements yet opposites. Economy can be prioritized, the usual case, and anything can be done to the environment, so long as the continuing development of the economy is not jeopardized thereby. The environment is kept in orbit with economics at the center. One ought to develop (since that increases wealth and social welfare), and the environment will constrain that development if and only if a degrading environment might undermine ongoing development. The underlying conviction is that the trajectory of the industrial, technological, commercial world is generally right—only the developers in their enthusiasm have hitherto failed to recognize environmental constraints.

If economics is the driver, we will seek maximum harvests, using pesticides and herbicides on land, a bioindustrial model, pushing for bigger and more efficient agriculture, so long as this is sustainable. This will push to the limits the environmental constraints of dangerous pesticide and herbicide levels on land and in water, surface and ground water, favoring monocultures, typically of annuals, inviting soil erosion and invasive species. The model is extractive, commodification of the land. Land and resources are "natural capital." The result of this model has been all those pollutants about which we were worrying, so we will have to be much more careful. But that is no reason to abandon the model, only reason to make it sustainable. What we must push for, according to the Royal Society of London (2009), the world's oldest scientific society, is "sustainable intensification" of reaping the benefits of exploiting the Earth.

In a second way of thinking about sustainability, the environment is prioritized. A "sustainable biosphere" model demands a baseline quality of environment. The economy must be worked out "within" such a policy for environmental quality objectives (clean air, water, stable agricultural soils, attractive residential landscapes, forests, mountains, rivers, rural lands, parks, wildlands, wildlife, renewable resources). Winds blow, rains fall, rivers flow, the sun shines, photosynthesis takes place, carbon recycles all over the landscape.

These process have to be sustained. The economy must be kept within an environmental orbit. One ought to conserve nature, the ground-matrix of life. Development is desired, but even more, society must learn to live within the carrying capacity of its landscapes. The model is land as community.

"Sustainable" is an economic but also an environmental term. The fundamental flaw in "sustainable development" is that it typically sees the Earth only as resource. What if the current trajectory of the industrial, technological, commercial world is generally wrong, because it will inevitably overshoot? The economic juggernaut is coupled with a political juggernaut to push for development, growth, more and more. That is always going to press the environment to a breaking point. But the environment is not some undesirable, unavoidable set of constraints. Rather, nature is the matrix of multiple values; many, even most of them are not counted in economic transactions. In a more inclusive accounting of what we wish to sustain, nature provides numerous other values (aesthetic experiences, biodiversity, sense of place and perspective), and these are getting left out. The *Millennium Ecosystem Assessment* (2005) explores this in great detail.

Yes, but economics is the overall governing driver; there is no escaping this—so economists will say. Washington and Wall Street call the shots. Decisions there are what make the world go round. But without air to breathe and water to drink, both Washington and Wall Street would soon be shut down. Every culture still depends on natural support systems. In fact, decisions based on the "command and control" mentality of Washington and Wall Street are more part of the problem than part of the answer.

Granted, the economists may continue. But development transcends Wall Street and Washington. Development is a perennial human drive. For all of human history, we have been pushing back limits. Especially in the West, we have lived with a deep-seated belief that life will get better, that one should hope for abundance, and work toward obtaining it. Economists call such behavior "rational"; humans will maximize their capacity to exploit their resources. What people want is prosperity, to be more and more prosperous. Moral persons will also maximize human satisfactions, at least those that support the good life, which must not just include food, health, clothing, and shelter, but an abundance, more and more goods and services that people want. Such growth is always desirable. There can and ought to be perpetual gains to human material well-being.

Here philosophers may enter the dialogue to claim that neither economists nor ecologists have any final competence in evaluating whether to give priority to economic development or to conserving nature. A people on a landscape will have to make value judgments about how much original nature they have, or want, or wish to restore, and how much culturally modified nature they want, and whether it should be culturally modified this way or that. Ecologists may be able to tell us what our options are, what will work and what will not, what is the minimum baseline health of landscapes. But there is nothing in ecology per se that gives ecologists any authority or skills at making these further social decisions. Science does not enable us to choose between diverse options, all of which are technologically possible.

Philosophers will go on to claim that neither do economists have any moral insight built into their economic science. Economists have no special competence in evaluating what rebuilding of nature a culture desires, or how far the integrity of wild nature should be sacrificed to achieve this. Economists, like the ecologists, may help tell us what our options are, what will work and what will not. But there is nothing in economics per se that gives economists any authority or skills at making these further social decisions. Economics does not enable us to choose between diverse options, all of which are economically possible. In fact, because economists typically value economic growth uncritically, they may be ill-suited to make such choices.

After four centuries during which science and economics have progressively illuminated us about how we can transform nature into the goods we want, the value questions are as sharp and as painful as ever. Both science and economics can, and often do, serve noble interests. Both science and economics can, and often do, become self-serving, a means of perpetuating injustice, of violating human rights, of making war, of degrading the environment. We will return to these issues, global scale, in Chapter 7, examining global capitalism.

We must have an ethics that asks about how to live justly. But the ethicists may soon find that, as did the ecologists and economists, they too have their problems: caring for persons versus caring for nature. In the West we have built development into our concept of human rights: a right to self-development, to self-realization. Today, such an egalitarian ethic scales everybody up and drives an unsustainable world. When everybody seeks their own good, there is escalating consumption. But equally, if one seeks justice and charity, when everybody seeks everybody else's good, there is, again, escalating consumption.

Is there any hope? People are attracted to appeals to a better life, to quality of life; and some progress is possible using an appeal to still more enlightened self-interest. Or perhaps better: to a more inclusive and comprehensive concept of human welfare. That will get us environmental health, sustainable development, even a realization that sustainable development must suppose a supporting, underlying bioregion.

Develop! Develop! Develop! Intensify! Intensify! Intensify! Maximize endless development? Is the future we want maximized development for human satisfaction? Perhaps when humans become more philosophical about their world, we will in the midst of our development also seek to sustain life on this wonderland planet. People and their Earth have entwined destinies; that past truth continues in the present, and will remain a pivotal concern in the new millennium—demanding an inclusive environmental ethics.

3. Domesticated Landscapes: "Man the Measure"

People work to domesticate their landscapes. Were we not saying that for thousands of years, people have been pushing back limits? Peoples have sought to manage their landscapes for millennia, with more or less success. They have grazed and plowed fields, cleared forests, planted crops, domesticated animals, built roads, canals, dams. Humans deliberately and extensively rebuild the spontaneous natural environment and make the rural and urban environments in which they reside. "Domesticated nature in its simplest form means nature exploited and controlled" (Karieva et al., 2007). Meanwhile, we do care about the quality of our life in these hybrids of nature and culture.

"Man is the measure of things," said Protagoras, an ancient philosopher (recalled in Plato, *Theaetetus*, 152). When we measure landscapes, we find that humans have a huge "ecological footprint." Human-dominated ecosystems now cover more of Earth's land surface than do wild ecosystems (McCloskey and Spalding, 1989; Foley et al., 2005). Nature now bears the marks of human influence more widely than ever before. Humans now consume from 30 to 40% of all terrestrial net primary production (Vitousek et al., 1986; Imhoff et al., 2004). Humans move more earth and produce more reactive nitrogen than all other terrestrial processes combined (Galloway, 2004). Human agriculture, construction, and mining move more earth than do the natural processes of rock uplift and erosion (Wilkinson and McElroy, 2007). These human activities alter the composition of the atmosphere, the soil, levels of biodiversity, energy flows within food webs, and threaten important ecosystem services. Perhaps a good way to sum this up is to look at a world map darkened by human influence (see Figure 2.1), the darker the more dominant the human influence (even the darkest areas are still in a one-third to three-quarters range).

The claim may now be that environmental ethics is mostly about intelligently domesticating landscapes (Fox, 2006). Nature as it once was, wild nature as it may continue, is not the main focus. Most of life for most people takes place on landscapes that are a hybrid tapestry of nature and culture, rural, agricultural, pastoral landscapes. More than 80% of all people live in densely populated rural, village, and urban landscapes, what may be called "anthropogenic biomes" (Ellis and Ramankutty, 2008). "Nature in itself" is diverse and often ambiguous; humans adapt wild landscapes to their liking. Nature now is inextricably entwined with human projects and self-understandings. For socially (re-)constructed, anthropogenic nature we need an adequate ethical perspective lest our practices go astray.

Wendell Berry raises this concern:

> The moral landscape of the conservation movement has tended to be a landscape of extremes.... On the one hand we have the unspoiled wilderness, and on the other hand we have scenes of utter devastation—strip mines, clearcuts, industrially polluted wastelands, and so on. We wish,

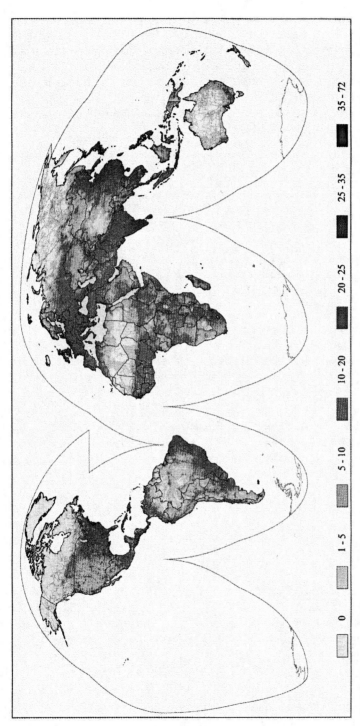

FIGURE 2.1 Human influence and wild nature. The darker an area, the more human influence, ranging from none (white, 0%), through shades of gray, to more intense (73%). (Sanderson et al., 2002)

0   1 - 5   5 - 10   10 - 20   20 - 25   25 - 35   35 - 72

say the conservationists, to have more of the one, and less of the other. To which, of course, one must say amen. But it must be a qualified amen, for the conservationists' program has been embarrassingly incomplete. Its picture of the world as either deserted landscape or desertified landscape has misrepresented both the world and humanity. If we are to have an accurate picture of the world, even in its present diseased condition, we must interpose between the unused landscape and the misused landscape a landscape that humans have used well.

(1995. p. 64)

According to a widely held account (descending from the philosopher John Locke), value arises when nature is mixed with human "labor" or "industry," with the human labor adding most of the value. A person finds little food or shelter hiking through a forest; a farmer cuts down the trees, builds a house with the wood, and plants a vegetable garden, which must be tended, else there will be mostly weeds. Raw petroleum is of little use, until refined into gasoline suitable for automobiles. A revealing word here is "resource." Where there is a natural "source" that has been or can be "re-directed" into channels of human interest and preference, nature is redone, "re-sourced," made over into an artifact that we can use. To use a more philosophical word, nature is "transformed," its form is transmuted into a more desirable humanized form. To use a scientific-engineering word, human values are "synthetic." Or if you prefer a biological word, human values and natural values are "symbiotic." If nature means absolutely pristine nature, totally unaffected by human activities, past or present, there is relatively little remaining on Earth. If culture means totally culturally de-natured, re-constructed, civilized with no dependence on natural systems, there is none of that on Earth either. What is all over the landscapes is nature linked with human identity. Environmental ethics is as social as it is natural.

So there is a synthesis of humans and nature, humans hoping to live well on their Earth. Still: "Human beings are at the centre of concerns…" So, the *Rio Declaration* begins, formulated at the United Nations Conference on Environment and Development (UNCED), and signed by almost every nation on Earth (UNCED, 1992). This document was once to be called the *Earth Charter*, but the developing nations were more interested in asserting their rights to develop, and getting more aid from the North to the South, and only secondarily in saving the Earth. The Rio claim is, in many respects, quite true. The human species is causing all the concern. Environmental problems are people problems, not gorilla or sequoia problems. The problem is to get people into "a healthy and productive life in harmony with nature" (UNCED, 1992).

An anthropocentric ethics claims that people are both the subject and the object of ethics. Humans can have no duties to rocks, rivers, nor to wildflowers or ecosystems, and almost none to birds or bears. Humans have serious duties only to each other. Anthropocentrists may wish to save various natural things—landscapes, mountains, rivers, wildlife—for the benefits they bring. But, they say, the environment is the wrong kind of primary target for an ethic. Nature is a means, not an end in itself. "Man is the measure of things," since Protagoras, has been setting the tone of philosophy, and this is still the proper measure in environmental ethics—at least by this account.

Environmental ethics, by this account, is sometimes founded on what we can call a human right to nature. The World Commission on Environment and Development claims: "All human beings have the fundamental right to an environment adequate for their health and well-being" (1987, p. 9). This includes the basic natural givens—air, soil, water, functioning ecosystems, hydrologic cycles, and so on. These could previously be taken for granted. But now the right must be made explicit and defended. Note that this is not any claim against or for nature itself; rather it is a claim made against other humans who might deprive some humans of such nature. But also note that this might still support the argument that humans need a sustainable biosphere that underlies any sustainable development.

Wilfred Beckerman and Joanna Pasek put it this way:

> The most important bequest we can make to posterity is to bequeath a decent society characterized by greater respect for human rights than is the case today. Furthermore, while this by no means excludes a concern for environmental developments—particularly those that many people believe might seriously threaten future living standards—policies to deal with these developments must never be at the expense of the poorest people alive today. One could not be proud of policies that may preserve the environment for future generations if the costs of doing so are borne mainly by the poorest members of the present generation.
>
> (2001, p. vi)

No one wishes to argue that the poorest should bear the highest of these costs, while the rich gain the benefits. We will return to issues of global environmental justice in Chapter 7. Nobody is proud of a conservation ethic that says: the rich should win, the poor lose. But what do we make of the claim that the poor (as well as the rich) have a right to exploit their environment, or at least to have their needs met, even if this destroys wildlife reserves? Look at how this plays out with World Health Organization policy:

> Priority given to human health raises an ethical dilemma if "health for all" conflicts with protecting the environment.... Priority to ensuring human survival is taken as a first-order principle. Respect for nature and control of environmental degradation is a second-order principle, which must be observed unless it conflicts with the first-order principle of meeting survival needs.
>
> (World Health Organization, Commission on Health and Environment, 1992, p. 4)

On this policy we measure people first, environment second. We measure people in healthy environments, but people always come first. That seems quite humane. But in India this policy certainly means no tigers. In Africa it means no rhinos. Both will only remain in Western zoos. To *preserve*, even to *conserve*, is going to mean to *reserve*. If there are biodiversity reserves, with humans on site or nearby, humans must limit their activities. Else there will always be some hungry persons, who would diminish the reserve. The continued existence in the wild of most of Earth's charismatic endangered species depends on some six hundred major reserves for wildlife in some eighty countries (Riley and Riley, 2005). If these are not policed, the animals will not be there.

Man is, and ought to be, the measure of things? Yes, humans are the only evaluators who can deliberate about what they ought to do conserving nature. When humans do this, they must set up the scales; and humans are the "measurers of things." But do we conclude that all we measure is what people have at stake on their landscapes? Cannot other species display values of which we ought to take some measure? Animals, organisms, species, ecosystems, Earth cannot teach us how to do this evaluating. But they can embody what it is that is to be valued. The valuational scales we construct do not constitute the value, any more than the scientific scales we erect create what we thereby measure. Humans are not so much lighting up value in a merely potentially valuable world, as they are psychologically joining ongoing planetary natural history in which there is value wherever there is positive creativity.

4. Anthropocene Epoch: Managed Earth and End of Nature?

By some accounts, we live now at a change of epochs, entering a new geological period: the Anthropocene (Crutzen, 2006; Zalasiewicz et al., 2010). Humans are now the most important geomorphic agent on the planet's surface (Wilkinson and McElroy 2007). "The decisions we and our children make are going to have much more influence over the shape of evolution in the foreseeable future than physical events" (Andrew Knoll, quoted in Zimmer, 2009). We are seeing "the end of nature" (McKibben, 1989; Wapner, 2010). For some that is cause for congratulation. Until now, the technosphere was contained within the biosphere; henceforth the biosphere will be contained within the technosphere. Evolutionary history has been going on for billions of years, while cultural history is only about a hundred thousand years old. But certainly from here onward, high-technology culture increasingly determines what natural history shall continue. Humans will manage the planet. A *Scientific American* special issue, *Managing Planet Earth*, claims that the two central questions today are: "What kind of planet do we want? What kind of planet can we get?" (Clark, 1989).

Figuring this out, many say, we will need adaptive management (Holling, 1980; Lee, 1993; Norton, 2005). Scientists turning to environmental policy often advocate ecosystem management. This promises to combine what eco-systems are, scientifically, with how we humans wish to employ them to serve our interests. This appeals alike to scientists, who see the need for understanding ecosystems objectively, and to applied technologists, also to landscape archi-tects and environmental engineers, who see nature as re-designed home, and to developers who like the idea of management. This seems balanced to politicians and environmental policy makers, since the combined ecosystem/management principle promises to operate at system-wide levels, presumably to manage for indefinite sustainability, alike of ecosystems and their outputs for human benefit. We examine ecosystem management in more detail in Chapter 6.

Those in the Judeo-Christian tradition, also desiring benefits for people, note that the secular word "manage" is a stand-in for the earlier theological word "steward," connecting with biblical "dominion" as caring for a good Earth. We have already heard (in Chapter 1) that scientists and theologians have disputed whether there is a commendable sense of human dominion that sees humans as trustees of Earth. They dislike thinking of humans as "earth commanders," but may favor thinking of peoples living on promised lands, on landscapes which they treasure and for which they care (and manage).

Those promoting adaptive environmental management are often leery about too much "command and control" from high-level government agencies. They may not be all that happy with "cost-benefit" analyses, worried that such a frame-work forces into monetary values what are more comprehensive kinds of ecosys-tem services that do not readily translate into market values. Decision makers, managers, need more flexibility in considering complex and often ambiguous, often shifting values. They need to be not so much principled (one ought always do x) as pragmatic about tradeoffs (a consensus about needing cleaner rivers), ones that move in desired directions (from fishable, to swimmable, to drink-able rivers). These directions are set by an ongoing dialogue between stakehold-ers negotiating their interests in a participatory community, a parliament where each advocacy group pushes its own agenda always realizing and respecting the interests of the whole—the whole human community at least, recognizing the feedback loops between human interests and ecosystem services.

Although adaptive and communitarian, this is still aggressive human man-agement. The root of "manage" is the Latin "manus," hand. Humans will handle the place. No one wishes to oppose intelligent management. Every-one wants to be "adaptive" (especially biologists, who want humans too to be adapted fits in their environments). But ought humans to place themselves at the center, claiming management of the whole in their human self-interest? This can even mean that *Homo sapiens* is the professional manager of an other-wise valueless world. The managers may call this "geoengineering." Is our only relationship to nature one of engineering it for the better? Perhaps what is as much to be managed is the human earth-eating, managerial mentality that has caused the environmental crisis in the first place.

On the larger planetary scales it is better to build our cultures in intelligent harmony with the way the world is already built, rather than take control and rebuild this promising planet by ourselves and for ourselves. Managing the planet for our benefit is not the best paradigm; it is a half truth which, when taken for the whole, becomes dangerous and self-defeating. "Hands" (the root of "manage," again) are also for holding in loving care. What kind of planet ought we humans wish to have? One we resourcefully manage for our benefits? Or one we hold in loving care? Yes. Manage. But what do you manage for? Will these managers produce either sustainable development or a sustainable biosphere? So far the "managers" seem mostly to have produced an environmental crisis—managing for escalating consumption, managing to make the rich richer, managing maximally to exploit natural resources.

American Indians had been on the North American continent 15,000 years, but with coming of the Europeans in 1492 a disruption was imminent. We are living at another of the ruptures of history, worried whether powerful European-Western civilization is self-destructing and, again, triggering disruptions around the globe. Earth is now in a post-evolutionary phase. Culture, pervasive on Earth, and increasingly technological, is the principal determinant of Earth's future, more than nature. The next millennium is the first of the Anthropocene. The native Americans were at a hinge point in their history five hundred years ago. We today are at a hinge point of in our history.

At this hinge point, do we want the future of Earth to turn entirely on us humans? Do we want "nature" to end? Perhaps we are post-evolutionary, but do we wish to be post-ecological? What kind of planet do we want? What kind of planet can we get? Maybe we also ought to ask: What kind of planet do we have? What kind of planet ought we to want? Maybe we ought to develop our capacities for gratitude, wonder, respect, and restraint. Maybe we live on a wonderland Earth that we ought to celebrate as much as to develop.

Environmental ethics ought to seek some complementarity. The world map of human influence that we considered above needs a theoretical ethical-policy model. Think of an ellipse with its twin foci (see Figure 2.2). Some events are generated under the control of one focus, *culture*; such events are in the *political* zone, where "polis" (town) marks those achievements in arts, industry, technology where the contributions of spontaneous nature are no longer evident in the criteria of evaluation. At the other end of the ellipse, a *wild* region of events is generated under the focus of spontaneous *nature*. These events take place in the absence of humans; they are what they are in themselves—wildflowers, loons calling, or a storm at sea. Although humans come to understand such events through the mediation of their cultures, they are evaluating events generated under the natural focus of the ellipse.

A domain of *hybrid* or *synthetic* events is generated under the simultaneous control of both foci, a resultant of integrated influences from nature and culture, under the sway variously of more or less of each. "Symbiosis" is a parallel

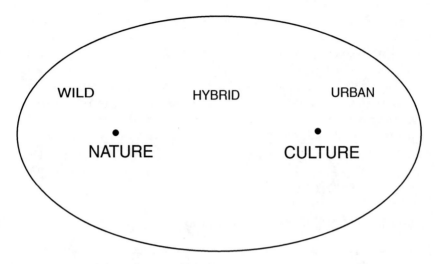

FIGURE 2.2 Ellipse—nature and culture

biological word. In the symbiosis zone, we have both, but we do not forget there remain event-zones in which the principal determinant is culture, and other zones in which the principal determinant remains spontaneous nature. We do not want the ellipse to collapse into a circle. We may be entering the Anthropocene era; we ought to choose not to enter the Anthropocentric era.

Nature as it once was, nature as an end in itself, is no longer the whole story. Nature as contrasted with culture is not the whole story either. An environmental ethic is not just about wildlands, but about humans at home on their landscapes, humans in their culture residing also in nature. This will involve resource use, sustainable development, managed landscapes, the urban and rural environments. Further, environmental ethicists, now and in the future, can and ought sometimes wish nature as an end in itself, a sustainable biosphere. That will prove an increasing challenge.

An additional paradox: When we face the decision whether to be apart from or to be a part of nature, our difference is revealed. We have to choose either the nature of our apartness, or the nature of our partness. In the defense of life on Earth since time immemorial, organisms have set up territorial boundaries. They defend their places, their resources. Else they cannot survive and reproduce. Humans can and ought to do this too. But now there is something new, never seen on Earth before during its billions of years of evolving species. Humans have begun to set conservation of the biodiversity on Earth as a moral and social goal. We set up boundaries (in biodiversity reserves, wilderness areas, national parks); and we set ourselves apart by consciously setting apart of bounded areas for others. Part of the planet is governed by culture; we also decide to set aside part to be governed by nature.

Roger DiSilvestro exclaims: "This is something truly new under the sun, and every protected wild place is a monument to humanity's uniqueness.... We not only *can* do, but we can choose *not to do*. Thus, what is unique about the boundaries we place around parks and other sanctuaries is that these boundaries are created to protect a region from our own actions.... No longer can we think of ourselves as masters of the natural world. Rather, we are partners with it" (1993, pp. xiv–xv). In, with, and under the Anthropocene, let there always be this unmanaged wild nature. Here (again, as concluded in Chapter 1) is the answer to the would-be planetary managers questions about what kind of life we want on what kind of planet: *We do not want a de-natured life on a de-natured planet. That would rupture history.*

5. Urban, Rural, Wild—Three-Dimensional Persons

Aristotle said that humans are by nature "political animals" (Greek *polis*, town, Aristotle, *Politics*, 1,2). We live in towns. Cultures shape our identities. He was right. Proof of that is your being in college and reading this book. But towns are not our only environment. Although our cities have grown enormously, worldwide still most persons live in rural environments, perhaps in villages with their farms nearby (as we earlier heard). In the United States in 1850 less than 20% of Americans lived in towns and cities. Today, resulting from our development, more than 80% are urban.

That brings a threat of being place-less, rather like sitting in front of a television, which takes you virtually everywhere in momentary flashes, and actually nowhere, or being in "digital space" on a computer. The jet set are in the air as much as on the ground, and on the ground their airports are all the same. There is little sense of place on an assembly line in a factory, in a research center, or at a business conference, or even in a university class, reading a textbook on physics, or ethics. Children stay glued to TV, play computer games, suffering from "nature deficit disorder." "The last child in the woods" is gone (Louv, 2005). Scientific studies show that adults who take walks for exercise and restoration get more benefits when they walk in natural areas rather than in town (Berman, Jonides, and Kaplan, 2008). These urban people today do have more mobility than in previous centuries, with opportunities to visit the rural and the wild.

The urban still requires the support of a rural environment for its food supply, so both are in our future indefinitely. But this is more than just vacations in parks and a reliable supply of wheat from the plains. People have a sense of place. Americans love the their landscapes: the Shenandoah Valley, the Chesapeake Bay, Cape Cod, the Great Lakes, the Ohio rivers, the Sierras, the Adirondacks, the desert Southwest, the Pacific Northwest, the Rocky Mountains (Rolston, 2008). Oklahomans sing: "We know we belong to the land, and the land we belong to is grand!" (Richard Rodgers and Oscar Hammerstein, *Oklahoma!*). Montana takes its name from its mountains. West Virginia is the "mountain mamma"—and her offspring hate to see their mountaintops blown away.

Yearning for a sense of place is a perennial human longing, of belonging to a community emplaced on landscape. All peoples need a sense of "my country," of their social communities in place on a sustaining landscape they possess in care and in love. The English love their countrysides. We earlier sang, with goose pimples, *America the Beautiful*. The promised land has been central in Hebrew faith. Ought not what we do in management of such places also be sensitive to values that are already "in place" before we humans arrive to dwell there? Part of the needed ethic does demand a constructed sense of place; but a person also needs an embodied sense of residence on a landscape.

Experience of the beauty in nature can be quite powerful and memorable. Ask people why save the Grand Canyon or the Grand Tetons, and the ready answer will be "Because they are beautiful; they are 'grand'." It is an easy move from "is" to "ought." One hardly needs commandments, certainly not laid onto otherwise unwilling agents. Take a drive to the mountains. Enjoy the view, look at the fields en route—the waving wheat, and think how air soil, water are basic human needs. One ought to celebrate—and conserve— beauty in nature. Aldo Leopold, famously, connected beauty and ethics in his land ethic. There is aesthetic stimulation in the sense of abyss overlooking the canyon, staring into space, or in following the sweep of the mountains up to the sky, then spotting an eagle in flight. Philosophers have elaborated the challenges and opportunities in environmental aesthetics (Berleant, 2002; Carlson and Lintott, 2008; Rolston, 2002; Hepburn, 1996). Whatever their debates, they are in consensus that life would be impoverished with reduced experience of natural beauty, rural and wild.

The rural environment is threatened, but even more threatened is that third environment that we can encounter: wild nature. We may love the rivers in which we fish, and care about the fish there. But there are areas that we ought to preserve that have nothing to do with our sense of place. Perhaps you contribute to save mountain gorillas, but have never seen them wild in Uganda. You might wish to save the vestimentiferans living at the deep-ocean hydrothermal vents, but these are no part of our ordinary experienced nature. The world is a plural place. Humans are residents of Earth, on six continents, but still there are wild places where we do not remain. And, of course, there is the seventh continent, which is virtually uninhabited.

Yet this wild nature too, as well as rural nature and urban environments is needed for our human well-being. John C. Hendee, George H. Stankey, and Robert C. Lucas, prominent leaders in wilderness conservation, put this strongly, too strongly:

> Wilderness is for people. This is a principle that bears restating. The preservation goals established for such areas are designed to provide values and benefits to society.... Wilderness is not set aside for the sake of its flora or fauna, but for people.

(Hendee et al., 1978, pp. 140–141)

We will be arguing that wilderness is set aside both for people and on account of intrinsic values there, and that the two are complementary. But humans do need experience of the wild. We need to value all three kinds of territories. Nature is much present in the hybrid habitats of rural landscapes. We need an ethic for agro-ecosystems. Much wildlife can remain on landscapes put to multiple use. We need an ethic for forests, for farmlands, for the countryside. Nature is present in, and a support of, our cities as well.

You may be thinking: Certainly humans need experience of the urban and rural, but why the wild. The short answer is that we need to wonder, and life on Earth is wonderful. We can start with a human-need answer. Although we cannot live there, the nature we encounter in wild nature, is the fundamental ground of our existence. True, by nature we are political animals. But by nature too, we are embodied creatures, residents on landscapes, earthlings, placed in a more inclusive, more comprehensive community of life and life support. In that sense, encounter with all three dimensions: urban, rural, and wild, protects a comprehensive experience of human identity.

For most of human history, people lived as hunters and gatherers on natural landscapes. Wildness is a living museum of our roots. The experiences humans have there are to be valued because we learn where we came from and who we are. We realize that nature is an originating source of value. We experience our roots, and this experiencing is to be valued. What the experiencing is of—these wild generative roots at work before humans arrived—has delivered to us much of value, processes the benefits of which are at work within us whether we are aware of them or not.

Beyond a healthy environment, which humans may think is their right, humans desire a quality environment, enjoying the amenities of nature—wildlife and wildflowers, scenic views, places of solitude—as well as the commodities—timber, water, soil, natural resources. If one insists on the word, one can call wild nature reserves *resources*, but in a deeper perspective these are the *sources* that define life. They are the life-support system, the ecosystems that humans inhabit. A wildland setting accentuates these touchstones, set off from the everyday life of town and commerce, but quite genuine and authentic, primordially natural.

In that sense a wilderness puts people in their place. We get taken out of culture into nature; we leave the city behind and go out into the country. The wildland visitor's first impression is that this is not where I live; the whole idea of being a visitor is being somewhere else from where you live. But a second, and deeper impression, is that this is where we do live, our cultures superposed on natural systems. First impressions may be that we have gone rustic, gone "back to" something past; we take the weekend off in a world that is unreal. But second impressions run deeper. We have not gotten away from it all; we have gotten back to it all. "Back to" metaphors, however, are always a little worrisome. We better say: "down to" it all. We reach a dimension of depth. We recontact the natural certainties.

We come to see forests, for example, as a characteristic expression of the creative process. In a forest, as on a desert or the tundra, the realities of nature cannot be ignored. The forest is both presence and symbol of forces in natural systems that transcend human powers and human utility. Like the sea or the sky, the forest is a kind of archetype of the foundations of the world. The central "goods" of the biosphere—forests and sky, sunshine and rain, rivers and earth, the everlasting hills, the cycling seasons, fauna and flora, hydrologic cycles, photosynthesis, soil fertility, food chains, genetic codes, speciation and reproduction, succession and its resetting, life and death and life renewed—were in place long before humans arrived, though they have lately become human economic and social resources. The dynamics and structures organizing the forest do not come out of the human mind; a wild forest is something wholly other than civilization. It is presence and symbol of the timeless natural givens that support everything else.

In the wild, in national parks or wilderness areas, one is immediately confronted with life persisting in the midst of its perpetual perishing. All the wild life is eating and being eaten, surviving through adapted fit. Wild nature is a vast scene of sprouting, budding, flowering, fruiting, passing away, passing life on. Birth, death, re-birth, life forever regenerated—that is the law, the nature of life.

Of course, we cannot escape this in town. There too people age and perish, and reproduce and prosper, generation after generation. But something about immersing oneself in a "nature reserve," confronts us more directly and intensely than usual with this life struggle and life support in primordial nature. We reach baseline nature. Survive. Adapt. Eat or be eaten. Life or death. The seasons are evident: spring with its flowering; fall with its dieback.

Wild nature brings benefits, but wild nature can threaten humans. That's bad, disastrous. Indeed wild nature can bring disaster; but even so, we have to think further. Floods, drought, tornadoes, hurricanes, hail, blizzards, earthquakes, avalanches—these have taken place across the eons of natural history. We might almost say that natural disasters did not appear until human civilization got in the way of these extreme events. Such events seldom do much harm to the plants or animals on the landscape, which are, for the most part, adapted to survive in such upsets (Rolston, 1992, 2003). One might say, yes, that is true on ecosystem scales, but there were the great catastrophic extinctions. Were they not truly catastrophic? For the moment, let's postpone an answer to Chapter 5.

On the scales of common human life, there do arise natural disasters—at least for affected humans, such as the earthquake in Haiti in 2010, or the South Asian tsunami in 2004. The occurrence, severity, and cost of natural disasters has increased in proportion to an escalating human population, which increases exposure to the effects of extreme events. Where humans choose to live also increases our vulnerability. Over 80% of the world's population lives near coastlines. Of the eighteen megacities on Earth, fifteen are on or near coastlines. Humans have often developed their civilizations in hazardous areas, such as floodplains or in earthquake zones, and built without regard for flood, hurricane, tornado, or earthquake.

We do need early warning systems, better education, and better preparedness for disaster response. In the 1976 Big Thompson Flood in a Colorado Canyon, over 140 people were killed, often trying to drive a road out of the canyon. Not one need have died, had each climbed to higher ground. Officials later posted signs: "In case of flood climb to safety." Get smarter about dealing with wild nature. Yes, but each year millions still annually come and drive over that now re-built road to see the majesties of Rocky Mountain National Park. In that park a large area has recently been designated wilderness—so people can experience primordial nature and perhaps take a few chances they do not take in town.

Life, including human life fitted to this planetary environment, is the principal mystery that has come out of nature. For several billion years, the ongoing development and persistence of that life, culminating in human life, have been the principal features of creativity manifest in nature. Humans, when they live strong and good lives, realize something of the strength and goodness that nature has disciplined into its creatures and is bequeathing to us.

6. Human Dignity on Earth: Part of or Apart from Nature?

Humans are a paradox on Earth, both a part of nature and apart from nature. We might say that, if contemporary biology, has taught us anything, it is that we humans are we part of nature. But there is cause for wonder. Maybe the emergence of humans was a rupture of natural history. We said above, with some emphasis, that humans do not want a de-natured life in a natured world. But maybe, in some sense, like it or not, humans must live de-natured lives, because we are by nature Aristotle's "political animals" and have made an exodus from nature.

You will be challenged throughout this book to think about values intrinsic to nature. The next two chapters will attempt appropriately to respect what animals and plants are. The two after that will emphasize values in species and in ecosystems. But we do have to reckon with ourselves, with humans on Earth. We need, we have been saying, a sense of place. But we also have to place humans on Earth. That is a major philosophical challenge, and getting environmental ethics right depends on figuring out who we are as much as it does figuring out where we are—especially if we think we are at a hinge point of history entering the Anthropocene Epoch!

Humans evolved out of nature; but, in important senses, they did just that, they evolved into culture, contrasted with nature. Humans are nurtured into an inherited culture. This cultural genius makes possible the deliberate and cumulative, and therefore the extensive, technological, rebuilding of nature. Humans reshape their environments, rather than being themselves morphologically and genetically reshaped to fit their changing environments. Humans are now a force of nature on the order of geological and climatic processes.

Yes, but nature, we have discovered, remains the milieu of culture. Using another metaphor, nature is the womb of culture, but a womb that humans never entirely leave. Nature can do much without culture—the several billion years of evolutionary history are proof of that. Culture, appearing late, can do nothing without nature as its ground. To use a word in some disfavor among philosophers, in this "foundational" sense, nature is the given. To turn a favored word on its head, rather than culture "constructing" nature, culture will always have to be constructed out of nature. Culture remains tethered to the biosystem and the options within built environments, however expanded, provide no release from nature as a life-support system. Humans depend on air flow, water cycles, sunshine, nitrogen-fixation, decomposition bacteria, fungi, the ozone layer, food chains, insect pollination, soils, earthworms, climates, oceans, and genetic materials. An ecology still lies in the background of culture, natural givens that underlie everything else. In any future that we can presently envision, some sort of inclusive environmental fitness is required. Nature is not gone. Nor are we post-natural; rather, nature is forever lingering around. Humans and this planet have entwined destinies.

Still, there is much that sets us apart and the scientists can be as insistent about this as they are that we are natural. We humans are the most sophisticated of known natural products. Michael Gazzaniga, a neuroscientist, speaks of "the explosion in human brain size":

> We are hugely different. While most of our genes and brain architecture are held in common with animals, there are always differences to be found. And while we can use lathes to mill fine jewelry, and chimps can use stones to crack open nuts, the differences are light years apart.... We humans are special.

> (2008, p. 13, pp. 1–3)

Bruce Lahn, leading a research team analyzing human genetics, concludes: "Humans occupy a unique position in the tree of life. Simply put, evolution has been working very hard to produce us humans" (Lahn, quoted in Gianaro, 2005). Craig Venter and his team of two hundred geneticists, concluded that, although humans do share far the most of their genes (95% or more) with chimpanzees, nevertheless, with the emergence of humans, there is "a massive singularity that by even the simplest of criteria made humans more complex in a behavioral sense" (Venter et al., 2001, p. 1347) So, the puzzle is how can a change of some few percent in DNA result in light years of mental explosion.

Animal brains are already impressive. In a cubic millimeter (about a pinhead) of mouse cortex there are 450 meters of dendrites and one to two kilometers of axons; human brains multiply that three thousand times. Despite the similarities of our genes with the chimpanzees, we have three times their cranial cortex. This cognitive development has come to a striking expression point in the hominid lines leading to *Homo sapiens*, going from about 300 to 1,400 cubic centimeters of cranial capacity. The connecting fibers in a human brain, extended, would wrap around the Earth forty times.

Some trans-genetic threshold seems to have been crossed. The human brain is of such complexity that descriptive numbers are astronomical and difficult to fathom. A typical estimate is 10^{12} neurons, each with several thousand synapses (possibly tens of thousands). Each neuron can "talk" to many others. The postsynaptic membrane contains over a thousand different proteins in the signal receiving surface. "The most molecularly complex structure known [in the human body] is the postsynaptic side of the synapse," according to Seth Grant, a neuroscientist (quoted in Pennisi, 2006). This network, formed and re-formed, makes possible virtually endless mental activity. The result of such combinatorial explosion is that the human brain is capable of forming thoughts numbering something in the range of $10^{70,000,000,000}$ thoughts a number that dwarfs the number of atoms in the visible universe (10^{80}) (Flannagan, 1992, p. 37; Holderness, 2001). On a cosmic scale, humans are minuscule atoms, but on a complexity scale, humans have "hyperimmense" possibilities in mental complexity (Scott, 1995, p. 81).

Although humans evolved from other primates, the human brain is not just a scaled up version of a chimpanzee brain. Humans are remarkable in their capacities to process thoughts, ideas, symbolic abstractions figured into interpretive gestalts with which the world is understood and life is oriented. This higher consciousness is a constitutive dimension of humans and is absent in all other species. Our ideas and our practices configure and re-configure our own sponsoring brain structures. Minds employ and reshape their brains to facilitate their chosen ideologies and lifestyles. In the vocabulary of neuroscience, we have "mutable maps." Michael Merzenich, a neuroscientist, reports his increasing appreciation of "what is the most remarkable quality of our brain: its capacity to develop and to specialize its own processing machinery, to shape its own abilities, and to enable, through hard brainwork, its own achievements" (2001, p. 418).

The surprise is that this intelligence becomes reflectively self-conscious and builds cumulative transmissible cultures. An information explosion gets pinpointed in humans. Humans alone have "a theory of mind"; they know that there are ideas in other minds, making linguistic cultures possible. The key threshold is the capacity to pass ideas from mind to mind. There is no clear evidence that chimpanzees attribute mental states to others. They do not know other minds are there with whom they might communicate, to learn what they know. Or, if you prefer to say that one chimp can know what another knows, chimps have a theory of immediate mind (one chimp sees that another chimp knows where those bananas are); humans have a theory of the ideational mind (one human teaches another the Pythagorean theorem).

"Humans have a whole system that we call theory of mind that chimps don't have" (Daniel J. Povinelli, quoted in Pennisi, 1999, p. 2076). Carl Zimmer concludes: "Of all the species on Earth, only humans possess what researchers call a 'theory of mind'—the ability to infer what others are thinking.... After decades of studies, no one has found indisputable signs that chimps or other nonhuman primates have a theory of mind." "Understanding that others think is a human exclusive" (Zimmer, 2003, p. 1079). Humans live in an ideational world, mind contemplating and contacting other minds. Christopher Frith shares his thoughts: "To get an idea from one brain into another, that's a deeply mysterious thing that we do" (quoted in Zimmer, 2003, p. 1079).

Kuniyoshi L. Sakai finds: "The human left-frontal cortex is thus uniquely specialized in the syntactic processes of sentence comprehension, without any counterparts in other animals" (2005, p. 817). The result is "massive differences in expressive capacities between human language and the communicative systems of other animals" (Anderson, 2004, p, 11). Ian Tattersall concludes: "We human beings are indeed mysterious animals. We are linked to the living world, but we are sharply distinguished by our cognitive powers, and much of our behavior is conditioned by abstract and symbolic concerns" (1998, p. 3).

What is missing in the primates is precisely what makes a human cumulative transmissible culture possible. The central idea is that acquired knowledge and behavior is learned and transmitted from person to person, by one generation teaching another. Ideas pass from mind to mind, in large part through the medium of language, with such knowledge and behavior resulting in a greatly rebuilt, or cultured, environment. Andrew Whitten finds:

> When we focus our comparative lens on culture, the evidence is all around us that a gulf separates humans from all other animals.... Ape culture may be particularly complex among non-human animals, yet it clearly falls short of human culture. An influential contemporary view is that the key difference lies in the human capacity for cumulative culture. In chimps, hints of cumulation exist, such as the refinement of using prop stones to stabilize stone anvils during nut cracking, but these remain primitive and fleeting by human standards.
>
> (2005, pp. 52–53)

Humans are only part of the world in biological, evolutionary, and ecological senses, their nature; but *Homo sapiens* is the only part of the world free to orient itself with a view of the whole, to seek wisdom about who we are and where we are, and to develop our lives on Earth by means of culture. Such cumulative, ongoing nurture determines outcomes in our uniquely historical behavior, making the critical difference. The determinants of animal and plant behavior are never anthropological, political, economic, technological, scientific, philosophical, ethical, or religious.

Humans live under what Robert Boyd and Peter J. Richerson (1985) call "a dual inheritance system," both genes and culture. They find "that the existence of human culture is a deep evolutionary mystery on a par with the origins of life itself." "Human societies are a spectacular anomaly in the animal world" (Richerson and Boyd, 2005, pp. 126, 195). The human transition into culture is exponential, non-linear, reaching extraordinary epistemic powers.

Without some concept of teaching, of ideas moving from mind to mind, from parent to child, from teacher to pupil, a cumulative transmissible culture is impossible. Humans learn what they realize others know; they employ these ideas and resulting behaviors; they evaluate, test, and modify them, and, in turn, teach what they know to others, including the next generation. So human cultures cumulate, but with animals there is no such cultural "ratchet" effect. Bennett G. Galef, Jr. concludes: "As far as is known, no nonhuman animal teaches" (1992, p. 161). "Given that imitation is rare in nonhuman primates and teaching is essentially nonexistent, it's hard to see how you are going to get the cumulative culture which is the hallmark of our culture" (Galef, quoted in Vogel, 1999, p. 2072).

By astronomical and evolutionary scales, the development of culture is many orders of magnitude more rapid, 5000 years of human historical memories against 13 billion years of universal history, or 3.5 billion years of life on Earth. In recent centuries, the explosive speed of cultural innovation has increased, with an ever-enlarging knowledge base making possible technological innovation, owing in large part to the powers of science. In recent decades, information accumulates and travels in culture at logarithmically increasing speeds. Today cultural development takes place digitized at megabytes per second over the internet. We seem to have reached a turning point in the long accumulating story of cognition actualizing itself.

A critical element in crossing into the human state is the emergence of morality. The uniquely rational animal is equally the uniquely ethical animal. Ethics is distinctively a product of the human genius, a phenomenon in our social behavior. To be ethical is to reflect on considered principles of right and wrong and to act accordingly, in the face of temptation. Such an emergence of ethics is as remarkable as any other event we know; in some form or other ethics is pervasively present in every human culture, whether honored in the observance or breach.

Animals are not moral agents. Marc Bekoff and Jessica Pierce (2009) claim that some mammals are moral beings, "know right from wrong" and "have a moral sense" including "a sense of justice." Peter Singer's *Ethics* has a section "Common Themes in Primate Ethics," including a section on "Chimpanzee Justice," and he wants to "abandon the assumption that ethics is uniquely human" (1994, p. 6). But many of the behaviors examined (helping behavior; dominance structures) are more pre-ethical than ethical; he has little or no sense of holding chimpanzees morally culpable or praiseworthy.

Frans de Waal finds precursors of morality, but concludes:

Even if animals other than ourselves act in ways tantamount to moral behavior, their behavior does not necessarily rest on deliberations of the kind we engage in. It is hard to believe that animals weigh their own interests against the rights of others, that they develop a vision of the greater good of society, or that they feel lifelong guilt about something they should not have done. Members of some species may reach tacit consensus about what kind of behavior to tolerate or inhibit in their midst, but without language the principles behind such decisions cannot be conceptualized, let alone debated.

(1996, p. 209)

Finding "ethics" in wild animals is partly a matter of discovering hitherto unknown behaviors but mostly a matter of redefining and stretching what the word "ethics" means to cover behavioral adjustments in social groups. After a careful survey of behavior, Helmet Kummer concludes, "It seems at present that morality has no specific functional equivalents among our animal relatives" (Kummer, 1980, p. 45). Jerome Kagan puts it this way: "What is biologically special about our species is a constant attention to what is good and beautiful and a dislike of all that is bad and ugly. These biologically prepared biases render the human experience incommensurable with that of any other species" (1998, p. 91).

After her years of experience with chimpanzees, and although she finds pair bonding, grooming, and the pleasure of the company of others, Jane Goodall writes: "I cannot conceive of chimpanzees developing emotions, one for the other, comparable in any way to the tenderness, the protectiveness, tolerance, and spiritual exhilaration that are the hallmarks of human love in its truest and deepest sense. Chimpanzees usually show a lack of consideration for each other's feelings which in some ways may represent the deepest part of the gulf between them and us" (van Lawick-Goodall, 1971, p. 194).

Human ethical concerns can become inclusive: cosmopolitan, global, transgenetic. But that might not yet be inclusive enough, if it remains devoted to one species. The deep gulf between the chimpanzees and us is splendidly embodied in Goodall herself, and in her concern first for appreciatively studying and later for the conservation of chimpanzees. We heard DiSilvestro (1993) praising humans when they set aside territories with boundaries that are created to protect the nonhumans. He saw that as ceasing to think of ourselves as masters of the natural world and becoming partners with it. But there is a double spin that can be put on this. This setting aside refuges for other species, which is only done by humans, *ipso facto* sets us apart. One has only to ask whether chimpanzees might ever study the rich biodiversity on Earth and become concerned to save it, to see that Gazzaniga was right: there is light years of mental distance between us. Could any monkey ever read this book now in your hands, wondering about the human obligations in environmental ethics?

True, *Homo sapiens* is the aristocratic species on Earth. Ethics to date has struggled with impressive, if also halting, success in an effort to evolve altruism in fit proportion to egoism. That has yielded a sense of ethical priority, often ethical exclusivism, toward humans. Humans are on top; only humans count. Love your (human) neighbors, as you do yourself. From a narrow, organismic perspective that can seem right, since in the prehuman world everything is making a resource of everything else, so far as it can. Culture is impossible except as built on value capture from nature. Every other living natural kind defends only its own kind; humans behave that way too, maximizing their own kind—and justifying (defending) their position by claiming to be the central species with and of moral concern. Always prefer humans.

From a wider, ecosystemic perspective such a rationale is oblivious to the way that the system has hitherto contained myriads of species in interdependent tension and harmony, with nothing maximizing itself except by optimizing a situated environmental fitness. From this more comprehensive perspective, persons operating with the prevailing humanistic focus are blind to most of their neighbors. All the rest of the products of the evolutionary ecosystem are counted as resources. That does not sound like *Homo sapiens* is being the wise species. Martin Luther described the essence of sinfulness with the Latin phrase *homo incurvatus in se*, the person curved in on himself or herself. Luther's insight is into the perennial temptation of human conceit.

Human ethicists who argue that humans always come first only halfway emerge from their environment. They are right about the human excellences. But they defend only their own kind, and in this respect, even when they become cosmopolitan, they do not *emerge*, they just *merge* and play by the rules of natural selection; they become moral agents in encounter with other humans, but they do not become moral agents in encounter with nature. Trying to defend the high human value, they act like beasts—looking out for themselves and their kind. In this aggressive attempt, these humane ethicists stunt humanity because they do not know genuine human transcendence—an overview caring for the non-human others.

Plainly, humans have expanded their territories all over the globe. But what is an appropriate lifestyle for residing in this globally occupied territory? Always to put themselves first? Nothing more? Rather than using mind and morals, hand and brain, as survival tools for defending the human form of life, the better answer is when mind forms an intelligible view of the whole and defends ideals of life in all their forms. *Humans* are cognate with the *humus*, made of dust (as Genesis teaches, long before any bioscience), yet unique and excellent in their aristocratic capacity to view the world they inhabit. They rise up from the earth and look over their world (Greek: *anthropos*, to rise up, look up). Persons have their excellences, and one way they excel is in this capacity for overview. They are made "in the image of God" (as Genesis also teaches).

The novelty in the human emergence is class altruism emerging to coexist with class self-interest, sentiments directed not simply at one's own species but at other species fitted into biological communities. Humans ought to think of Earth as an evolutionary ecosystem out of which they have evolved, which continues and remains as their life support, and which they ought appropriately to respect. In occupying this position, humans play roles in the storied achievements on Earth. Interhuman ethics has spent the last two millennia waking up to human dignity. As we expand ethics in this new millennium, environmental ethics invites awakening to the greater story of which humans are a consummate part.

This is what human dominion potentially meant in Genesis, or should have meant. This is what living in a God-given land of promise offers for a land ethic. This takes humans past *resource* use to *residence* and constrains their policy, economics, science, technology. Being a "resident" is something more than maximum exploitation of one's environment, though it requires resourceful use. Being a "resident" is more than being a "citizen." Such residing takes us past management questions to moral questions. Humans can get "let in on" more value than any other kind of life. They can share the values of others and in this way be altruists. Humans are of capstone value because they are capstone evaluators.

Seen this way, in earlier eras humans needed an exodus out of nature into culture, but now they want to be liberated out of egoism, out of humanism, into a transcending overview that sees Earth as a blessed land, exuberant with life, a land filled with integrity, beauty, dynamic achievement, and storied history. This is exodus within a promised land.

Without denying that there is value superiority *within* humans, an enlightened environmental ethics says more. It not just our capacity to *say I*, to actualize a self, but our capacity to *see others*, to oversee a world, that distinguishes humans. Environmental ethics calls for seeing nonhumans, for seeing the biosphere, the Earth, ecosystem communities, fauna, flora, natural kinds that cannot say "I" but in which there is formed integrity, objective value independent of subjective value. Environmental ethics advances beyond humanistic ethics, in that it can treat as ends others besides humans. Environmental ethicists see further morally. In this sense the capacity for thoughtful residence, for experiencing community with nonhuman others is as requisite for ethics as any capacity for human self-actualizing. That very self-actualizing in this ethic seeks human self-transcending.

It is commendable to be altruists humanistically speaking. But a really exciting difference between humans and nonhumans is that, while animals and plants can count (defend) only their own lives, with their offspring and kind, humans can count (defend) life and even nonlife with vision of greater scope. Humans can be genuine altruists; this begins when they recognize the claims of other humans, whether or not such claims are compatible with their own self-interest. But the evolution of altruism is not complete until humans can recognize the claims of nonhumans—ecosystems, species, landscapes. In that sense environmental ethics is the most altruistic form of ethics. It really loves others. It transforms residual egos into resident altruists. This ultimate altruism is, or ought to be, the human genius. In this sense the last becomes the first; this late-coming species with a latter day ethics is the first to see the story that is taking place. This late species takes a leading role.

References

Abbott, Alison, and Helen Pearson. 2004. "Fear of Human Pandemic Grows as Bird Flu Sweeps through Asia," *Nature* 427(5 February):472–473.

Aguire, A. Alonso, Richard S. Ostfeld, Gary M. Tabor, Carol House, and Mary C. Pearl. 2002. *Conservation Medicine: Ecological Health in Practice.* Oxford, UK: Oxford University Press.

Anderson, Stephen R. 2004. *Doctor Doolittle's Delusion: Animals and the Uniqueness of Human Language.* New Haven, CT: Yale University Press.

Beckerman, Wilfred, and Joanna Pasek. 2001. *Justice, Posterity, and the Environment.* New York: Oxford University Press.

Bekoff, Marc, and Jessica Pierce. 2009. *Wild Justice: The Moral Lives of Animals.* Chicago: University of Chicago Press.

Berleant, Arnold, ed. 2002. *Environment and the Arts: Perspectives on Environmental Aesthetics.* Aldershot. Hampshire, UK: Ashgate.

Berman, Marc G., John Jonides, and Stephen Kaplan. 2008. "The Cognitive Benefits of Interacting with Nature," *Psychological Science* 19:1207–1212.

Berry, Wendell. 1995. "The Obligation of Care," *Sierra* 80(no. 5):62–67, 101.

Boyd, Robert, and Peter J. Richerson. 1985. *Culture and the Evolutionary Process.* Chicago: University of Chicago Press.

Carlson, Allen, and Sheila Lintott, eds. 2008. *Nature, Aesthetics, and Environmentalism.* New York: Columbia University Press.

Clark, William C. 1989. "Managing Planet Earth," *Scientific American* 261 (no. 3, September): 46–54.

Crutzen, Paul J. 2006. "The 'Anthropocene'." Pages 13–18 in Eckart Ehlers and Thomas Kraft, eds., *Earth System Science in the Anthropocene.* Berlin: Springer.

de Waal, Frans. 1996. *Good Natured: The Origins of Right and Wrong in Humans and Other Animals.* Cambridge, MA: Harvard University Press.

DiSilvestro, Roger L. 1993. *Reclaiming the Last Wild Places: A New Agenda for Biodiversity.* New York: Wiley.

Dobson, Andrew P. 2005. "What Links Bats to Emerging Infectious Diseases?" *Science* 310:628–629.

Ellis, Erle C., and Navin Ramankutty. 2008. "Putting People in the Map: Anthropogenic Biomes of the World," *Frontiers in Ecology and the Environment* 6 (no. 8):439–447.

Ferry, Luc. 2007. "Protéger l'espèce humaine contre elle-même" [Protect the human race against itself]. Interview with Luc Ferry in *la Revue des Deux Mondes* (October–November):75–79.

Flannagan, Owen. 1992. *Consciousness Reconsidered.* Cambridge, MA: MIT Press.

Foley, Jonathan A., Ruth DeFries, Gregory P. Asner, et al. 2005. "Global Consequences of Land Use," *Science* 309(22 July):570–574.

Fox, Warwick. 2006. *A Theory of General Ethics: Human Relationships, Nature, and the Built Environment.* Cambridge, MA: The MIT Press.

Galef, Bennett G., Jr. 1992. "The Question of Animal Culture," *Human Nature* 3(no. 2):157–178.

Galloway, J. N. 2004. "The Global Nitrogen Cycle." Pages 557–583 in W. H. Schlesinger, ed., vol. 8, *Biogeochemistry,* in H. D. Holland and K. K. Turekian, eds., *Treatise on Geochemistry.* Oxford, UK: Elsevier-Pergamon.

Gazzaniga, Michael S. 2008. *Human: The Science Behind What Makes Us Unique.* New York: Ecco, Harper Collins.

Gianaro, Catherine. 2005. "Human Cognitive Abilities Resulted from Intense Evolutionary Selection, Says Lahn," *The University of Chicago Chronicle* 24(no. 7, January 6):1, 5.

Hendee, John C., George H. Stankey, and Robert C. Lucas. 1978 *Wilderness Management,* USDA Forest Service Miscellaneous Publication No. 1365. Washington, D.C.: U.S.Government Printing Office.

Hepburn, Ronald. 1996. "Contemporary Aesthetics and the Neglect of Natural Beauty." Pages 285–310 in Bernard Williams and Alan Montefiore, eds., *British Analytical Philosophy.* London: Routledge and Kegan Paul.

Holderness, Mike. 2001. "Think of a Number," *New Scientist* 170(16 June):45.

Holling, C. S., ed. 1980. *Adaptive Environmental Assessment and Management.* New York: Wiley.

Imhoff, Marc L., Lahouari Bounoua, Taylor Ricketts, et al. 2004. "Global Patterns in Human Consumption of Net Primary Production," *Nature* 429:870–873.

Kagan, Jerome. 1998. *Three Seductive Ideas.* Cambridge. MA: Harvard University Press.

Kareiva, Peter, Sean Watts, Robert McDonald, and Tim Boucher. 2007. "Domesticated Nature: Shaping Landscapes and Ecosystems for Human Welfare," *Science* 316(29 June):1866–1869.

Karesh, William B., and Robert A. Cook, 2005. "The Human-Animal Link," *Foreign Affairs* 84(4):38–50.

Kummer, Helmut. 1980. "Analogs of Morality Among Nonhuman Primates." Pages 31–47 in Gunter Stent, ed., *Morality as a Biological Phenomenon.* Berkeley: University of California Press.

Lee, Kai N. 1993. *Compass and Gyroscope: Integrating Science and Politics for the Enviropnment.* Washington, D.C.: Island Press.

Louv, Richard. 2005. *The Last Child in the Woods: Saving Our Children from Nature-Deficit Disorder.* Chapel Hill, NC: Algonquin Books of Chapel Hill.

McCloskey, J. M., and H. Spalding. 1989. "A Reconaissance Level Inventory of the Amount of Wilderness Remaining in the World," *Ambio* 18:221–227.

McKibben, Bill. 1989. *The End of Nature.* New York: Random House.

Merzenich, Michael. 2001. "The Power of Mutable Maps," p. 418 in Bear, Mark F., Connors, Barry W., and Paradiso, Michael A. 2001. *Neuroscience: Exploring the Brain,* 2nd ed. Baltimore: Lippincott Williams and Wilkins.

Millennium Ecosystem Assessment. 2005. Online at http://www.maweb.org/en/index.aspx.

Morens, David M., Gregory K. Folkers, and Anthony S. Fauci, 2004. "The Challenge of Emerging and Re-emerging Infectious Diseases," *Nature* 430:242–249.

Norton, Bryan G. 2005. *Sustainability: A Philosophy of Adaptive Ecosystem Management.* Chicago: University of Chicago Press.

Pennisi, Elizabeth. 1999. "Are Our Primate Cousins 'Conscious'?" *Science* 284:2073–2076.

———. 2006. "Brain Evolution on the Far Side," *Science* 314(13 October):244–245.

———.2010. "Body's Hardworking Microbes Get Some Overdue Respect," *Science* 330:1619.

Richerson, Peter J., and Robert Boyd. 2005. *Not by Genes Alone: How Culture Transformed Human Evolution.* Chicago: University of Chicago Press.

Riley, Laura, and William Riley. 2005. *Nature's Strongholds: The World's Great Wildlife Reserves.* Princeton, NJ: Princeton University Press.

Rolston, Holmes, III, 1992. "Disvalues in Nature," *The Monist* 75:250–278.

———. 2002. "From Beauty to Duty: Aesthetics of Nature and Environmental Ethics" Pages 127–141 in Arnold Berleant, ed., *Environment and the Arts: Perspectives on Environmental Aesthetics.* Aldershot, Hampshire, UK: Ashgate.

———. 2003. "Naturalizing and Systematizing Evil." Pages 67–86 in Willem B. Drees, ed., *Is Nature Ever Evil? Religion, Science and Value.* London: Routledge.

———. 2005. "Panglobalism and Pandemics: Ecological and Ethical Conserns," *Yale Journal of Biology and Medicine* 78:309–319.

———. 2008. "Mountain Majesties above Fruited Plains: Culture, Nature, and Rocky Mountain Aesthetics," *Environmental Ethics* 30(2008):3–20.

Royal Society of London. 2009. *Reaping the Benefits: Science and the Sustainable Intensification of Global Agriculture.* Royal Society, London. Online at: http://royalsociety.org/Reapingthebenefits/

Sakai, Kuniyoshi L. 2005. "Language Acquisition and Brain Development," *Science* 310(4 November):815–819.

Sanderson Eric W., Malanding Jaiteh, Marc A. Levy, et al. 2002. "The Human Footprint and the Last of the Wild," *BioScience* 52:891–904.

Schwartzman, Megan R., and Michael P. Wilson. 2009. "New Science for Chemicals Policy," *Science* 326(20 November):1065–1066.

Scott, Alwyn. 1995. *Stairway to the Mind: The Controversial New Science of Consciousness.* New York: Copernicus; Springer-Verlag.

Singer, Peter. 1994. *Ethics.* New York: Oxford University Press.

Tabor, Gary M. 2002. "Defining Conservation Medicine." Pages 8–16 in A. Alonso Aguire, Richard S. Ostfeld, Gary M. Tabor, Carol House, and Mary C. Pearl, *Conservation Medicine: Ecological Health in Practice.* Oxford: Oxford University Press.

Tattersall, Ian. 1998. *Becoming Human: Evolution and Human Uniqueness.* New York: Harcourt Brace.

United Nations Conference on Environment and Development (UNCED). 1992. *The Rio Declaration.* UNCED Document A/CONF.151/5/Rev. 1, 13 June. Online at: http://www.un.org/documents/ga/conf151/aconf15126-1annex1.htm

United Nations Department of Economic and Social Affairs (DESA), 2007. *Indicators of Sustainable Development: Guidelines and Methodologies.* New York: United Nations. Online at: http://www.un.org/esa/sustdev/natlinfo/indicators/guidelines.pdf

United Nations World Commission on Environment and Development, 1987. *Our Common Future.* New York: Oxford University Press.

U.S. Congress, 1976, Toxic Substances Control Act. Public Law 94-469. 90 Stat. 2003.

———. 1977. Clean Air Act. Public Law 88-206 77 Stat. 392.

———. 1977. Clean Water Act. Public Law 92-500. 86 Stat 816.

———. 1980. Comprehensive Environmental Response, Compensation, and Liability Act. Public Law 96-510. 94 Stat 2767.

van Lawick-Goodall, Jane. 1971. *In the Shadow of Man.* Boston: Houghton Mifflin.

Venter, J. Craig et al. 2001. "The Sequence of the Human Genome," *Science* 291(16 February):1304–1351.

Vitousek, Peter M., Paul R. Ehrlich, Anne H. Ehrlich, and Pamela A. Matson. 1986. "Human Appropriation of the Products of Biosynthesis," *BioScience* 36:368–373.

Vogel, Gretchen. 1999. "Chimps in the Wild Show Stirrings of Culture," *Science* 284(24 June):2070–2073.

Wapner, Paul. 2010. *Living Through the End of Nature: The Future of American Environmentalism.* Cambridge, MA: MIT Press.

Whitten, Andrew, 2005. "The Second Inheritance System of Chimpanzees and Humans," *Nature* 437(1 September):52–55.

Wilkinson Bruce H., and Brandon J. McElroy, 2007. "The Impact of Humans on Continental Erosion and Sedimentation," *Geological Society of America Bulletin* 119:140–156.

Wilson Michael, 2005. *Microbial Inhabitants of Humans: Their Ecology and Role in Health and Disease.* Cambridge, UK: Cambridge University Press.

World Health Organization, Commission on Health and Environment, 1992. *Our Planet, Our Health: Report of the WHO Commission on Health and Environment.* Geneva: World Health Organization.

Zalasiewicz, Jan, Mark Williams, Will Steffen, and Paul Crutzen, 2010. "The New World of the Anthropocene," *Environmental Science and Technology* 44:2228–2231.

Zimmer, Carl, 2003. "How the Mind Reads Other Minds," *Science* 300(16 May):1079–1080.

———. 2009. "On the Origin of Tomorrow," *Science* 326(4 December):1334–1336.

3

ANIMALS

Beasts in Flesh and Blood

Ethics is for people, but is ethics only about people? Wild animals do not make man the measure of things at all. There is no better evidence of non-human values and valuers than spontaneous wild life, born free and on its own. Animals hunt and howl, find shelter, seek out their habitats and mates, care for their young, and flee from threats. They suffer injury and lick their wounds. Animals maintain a self-identity that they value as they cope through the world. They defend their own lives because they have a good of their own. Their lives matter to them.

An animal values its own life for what it is in itself, without further contributory reference, though, of course, a wild animal inhabits an ecosystem on which its life-support depends, and other animals may depend on it. Domestic animals, descended from wild animals, also value their own lives, whether livestock or pets, even if such animals are not on their own but dependent on human support. Animals are value-able, able to value things in their world, their own lives intrinsically and their resources instrumentally.

Confronted with such facts, we have to philosophize over them. What sort of nonhumans are "morally considerable" (Goodpaster, 1978)? The conclusion seems to follow that, whatever our unique differences as *Homo sapiens*, given our kinship with these animal others, there ought to be some moral concern for them. Even if such animals are not "moral agents," they should be "moral patients." Environmental ethics ought to include some concern for individual animals, such as animals hunted. By parity of reasoning, it seems that what humans value in themselves, if they find this elsewhere, they ought also to value in non-human others. We value what does not stand directly in our lineage but is like enough ourselves that we are drawn by spillover to shared phenomena manifest in others. Concern for animals, we found in Chapter 1, has been one of the driving motifs of the environmental turn.

The principle of universalizability demands that an ethicist recognize corresponding values in fellow persons. Growth in ethical sensitivity, or virtue, has often required enlarging the circle of neighbors to include other races and cultures. But these widening circles do not end with reciprocating moral agents. A communitarian ethics finds enlarging concentric circles around the moral self: family, local community, nation, humankind, and—in a surrounding though more remote circle—animals. Sometimes, people may care more about their nearby animals (horses, pets) than they do about distant humans (the Ethiopians). Since animal values similar to human values are at stake, it seems that there can and ought to be an ethic about animals. Or, since many of these animals are domestic, some prefer to say that, parallel to environmental ethics, there ought to be an ethic about animals, wherever they are, alike in rural and wild ecosystems and in feedlots, battery farms, zoos, and pets at our feet lying on the kitchen floor (Armstrong and Botzler, 2008; Sunstein and Nussbaum, 2004; Kaloff and Fitzgerald, 2007; Bekoff and Meaney, 1998).

Such an ethic is even written into laws prohibiting animal cruelty. Anyone who doubts this needs only to recall a recent case. Michael Vick is a quarterback for the Philadelphia Eagles and earlier played for the Atlanta Falcons, setting National Football League records. He also served time in prison for his involvement in dog fighting, involving an illegal interstate dog fighting ring of seventy dogs and gambling. He was suspended from playing by the NFL for conduct that was illegal, cruel, and reprehensible, including killing by hanging or drowning dogs that did not fight well. The loss of his salary and income from product endorsements, added to financial mismanagement and once lavish living, threw him into bankruptcy. Reinstated with the Eagles, he continues as a spectacular player, now greatly regretting his former behavior (BET, Black Entertainment Television, aired a series on Vick, spring 2010).

1. Somebody There? Encountering Individual Animals

Yes, many agree. Animal pains and pleasures ought to count, and this is an ethics based on sentience. This is variously called an animal rights ethics, an animal welfare ethics, perhaps animal liberation. These ethicists claim that value exists where a subject has an object of interest, which is evidently so with humans, but we must also consider the pleasures and pains of non-human subjects. Common sense first and science later teaches that we human animals have many similarities with non-human animals. No one doubts that animals grow hungry, thirsty, hot, tired, excited, sleepy. The protein coding sequences of DNA for structural genes in chimpanzees and humans are more than 95% identical. Ethics is about the sorts of things people value; and some, but not all, of these values are present in nonhumans, so we need to extend ethics there.

That extends ethics beyond humans but, if this kindred sentience is our only ethical principle, this also stops ethics where these similarities stop. Tom Regan says that ethics extends to any living organism that is "the subject-of-a-life," meaning that the organism is capable of felt experience, which for him is mostly mammals (Regan, 2004, p. 243). Peter Singer says that ethics stops "somewhere between a shrimp and an oyster" (Singer, 1990, p. 174). After that, Singer insists, "there is nothing to be taken into account" (Singer, 1990, p. 8). He may be choosing his examples because shrimp have eyes and oysters do not. Having eyes tends to register a conviction that there is "somebody there" who might feel pain behind those eyes in shrimp and nobody there inside the oyster. Beings with eyes can take an interest in what is going on. Ethics directly arises confronting sentience in the presence of animals that can suffer pleasure and pain. That is what is similar in both human animals and nonhuman animals.

Humans are discovering in nature their animal roots, their neighbors, and also alien forms of life with experiences that we cannot share. So much of what we most radically value arose anciently in spontaneous wild nature (hearing, sight, fingers), and we re-awaken to it when we encounter such sentience in the wild. Such sentience, although ancient and prehuman, does not merely lie behind, it remains in our embodiment. We recognize this, when laden with a pack, moving briskly along, breathing heavily, we spook a coyote who races away, needing to use lungs, legs, muscles as much as do we to make our way. Visceral, intimate bodily experience of animals helps us to appreciate these phenomena as larger than ourselves, natural givens which we share with other forms of life. (Such experience will be worth recalling when we hear about the end of nature and its social construction.)

This kind of experience requires sentience, but permits differences in sentient capacities. Humans cannot fully share the experience even of other humans, and wild animals (bats with their sonar, wolves with their keen noses, elephants with their low frequency communication) will have experiences that we have to appreciate indirectly. Experienced values grow wilder, if you will, but they still do require an experiencer, somebody there. Nature is often a strange place. Our human roots may lie in wild nature, but wild nature also turns out often to be a radically different place.

There are phylogenetic lineages far removed from our own. Here is a new challenge. We do not want to measure nonhumans by human standards, though we sometimes want to measure nonhumans and humans by comparable standards. We also frequently run past our capacity to argue by analogy from the value of our experience. For there are quite alien forms of life, with whom we can hardly identify experientially.

> *Octopus* is a mollusc that a primate can recognize as a fellow creature. It is very easy to identify with *Octopus vulgaris*, even with individuals, because they respond in a very "human" way. They watch you. They come to be fed and they will run away with every appearance of fear if you are beastly to them. Individuals develop individual and sometimes irritating traits ... and it is all too easy to come to treat the animal as a sort of aquatic dog or cat.
>
> Therein lies the danger. It is always dangerous to interpret an animal's reactions in human terms, but with dogs or cats there is a certain reasonableness in doing so. We are mammals too ... The octopus is an alien. It is a poikilotherm, never had a dependent childhood, has little or no social life. It may never know what it is to be hungry.... The animal, it is true, learns under conditions that would lead to learning in a mammal but the facts that it learns about its visual and tactile environment are sometimes very different from those that a mammal would learn in similar circumstances. Simply because it is evidently intelligent and possessed of eyes that look back at us, we should not fall into the trap of supposing that we can interpret its behavior in terms of concepts derived from birds or mammals. This animal lives in a very different world from our own.
>
> (Wells, 1978, pp. 8–9)

Those who take one evolutionary route in sentient experience are precluded from the direct experience of alien routes, which also have their integrity. Humans can recognize that integrity, even though participation in it remains foreign to us. We can grant that the octopus is a center of experience, a subject (while we doubt that a mussel is), and respect a marine life form with which we cannot empathize. Some may think it logically or psychologically impossible to value what we cannot share, but this underestimates the human genius for appreciation. Some respect for alien forms of life seems plausible, even if we are slipping away into realms of experience that we cannot reach, even if these are realms it will be difficult to evaluate. Humans do have remarkable capacities for appreciating these unshared experiences. Human experience would be the poorer for ignoring or scorning what exceeds our powers of sentience.

2. Environmental Ethics and Animal Welfare

But people who join the Humane Society do not have the same concerns as those who join the Sierra Club. Now the claim will be that compassion for animal suffering or concern for their rights may be a good thing, but looking for "somebody there" is only a fragment of a more comprehensive environmental ethics. Concern for animals is far too simple, the environmental ethicists will reply, and one way to see this is to look at the differences (Callicott, 1980). Animal lovers do not want to hunt, but ecologists may hunt. Animal lovers wish to feed starving deer in the winter; ecologists may advocate shooting the deer to cull them. Animal ethicists may wish to rehabilitate injured animals hit by cars or birds that fly into power lines, but (unless they are rare species) environmental ethicists may have little interest in this, thinking time and effort better spent in restoring forests or wetlands. Animal ethicists and environmentalists disagree over what to do with feral mustangs, burros, or goats. Ecologists only worry about fur coats if this is depleting seal or mink population in the wild—not if there is fur trade in captive animals. Animal ethicists think it wrong to harvest and eat whales, common or rare. Ecologists only worry if the species is endangered.

Mark Sagoff found these differences so great that he concluded that animal welfare ethics and environmental ethics are not only different, they are incompatible:

> Environmentalists cannot be animal liberationists. Animal liberationists cannot be environmentalists. The environmentalist would sacrifice the lives of individual creatures to preserve the authenticity, integrity and complexity of ecological systems. The liberationist—if the reduction of animal misery is taken seriously as a goal—must be willing, in principle, to sacrifice the authenticity, integrity, and complexity of ecosystems to protect the rights, or guard the lives, of animals.... Moral obligations to nature cannot be enlightened or explained—one cannot even take the first step—by appealing to the rights of animals.
>
> (1984, pp. 304, 306)

Shared experience. Kindred experience. Alien experience. But what if there is no experience at all? Environmental ethics will object that in an ethic based on sentience, and stopping there, most of the biological world has yet to be taken into account: lower animals, insects, microbes, plants, species, ecosystems and their processes, and the global system of life on Earth. An animal-based ethics can value everything else only instrumentally with reference to higher animals, who form only a small fraction of living things. So Singer, stopping between a shrimp and an oyster, does add that there is a lot more to be taken into account instrumentally, since animals (and humans) depend on a life support system, which includes all these other creatures. Animals live at the top of what ecologists call trophic pyramids, food chains, and they need the pyramids.

Environmental ethicists agree but still think that this is too short-sighted. From a biological point of view, this is little better than humans valuing everything else, higher animals included, as their own resources. A deeper respect for life must value more directly all living things and the generative processes that sustain life at all its levels, from the genetic to the global. An animal rights or welfare ethic, if it stops there, is blind to the still larger effort in environmental ethics to value life at all its ranges and levels; indeed to care for a biospheric Earth.

Animal welfare advocates build their case by insisting that animals suffer and that, by parity of reasoning, we humans concerned about suffering in ourselves cannot logically and ought not morally fail to count their suffering. But this focus, even if it persuades people to be more concerned about the animals, leaves these ethicists nothing further to say than that "animals need these resources" about insentient life, all the plants, and also most of the animals, if we remember the mollusks, crustaceans, nematodes, beetles, and the like. An animal welfare ethic is mostly for vertebrates, who form only 4% of living things by species and only a tiny fraction of a percent by numbers of individuals. Really, their concern is almost entirely for the mammals, and declines rapidly with decreasing complexity in the central nervous system. They don't stop between shrimp and oysters because they never get that far. Tom Regan defends his ethic as a "case for animal rights," and his focus in on the familiar animals, beasts with flesh and blood, with whom humans interact when they eat them, kill them for fur coats, use them in scientific research, or keep them as pets.

Environmental ethicists may say, perhaps being deliberately provocative, that those who love the soft, furry deer with big eyes have an overly sentimental "Bambi ethic," and are out of touch with the real wild world. This is just an ethic for our close animal cousins. Nevertheless, many do combine an environmental ethics and an animal welfare ethic (Jamieson, 1995, 2008; Varner, 1995; 1998; Rawles, 1997; Hargrove, 1992; Callicott, 1989; Post, 2004). Emotional responses to suffering animals are not out of place; even sport hunters seek a clean kill and will track an injured animal to kill it, not simply to have their game, but lest it suffer a slow, agonizing death. Almost nobody is really indifferent to severe animal pain, even those who think it is not our duty to save drowning bison in Yellowstone (see below).

3. On the Hunt: Killing, Eating, Respecting Wild Beasts

Wild beasts have filled the Earth in great numbers and diverse kinds over evolutionary history. There are predators and prey, herbivores, carnivores, omnivores. This has been going on over a billion years and humans evolved from such roots. Humans evolved as omnivores; they were from their origins hunters and gatherers, or (the feminists may say) gatherers and hunters. Chimpanzees gather and also hunt; they hunt in teams and share the kill, which developed their social skills (Stanford, 1999). Since our ancestors have been killing and eating meat for more than five million years, nothing seems more natural than that humans should continue to hunt—and gather.

Yes, comes a reply but humans no longer gather much of their food; agriculture has replaced gathering wild food during the past five to ten thousand years (the time differs in different regions of Earth). Equally, agriculture has replaced hunting for most of our meat. In few cultures or none do humans still depend on getting most of their food hunting or gathering. Depending on wild meat brings disaster to hunted animals. Bushmeat hunting is a multi-billion dollar trade in the tropics (Carey, 1999; McNeil, 1999). The fact that hunting looms large in our past need not mean that it ought to continue today. Men have dominated women for thousands of years; should that continue? So, it is time to reconsider hunting.

The debate between hunting apologists and anti-hunting antagonists is ongoing. There is a wide spectrum of views (Kowalsky, 2010; Evans, 2005; Pauley, 2003; Wood, 1997; Cartmill, 1993; Causey, 1989). The central debate spirals about two main axes. When animal activists condemn hunting, and hunters see their hunting as human participation in predation, this suggests that these activists, though they may love animals, also hate real nature, the wild, raw world in which these animals live. The challenge for the critics of hunting is to show that one can properly appreciate natural predation while consistently objecting to human participation in it. Some have frankly lamented predation in the wild (Raterman, 2008), even wondering if humans should genetically modify currently carnivorous species into herbivorous ones—so that lions eat straw (McMahan, 2010).

On the other hand, the challenge for the hunters is to show that humans do still need to, or are permitted to, kill and eat wild beasts. Hunters seek food, at the same time that they have easier (and maybe more humane) alternatives available at the grocery store or on the farm (with uncommon exceptions, such as Eskimos' subsistence hunting). Some defend hunting as part of a cultural tradition, although the more hunting is "cultural," the less it is "natural" (Hawkins, 2001). There are often claims that the psychological well-being of the hunter needs this ancient ritual. These merge with claims that hunters deeply connect with nature. Man is a natural-born hunter.

In a book widely used in hunter education classes, Jim Pozewitz, a Montana hunter, writes:

> As hunters we enjoy the rare privilege of participating in the natural process rather than only observing it from a distance. We become, for a time, a predator like the human hunters of our distant origins.
>
> A hunter is a predator participating in a world where predation belongs.... You need to be familiar with the field, the woods, the marsh, the forest, or the mountains where you hunt. If you work hard and long at this aspect of hunting, you can *become a part* of the place you hunt. You will sense when you start to belong to the country. Go afield often enough and stay out long enough and it will happen. Little by little you will become less of an intruder. More animals will seem to show

themselves to you. You are no longer a stranger in their world; you have become part of it. Many people hunt for a lifetime without learning this, and they miss the most rewarding part of being a hunter.

(1994, pp. 109–110, 20, 23)

Becoming a natural-born hunter, at least in our modern, technologized, urbanized world, takes some working at it. Nearly all hunters accept that hunting must be done according to "sporting" rules, which involves both conservation and killing as humanely as possible. For several decades there was an effort to get waterfowl hunters to switch from lead to steel shot. Ducks feed on spent shot that fall into their ponds, needing grit for their gizzards, and afterward die slowly from lead poisoning. Two to three million ducks and geese were dying this way each year. Steel shot are a little more expensive, wear the bore a little faster, and were unfamiliar to hunters, who must adjust for the weight difference. Weapons manufacturers mostly resisted steel shot; federal agencies eventually required their use. So it seems that there is an ethic that must be learned in culture for the natural-born hunter (Thomas, 1997).

Hunting for meat and simultaneously for sport typically combine (deer hunting), though when this becomes mere hunting for sport, with little interest in the meat (bear hunting), this becomes harder to justify (List, 2004; Loftin, 1984). Montana and Idaho elk hunters hunt for both food and sport. In recent years, with wolves delisted and legal to hunt, thousands of these elk hunters also buy a wolf tag, just in case they get a shot at a wolf. None of these hunters intends to eat a wolf, should they kill one. This seems to reveal another aspect of the drive to hunt—like that of the trophy hunters to which we next turn. Predators kill for food, not for sport, and the claim that sport hunting is "natural" is implausible, even if wild predators enjoy their kill.

Justifying killing a trophy animal is even harder (Gunn, 2001). If trophy hunting is ever accepted by environmental ethicists, this is typically with misgivings (wealthy elephant hunters supplying income to local villagers, encouraging the locals to conserve their profitable elephants). More frankly, it seems that the big gun-slingers, the great white hunters, are driven by macho pretensions. They may talk about "respect" for the big game they kill and getting immersed in primordial realities—cycles of decay, death and rebirth (Magnuson, 1991). In fact, killing the trophies, they want to prove themselves he-men.

But with a little psychoanalysis, deeper down, such archaic behavior is, in fact, primitive and childish and they ought to grow up. The romantics are not the animal lovers. The romantics are the masculine hunters who cling to a mythological past. Among the beasts, females hunt as much or more than the males, even if, among humans, the women who bear and nurse children hunt less than men (Stange, 1997). Hunting belongs with bullfighting. Get heroic on the athletic field, cycling, or backpacking; prove your masculinity, tenacity, discipline, courage in ways that do not require violent killing of animals for sport.

Even if you do not hunt, but do fish, some of these counter arguments will still face you. You too seem to put sentient animals to stress and pain for their sport. Fishermen like for the fish to fight and pride themselves on pulling it in. They may "catch and release" and think themselves good conservationists for releasing the fish. Then they do it all over again, torturing another fish. By some accounts "catch and eat" is a better ethic. Catch enough for supper, then quit and enjoy the woods (de Leeuw, 1996).

Humans do not just hunt and kill wild animals. Sometimes they save them. Sometimes they take compassion on them. If one seeks appropriate respect for wild beasts, the ethic now takes an about face: "Be humane!" But then again these beasts are not humans, so maybe we should not be humane.

Save the whales! The world cheered in the fall of 1988 when we rescued two gray whales from the winter ice off Point Barrow Alaska. The whales were stranded for three weeks several miles from open water, rising to breathe through small—and shrinking—holes in the ice. Chainsaws cut pathways through the ice and a Russian icebreaker broke open a path to the sea. We spent more than a million dollars to save them; they drew the sympathy of millions of people. A polar bear, coming in to eat the whales, was chased away. Television confronted the nation with the plight of the suffering whales. Seeing them sticking their heads out of the ice and trying to breathe, everybody wanted to help. We saved the whales. People felt good about it (Shabecoff, 1988; Clayton, 1998).

But was that really the right thing to do? Maybe it was too much money spent, money that could have been used better to save the whales—or to save people. Maybe money is not the only or even the principal consideration. Maybe our compassion overwhelmed us, and we let these two whales become a symbol of survival, but they do not really symbolize our duties in conservation and animal welfare. Maybe we needed not to help the whales, but to let the fittest survive.

Let the bison drown! One February morning in 1983 a bison fell through the ice into the Yellowstone River, and, struggling to escape, succeeded only in enlarging the hole. Toward dusk a party of snowmobilers looped a rope around the animal's horns and, pulling, nearly saved it, but not quite. It grew dark and the rescuers abandoned their attempt. Temperatures fell to twenty below that night; in the morning the bison was dead. The ice refroze around the dead bison. Coyotes and ravens ate the exposed part of the carcass. After the spring thaw, a grizzly bear was seen feeding on the rest, a bit of rope still attached to the horns (Robbins, 1984).

The snowmobilers were disobeying park authorities who had ordered them not to rescue it. One of the snowmobilers was troubled by the callous attitude. A drowning human would have been saved at once; so would a drowning horse. The Bible commends getting an ox out of a ditch, even if this means breaking the Sabbath (Luke 14.5). It was as vital to the struggling bison as to any person to get out; the poor thing was freezing to death. A park ranger replied that the incident was natural and the bison should be left to its fate.

A snowmobiler protested, "If you're not going to help it, then why don't you put it out of its misery?" But mercy-killing too was contrary to the park ethic, which was, in effect: "Let it suffer!" That seems so inhumane, contrary to everything we are taught about being kind, doing to others as we would have them do to us, or respecting the right to life. Isn't it cruel to let nature take its course?

The snowmobilers thought so. One contacted radio commentator Paul Harvey, who made three national broadcasts attacking park service indifference. "The reason Jesus came to earth was to keep nature from taking its course." Was the Yellowstone ethic too callous, inhumane? This ethic seems rather to have concluded that a simple extension of compassion from human ethics or humane society ethics to wildlife is too nondiscriminating. To treat wild animals with compassion learned in culture does not appreciate their wildness. That was the trouble with rescuing those whales. Or, animal activists will say, we are carrying this let-nature-take-its-course ethic to extremes.

Let the lame deer suffer! In April 1989 in Glacier National Park a wolverine attacked a deer in deep snow but did not finish the attack, possibly interrupted by two workmen who saw the event from a distance, a rare sighting of an endangered species. The injured deer struggled out onto the ice of Lake McDonald, but, hamstrung, could move no further. Many visitors saw it; a photograph appeared in the local newspaper. Park officials declined to end its suffering. Possibly the wolverine would return. So, the lame deer suffered throughout the day, the night, and died the following morning (*Hungry Horse News*, 1989). Can this be the right ethics for a wild animal, so inhumane and indifferent? Or has ethics here somehow gone wild in the bad sense, blinded by a philosophy of false respect for cruel nature? Park officials can sometimes be compassionate. The same spring that the lame deer was left to its fate a bear was injured when hit by a truck, and Glacier Park officials mercy-killed the bear.

Let the blinded bighorns starve! The bighorn sheep of Yellowstone caught pinkeye (conjunctivitis) in the winter of 1981–82. On craggy slopes, partial blindness can be fatal. A sheep misses a jump, feeds poorly, and is soon injured and starving in result. More than three hundred bighorns, over 60% of the herd, perished (Thorne, 1987). Wildlife veterinarians wanted to treat the disease, as they would have in any domestic herd, but the Yellowstone ethicists left them to suffer, seemingly not respecting their life. Their decision was that the disease was natural, and should be left to run its course. Had they no mercy? Was this inhumane?

A human being in a frozen river would be rescued at once; a human attacked by a wolverine would be flown by helicopter to the hospital. Bison and deer are not humans and we cannot give them identical treatment; still, if suffering is a bad thing for humans, who seek to eliminate it, why is suffering not also a bad thing for bison? After all, the poor bison was struggling to get out of the ice. We cannot give medical treatment to all wild animals; we should not interrupt a predator killing its prey. But when we happen upon an opportunity to rescue an animal with the pull of a rope, or mercy-kill it lest it suffer, why not? If we can treat a herd of blinded sheep, why not? That seems to be what human nature urges, and why not let human nature take its course? Sympathy toward suffering animals is appropriate, wild as well as domestic (Fisher, 1987). That seems to be doing to others as you would have them do to you.

But perhaps mercy and humanity are not the criteria for decision here. The ethic of compassion must be set in a bigger picture of animal welfare, recognizing the function of pain in the wild. The Yellowstone ethicists knew that, while intrinsic pain is a bad thing whether in humans or in sheep, pain in ecosystems is instrumental pain, through which the sheep are naturally selected for a more satisfactory adaptive fit. Pain in a medically skilled culture is pointless, once the alarm to health is sounded and heeded, but pain operates functionally in bighorns in their niche, even after it becomes no longer in the interests of the pained individual. To have interfered in the interests of the blinded sheep would have weakened the species. Simply to ask whether they suffer is not enough. We must ask whether they suffer with a beneficial effect on the wild population.

Of course, we treat our children who catch pinkeye. We put them to bed, draw the curtains, and physicians prescribe eyedrops with sodium sulfacetamide. The *Chlamydia* microbes are destroyed and the children back outside playing in a few days. But they are not genetically any different than before the disease, nor will the next generation be different. When the grandchildren catch pinkeye, they will get eyedrops too. But that is an ethic for culture, where humans interrupt and relax natural selection. The welfare of the sheep still lies under the rigors of natural selection. As a result of the park ethic, only those sheep that were genetically more fit, able to cope with the disease, survived; and this coping is now coded in the survivors. What we *ought* to do depends on what *is*. The *is* of nature differs significantly from the *is* of culture, even when similar suffering is present in both.

Compassion is not the only consideration in an ethic, and in environmental ethics it plays a different role than in a humanist ethics. Animals live in the wild, where they are still subject to the forces of natural selection, and the integrity of the species is a result of these selective pressures. To intervene artificially in the processes of natural selection is not to do wild animals any benefit at the level of the good of the kind, although it would benefit an individual bison or deer. Human beings, by contrast, are no longer simply subject to the forces of natural selection. They live in culture, where these forces are relaxed, and the integrity of *Homo sapiens* does not depend on wild nature.

In that sense, these compassionate feelings innate in us and the imperatives urged by our moral education are misplaced when they are transferred to the wilds. We ought not to treat the bison as we would a person, because a bison in a wild ecosystem is not a person in a culture.

Pain in any culture ought to be compassionately relieved where it can be with an interest in the welfare of the sufferers. But pain in the wild ought not to be relieved if and when it interrupts the ecosystemic processes on which the welfare of these animals depends.

Having said this, we must also recognize that suffering in natural systems is often contingent. We do not have any evidence that the drowning bison was genetically inferior. We might suppose that the lame deer was a weaker one but we do not know that. These animals could have just been unlucky. In the zig-zag of chance and mischance, each zigged when a zag would have saved it—the bison crossing the river, the deer with its tendons severed by a wolverine claw. Now, alas, each lies suffering. Have we any duty to respect that rotten luck?

This is wildness once again, not so much the survival of the fittest, a process that we can respect, but the death of the unfortunate, whose carcasses will be exploited by opportunist scavengers. Ethics can really seem to have gone wild when it respects even this contingent element in nature and refuses to end for-tuitous pain. Sometimes it seems that an environmental ethics takes us nearer than we wish toward a tragic view of life. Yet, even tragic contingency is pulled into ecosystem integrity. Scavengers too have adapted fits in ecosystems and enrich the biodiversity.

Treat the bighorns with lungworm! Colorado wildlife veterinarians have made extensive efforts to rid the Colorado bighorns of lungworm (genus: *Pro-tostrongylus*), concerned about the welfare of the sheep, respecting their right to life. We let the blinded bighorns starve in Wyoming, but we fed the Colo-rado bighorns apples laced with Fenbendazole (Schmidt et al., 1979; Miller et al., 1987). Were the Colorado veterinarians more moral than the Wyoming ones? But we have to consider that the lungworm parasite was contracted (most think) from imported domestic sheep and that such human interruption yields a duty to promote welfare not present in the Yellowstone case. Others say that the parasite is native but that the bighorns' natural resistance to it is weakened because human settlements in the foothills deprive sheep of their winter forage and force them to winter at higher elevations. There, undernourished, they contract the lungworm first and later die of pneumonia, caused by bacteria, generally genus *Pasteurella*. Also the lungworm is passed to the lambs who die of pneumonia when they are a few months old.

The difference is this. The introduced parasite, or the disrupted winter range, or both, mean that the original processes of natural selection that had shaped the sheep were no longer taking place. The sheep were being exposed to conditions with which they had no evolutionary experience. We were run-ning the risk of human interferences causing a species to go extinct. Letting the lungworm disease run its course really was not letting nature take its course; and, both in concern for the species and in concern for suffering individuals, treatment was required.

If we move this principle with populations back down to the individual level, we see why the lame deer should not be mercy-killed but why the bear hit by a truck was. The logic is that encounter with a truck (an artifact) is no part of the forces of natural selection that have operated historically on bears. Where humans cause the pain, they are under obligation to minimize it. If we had thought that the wolverine failed to kill the deer because humans interrupted the attack, that might have been cause to dispatch it, although even here consideration for the wolverine, as an endangered species, would probably have meant that the deer should be left in case the wolverine returned.

4. Domestic Animals: From Cows to Poodles

Humans have domesticated a large number of animals, from cows to poodles. Over the centuries, civilization in Europe and Asia is hardly imaginable without horses, donkeys, mules. We still race horses. We raise to kill and eat the beef cows; we pet the poodles and attend to their needs almost as though they were children. In industrial agriculture, when we exploit animals for human interests, what ethical obligations do humans have to reduce the suffering of animals? Perhaps humans should become vegetarians and not eat meat at all. Perhaps we can eat meat but only if we minimize animal suffering. Or perhaps we ought to treat the animals so that they do not suffer any more than they might have if they were not domesticated and had continued in wild nature, where they might be prey for predators and certainly would have to struggle to survive.

An ethic of respect for nature does not seem to bind humans to inflict no innocent suffering. That seems rather to be inevitable in the food chains in nature, or in the struggles for survival. In the clash and interweaving of goods in an ecosystem, pain goes with the defending and capturing of goods that characterizes all sentient life. Nothing lives autonomously; not even autotrophs (plants). Everything competes with neighboring life. One good must spoil another. Heterotrophs (animals) sacrifice other lives for their own. Sentient lives both suffer and cause pain. No predator can live without causing pain.

Humans evolved out of such environments. Even yet (by account of the hunter's ethic) they may hunt in such environments. When humans now domesticate (capture) animals, they may continue to inflict innocent suffering, particularly in the regimens of securing food, shelter, and basic physical comforts. Human predation on nature, more or less within the natural patterns, cannot be condemned simply because humans are moral agents, not if nonhuman predation has been accepted as a vital component in the wild system. The wild animal has no right or welfare claim to have from humans a kinder treatment than in nonhuman nature. What should happen morally when encountering nature (distinguished from what happens within culture) is a function of what has happened naturally. Nearly all meat-eaters claim that their meat-eating is "natural."

Meanwhile, culture ought not to amplify the cruelty in nature, certainly not without showing that greater goods come of it. The way to judge whether an intervention introduces needful suffering is to ask whether the suffering is analogous to functional, baseline suffering in the ecosystemic routines. At this point, right in culture means no more than right in nature, that is, in continuity with the satisfactory fit that such an animal had in the ecosystem from which it was taken. What *is* in nature is taken as a criterion for what *ought-to-be* when culture overtakes nature. Making a resource of something else is pervasive in the system, even when this inflicts suffering; and, when humans do this too, they simply follow nature. There is nothing immoral about participating in the logic and biology of one's ecosystem.

In this sense the claim may now be that those who sympathize with the pains of animals and wish to eliminate these pains (by being vegetarians, for instance) are not biologically sensitive but insensitive. Pain is a pervasive fact of life, not to be wished away by a kindly ethic, neither in natural systems, nor in agricultural overlays on these systems. Eating plants and animals is the way mammalian nature works. Humans continue this pattern with their interruptions of the natural order. This shows no disrespect for animal life; to the contrary it respects natural processes. We follow nature and set norms accordingly.

It might first be thought that pain is an evil wherever it occurs, in nature or in culture, and so it does not matter whether the injury is in a human or a cow. The evil is that it hurts, and the cow has as much right to painless life as does the human. But pain operates functionally in meat-eating, whether a cougar is eating a deer or a human eating a cow. Pain in nature is situated, instrumental pain. The pain is not pointless in the system, even after it becomes no longer in the interests of the pained individual. The profit in the pain has vanished for persons undergoing medical treatment, but it remains in meat-eating. Animals have no right to be removed from their niche, nor have we a duty to remove them, nor a duty to reform nature when we superpose agriculture and industry on it.

We can add that where pain in agricultural or industrial animals has also become pointless, because they too have been removed from the environment of natural selection, humans have a duty to remove it, as far as they can. Where humans elect to capture animals for food, domestication, research, or other utility, our duties to them, if any arise, are generated by these animals' encounters with culture, and are not simply a matter of the animals' *capacity* to suffer pains but of their *context* (Palmer, 2010). That context is both natural and cultural; it is a hybrid of the two.

The animals do not participate cognitively in human culture; on the other hand they are not in the wild, but domesticated. Judgments about duties are not merely to sentience, but to sentience in niche in ecosystem, now modified by agriculture. In the capturing of values in nature, pain is often present, even in innocent life, and when culture captures values in nature, there is only a weak duty to subtract from the pain. Such pain is no longer in the context of natural selection, but it remains in the context of the transfer of ecological goods, inherited from the wilds.

Now the claim is not based on capacity to suffer alone, but on more systemic, ecosystemic considerations. Meat-eating in culture exploits animals, but this also fits into the natural givens, where pain is inseparable from the transfer of values between sentient lives. Culturally imposed suffering must be comparable to ecologically functional suffering. Humans ought to introduce no inordinate, unnatural suffering, though they may substitute variant forms in their interests. If we wish to use rights language, we can say that animals gain that much right in their encounter with humans. Ethics does not require us to deny our ecology, but rather to affirm it, even as we domesticate and rebuild our environment. Ecology, not charity or justice, provides the benchmark, or at least the floor. Going further can be commended, but not required.

Reduce suffering as far as it is pointless. Above any ecosystem base, or following nature, this ethic has a hedonist concern for pointless pain. There is a long tradition of concern for animals under human care, often with laws about cruelty to animals (the rancher who lets his horses starve). Some of this goes back to biblical times. "A righteous man has regard for the life of his beast" (Proverbs 12.10). Oxen are to be rested on the sabbath (Exodus 20.10); the ox in the pit requires rescue, even at breach of the sabbath (Luke 14.5). The ox that treads out the grain is not to be muzzled (Deuteronomy 25.4), nor are animals to be unequally yoked (Deuteronomy 22.10). Such concerns urge compassionate treatment of domestic animals.

Earlier we seemed to be arguing that, by parity of reasoning, if pain is bad for humans, then pain is also bad for animals. Humans ought not to cause it. We would not want ourselves to be eaten by lions or bears; so we ought not to eat deer or cows. But now there is disparity; we humans can eat animals and cause them pain. We might call that a farmer's ethic. Keep and eat animals, but show as much respect as you can for their welfare; treat them as humanely as possible, given that beef cows are raised to be eaten. Similarly with pigs, chickens, turkeys, and other domestic food animals. This may be called "free-range" farming, where the cows are in pastures, the chickens roam the barnyard, in contrast with the confinement to which we next turn. Where this is combined with concern for how vegetables are raised, this is often called "organic food," and those who shop for foods may patronize such natural products.

Now the objection will be raised that, even if such a farmer's ethic is plausible on rural lands, or even if a few can buy such now-specialty organic foods (once common to our great-grandfathers), most of our meat comes from modern factory farms where such animals are treated quite differently, or indifferently. Developing in the last half century, factory farming is the practice of raising confined livestock or other food animals (chickens, turkeys) in high density operations, usually indoors. Some may be called concentrated animal feeding operations (CAFOs), indoors or out. A farm operates as a factory, an industrial agribusiness. The main product of this industry is meat, milk, or eggs for human consumption, with a systematic effort to produce the highest output at the lowest cost by relying on economies of scale, modern machinery, biotechnology, and modern (even global) transportation.

Factory farming does get its products in the markets and on the table at lower prices, but there is ongoing debate about whether organic or free range farming could do as well, if it too were high volume. Perhaps consumers ought to be willing (or even required by law) to pay higher prices if this reduces animal suffering. There is debate about the motivations of the factory farmers. Are such agri-industrialists really motivated to benefit humans with cheaper food, or are they driven by profit, heedless of animal pain, and selling as high as they can where they can?

Factory farming advocates often claim that they must attend to animal health; animal health and economic profitability are complementary goals. The high density requires antibiotics and pesticides to prevent the spread of disease and pestilence exacerbated by these crowded living conditions. Antibiotics are also used to stimulate livestock growth by killing intestinal bacteria (possibly also creating "superbugs"). Disposal of animal wastes is often a problem, especially when pollutant run-off escapes into surrounding streams or groundwater. Although factory farming began in developed countries, over 40% of meat worldwide is produced on factory farms (Nierenberg, 2005, p. 5). So the claim may be that, in the light of increasing human populations and future demands for food, factory farming is necessary.

Factory farming is one cause, though not the only cause, of the declining number of persons who live on farms. Agricultural production has escalated, but the number of people involved in farming has dropped as the process has become more automated. In the 1930s, 24% of the American population worked in agriculture compared to 1.5% in 2002; in 1940, each farm worker supplied eleven consumers, whereas in 2002, each worker supplied ninety consumers (Scully, 2002, p. 29). In the United States, four companies produce 81% of cows, 73% of sheep, 57% of pigs and 50% of chickens.

In the United States, farmed animals are excluded from the Animal Welfare Act (see below on research animals), also by many state animal cruelty laws. There is a Twenty Eight Hour Law, enacted in 1873 and amended in 1994 (Public Law 103-272; 49 U.S.C. 80502), which states that when animals are being transported for slaughter, the vehicle must stop every 28 hours and the animals must be let out for exercise, food, and water. The United States

Department of Agriculture claims that the law does not apply to birds. The Humane Methods of Livestock Slaughter Act, originally passed in 1958 (Public Law 85-765, 7 U.S.C. 1901 ff), requires that livestock be stunned into unconsciousness prior to slaughter. Individual states all have their own animal cruelty statutes; however many states have a provision to exempt standard agricultural practices. The Michigan State University College of Law maintains an Animal Legal and Historical Center, with information about laws pertaining to animals (http://www.animallaw.info).

In the United Kingdom, there is a Farm Animal Welfare Council, which was set up by the government to act as an independent advisor on animal welfare in 1979. For farmed animals, they advocate five freedoms: from hunger and thirst; from discomfort; from pain, injury or disease; to express normal behavior; and from fear and distress (http://www.fawc.org.uk) (Brooman and Legge, 1997).

Some issues have been the de-beaking of chickens, to keep them from fighting, poor air quality, the lack of daylight, of freedom of movement (animals may be confined to crates no larger than themselves), about social stress due to crowding, about discarding useless animals. There has been particular concern about the close confinement of sow pigs with piglets (gestation crates), and this is being phased out in the United States and the European Union. There is concern about the use of drugs to stimulate growth, about breeding for passive animals that can live in these conditions.

There is concern about intensifying animal diseases, which not only causes animals to suffer, but might spread some of these diseases to humans, or even create pandemic pathogens, for example avian flu. On global scales, the "just-in-time" delivery system transports millions of animals in a few days time, inviting poor inspection and the unexpected transmission of animal diseases in crowded conditions. Fresh meat (and other produce) is flown across oceans and delivered the day before it is sold. The customer is satisfied; the wholesaler saves cost of inventory and warehousing. Stressed animals, some of whom have travelled long distances, will be more susceptible to diseases, and these stressed animals are likely to be mixed in pens and batteries with local and healthy animals.

Consumer desires for cheap and tasty food override caution and care in production—coupling with producers desires to maximize profit. This will stress inspection systems that need time to be more cautious. Developed nations can monitor livestock and food commerce within their borders, but not overseas origins, which is not within their jurisdiction. Agencies have to respect national borders; pathogens do not. This situation is likely to generate mismatches between free market economics and the biology of pathogens. Surveillance, domestic or international, is piecemeal; nobody has this scope of vision or authority.

Ever more massive power to manipulate these animals will sooner or later have far-reaching, amplifying adverse consequences, both for the animals and the humans they feed. As the depth of upset advances across the spectrum from global to microbial processes, unintended consequences accompany the intended consequences. Human power to produce changes overshoots increasingly human power to foresee all the results of these changes.

A disease of cattle, BSE (bovine spongiform encephalopathy), which may cause Creutzfeldt-Jacob disease in humans, was found in the United Kingdom. The United Kingdom *BSE Inquiry Report* to the House of Commons concluded that those who authorized feeding cattle recycled meat and bone meal (MBM) remains from sheep and cattle, ought to have anticipated trouble with the effort "to turn grass-eaters into cannibals," feeding them food that cattle did not evolve to eat. They ask "why those responsible for the practice of using MBM in cattle feed did not foresee that this might be a recipe for disaster." "What went wrong was that no one foresaw the possibility of the entry into the animal feed cycle of a lethal agent far more virulent than the conventional viral and bacterial pathogens, and one which would be capable of infecting cattle despite passing through the rendering process" (Phillips, Bridegman, and Ferguson-Smith, 2000, vol 1, pp. 226–227). To put this bluntly: if—to push your profits—you try to make carnivores out of herbivores, you can expect upsetting surprises. Capitalists want to operate, as economists say, "at the margin." Although in commerce that has a technical meaning, it also means that capitalists will stress the limits of their productive systems.

Despite the UK experience, the U.S. Food and Drug Administration, though it has proposed some prohibitions, particularly of brain and spinal materials, still permits feeding animal proteins to livestock. The F.D.A. and the meat industry remain "totally committed to continuing the practice of feeding slaughterhouse waste to cows." A ban on feeding all animal protein to livestock, an F.D.A. spokesperson says, would be "a big expense for the industry." This comes, of course, with simultaneous F.D.A. reassurances that the new prohibitions will "remove 90 percent of potentially infectious matter from all animal feed" and that this "reduces a very, very low risk even lower" (McNeil, 2005). Remembering how, as one critical summary of the UK Phillips report put it, the cattle were fed the animal protein, the "nation fed a diet of reassurances" (Connor, 2000), one wonders whether to trust the experts and, if they are right, whether low, low risk of a pandemic disease is acceptable. That worry increases with the fear that the industry in its drive for profits is unwilling to consider any big expense in the interests of food safety.

To economic concerns, we can add political ones. Once a disease is found unexpectedly in the animals, the danger hits the press, and the regulatory authorities decide to go safe, there is likely to be overkill. Perhaps the overkill is justified by the safety caution, given the unknown dangers. But notice that, after the alarm, government authorities, now embarrassed, are likely to wish to show their muscle, as much to impress citizens, as to control the epidemic. They are now watching the spread of public opinion as much as of the disease (Phillips et al., 2000, vol. 1, pp. 98, 127–129). In choosing their strategies, they want to re-assure the public, and also to re-assure customers at home and abroad. This keeps the economic profits going and the politicians and regulators in office.

In any mass slaughter program to prevent the spread of a newly found and feared disease, far the vastest number of the slaughtered will be quite healthy animals. Most of the slaughter will be on suspicion or "just in case," a thousand cows for every one that has foot and mouth disease. If the cull includes all the animals on nearby farms as well (within three kilometers in Britain), that will result in devastating hardship on innocent owners, to say nothing of the innocent cows. Innocent owners may have little choice once the cull policy is in place; the policy is dictated. Or if not dictated, any farmer with misgivings is shunned as being unpatriotic; their cows may be killed willy-nilly.

Such mass slaughter programs kill, probably by less than the most humane methods, large numbers of perfectly healthy animals. Most of the animals were destined to be killed and eaten, of course. But at least then some good would have come of their deaths. In the cull, the animals are wasted. The UK killed six million animals in the 2001 outbreak of foot and mouth disease. In the BSE (bovine spongiform encephalopathy) epidemic 170,000 cows died from BSE, and another 4.7 million were killed in a precautionary slaughter, and over 140 persons died from a new variant of Creutzfeldt-Jacob Disease (VCJD), contracted as a result of exposure to contaminated meat. One kind of pressure, to have food fast and cheap, pushed too far, results in another extreme, massive slaughter and waste. Fear of Asian flu led to culling of 20 million chickens in eight nations (Abbott, 2004). Public health is at stake, as authorities will correctly claim. But what drives the overkill may as much be economic fears of industry collapse. Certainly minimal killing and concern for animal suffering is not an issue.

People don't just eat or do research on animals. They keep pets. The dog is man's best friend. Horses today are almost entirely recreational animals. Is there a different ethic for companion animals? (Spencer et al., 2006). One may first think that with pet animals humans are at their best caring for nature (Beck and Katcher, 1996). The animals are well fed, sheltered, kept healthy, and have an easy life. They are members of the family. Over half of dog owners sign for the pets too when they send Christmas cards. The dogs enjoy their relationship with their owners. Haven't you ever played fetch throwing a stick that the dog enthusiastically retrieves? These animals are not wild; they are lucky. The more of this the better. There are about as many dogs and cats in the United States as there are adult humans, sixty million dogs and seventy million cats. The number of pets in Europe is similar. Although people kept pets in earlier centuries (often as much working dogs: hunting, guard, or sheep dogs), the huge number of companion animals is relatively recent in human history (Ritvo, 1987).

But there are critics. Pets, even as companion animals, are being used for human ends. You are a "pet owner." Would you consider your husband, wife, or child a pet you own? That would be demeaning. But these are animals, pet owners reply, and that is different. They are loved, petted, which makes them radically different from laboratory or farm animals. Even for farm animals, there was concern that they be free to express their natural behavior, but pets often do not, and cannot. Dogs may be kept in houses for most of the day; some cats never go outdoors at all. Pet rabbits are kept in hutches, guinea pigs and birds in cages. They are, in effect, in prison. Dogs may have their tails docked, be forced into shampooing, poodles will have their hair cut and nails painted, may be shock-collared to prevent their barking. Dog lovers push specialist breeding that warps the dog's natural tendencies, as for example, in dogs bred to be ornamental movie-star lapdogs, in St. Bernards or in Boxers with breathing troubles). In fact, it may be claimed that dogs (descended from wolves) have been bred for so long that they no longer have any original "nature" in them. They are artifacts of civilization. There are feral dogs, but no Cocker Spaniel could survive if turned loose in a wilderness.

Another problem has been unwanted horses, too old, unruly, or expensive to keep. In the past, these were "put out to pasture," but this is often not an option. One might say just euthanize the horse, and bury it, but that proves expensive too. Such horses were slaughtered, up to 100,000 a year, and the meat shipped overseas to Asian and European markets, but horse lovers have complained that this typically was done inhumanely, and such slaughterhouses were shut down by Act of Congress in 2007. After that, many were shipped to Mexico and slaughtered in plants there, sometimes under even more inhuman conditions. Recently animal welfare activists have been asking whether it is not better to do the slaughter humanely in the United States (Simon, 2011).

The very existence of humane societies, such as The Humane Society of the United States, results from problems people have with their pets, which often become unwanted animals. The Royal Society for the Prevention of Cruelty to Animals in the United Kingdom (RSPCA) has long been concerned with mistreatment of pets. In England and Wales, the Animal Welfare Act, coming into force in 2007, updated a number of pet abuse laws. This Act does ban tail-docking of dogs for cosmetic purposes (with exceptions for military and police dogs). It also bans ear-cropping. In Scotland the Animal Health and Welfare Act came into force in 2006. Those concerned for human poverty will note that the amount of money spent on pet food in developed countries, if it could be transferred, would go a long ways toward sustaining starving children in the poorer developing countries. Pets increasingly get high-tech medicine at high costs (Nordheimer, 1990).

5. Zoos: Caged Beasts on Display

People enjoy seeing wild animals, but animals in the wild are inconvenient to see. Some of the commoner kinds can be seen in outdoor recreation, and people go to national parks to see wildlife. Still, animals may live far away, or be active at night, or easily spooked, or rare; they do not accommodate our wishes to see them. A solution to this is to cage them for observation, and the result is a zoo. But this is a problematic solution. A wild animal in a zoo is not really a wild animal anymore; the wildness has been caged.

A lion in a zoo is still a lion from the skin in; the morphology and metabolism is there, but the lion from the skin-out is gone. It can't behave like a lion; it can't be a lion. A species in the wild is an adapted fit in an ecosystem; it is *what* it is *where* it is. Species are processes, dynamic historical lines, and not just the products, individuals. In an ecological view of the world, things belong in their natural environments; they are what they are in their niches. In zoos, lions' brains even degenerate because they do not have to use them.

Still, a zoo might be, on balance, a good thing, even though some animal values are sacrificed. There are four main justifications: recreation, education, scientific research, and conservation (Hutchins, Smith, Allard, 2003). Zoos are also a refuge for injured animals that cannot be released into the wild. The degree to which zoos do in fact provide such benefits is an empirical question, and no doubt different zoos succeed in different proportions. Sufficient amounts of these benefits might indeed override the loss of minimal animal values. But insufficient amounts would not. Some factors to consider will be whether the recreation is mostly amusement, which could be as well obtained in other forms of amusement, or whether there is some unique recreational benefit here. Perhaps, for instance, children have a special need for first-hand encounter with wild animals, as in some "petting zoos."

Likewise, the educational benefits must be evaluated: do zoo visitors learn the right things about animals? Do they learn anything that they could not better learn by watching nature shows on television? Or by visiting national parks? Does the menagerie of animals caged for amusement teach the wrong thing about animals so loudly that other educational efforts toward the appreciation of wild animals can hardly be heard? Surveys indicate that zoo-goers do not learn much; they are mostly there for causal amusement.

Certainly there are some scientific benefits. The animal keepers can learn the nutritional requirements of the animals, veterinarians can observe animal diseases and experiment with treating them. Perhaps there will be some medical benefits for people. But there will be few ecological or behavioral facts learned, since the animals are in a highly artificial context. In fact, few zoos conduct any scientific research; what there is could be accomplished in half a dozen zoos, instead of the thousands of zoos there are in the world. Sometimes animals can be kept temporarily in zoos and later released into the wild. Or animals can be bred for restoration into the wild. Or the interests of visitors can be enlisted to support conservation research and restocking. But neither the scientific nor the conservation justifications require the use of animals recreationally; these might not be compatible at all. The capture of animals for zoos might endanger wild populations. Typically, ten chimpanzees are killed or die in transport to bring one into the United States. So the issues are complex.

On the one hand, the great zoos of the world have, over the years, kept wildlife in the public eye and generated much appreciation for wildlife. On the other hand, they compromise wildlife by caging it, often frustrating wild lives, demeaning those "born free" to lives in capture, relatively comfortable and well nourished though these lives may be. Zoos can be modified so that animals are less caged; they may have more freedom of movement in an enclosure that mimics their natural environment. With small animals in large enough environments, the animals might hardly know they are caged. With larger animals, an animal can have a simulated natural environment only to a limited extent even in the most ideal situation, and few zoos have done much in practice to achieve this.

Shifting perceptions, changing values, and deeper sensitivities to the integrity of wild lives has led to steadily increased efforts either to redesign zoos to minimize the invasion of animal lives, or to phase out zoos entirely. In the early 1990s, this attitude, for instance, coupled with the increasingly high costs of operating zoos, led to the threatened closing of the world's largest and most famous zoo, the London Zoo. Critics said that Londoners ought to move past entertaining themselves by staring at animals pacing about in cages and pens. Shutting down the London Zoo would be a step forward, teaching that the proper place for animals is their own natural setting. But the London Zoo continues and cages 15,000 animals for the pleasure of Londoners, unable or unwilling to see them in the wild.

"Zoo professionals like to say that they are the Noahs of the modern world and that zoos are their arks. But Noah found a place to land his animals where they could thrive and multiply. If zoos are like arks, then rare animals are like passengers on a voyage of the damned" (Jamieson, in Norton et al, 1995, p. 62). Noah took the animals on the legendary ark to protect them during a calamity, and after two months let them all off again. But zoos are arks which most animals never get off; the ark is a euphemism for a prison (Jamieson, 1985).

What is the justification for and the future of zoos? What are they doing? Entertaining the public? Educating the public? What are the targets of protection—genes, individuals, populations, species, ecosystems? What is the relationship between captive breeding and wild populations? What are the protocols of humane captive care and maintenance? How do zoos raise funds and how is their treatment of captive animals affected by their need to please the zoo public? Critics of zoos, especially those alert to the philosophical debates about animal welfare, register troubling concerns that zoo advocates have had difficulty answering (Norton et al., 1995; Bostock, 1993; Hancocks. 2001).

Zoos claim repeatedly that the first priority of the reinvented, modern zoo is wildlife conservation. "Wildlife conservation has been identified as the highest priority of the AZA (American Zoo and Aquarium Association)" "Reintroduction is a primary goal of keeping animals in captivity" (Norton et al., 1995, p. 148, p. 127, 181). After that comes science, education, and recreation. But the plain fact is that zoos do not, and probably cannot, practice what they preach. In fact, zoos contain tens of thousands of animals which they have no intention of returning to the wild. They are there for public recreation. Millions of people visit zoos each year. If, during the recreation, there can be education, so much the better. That might justify recreation requiring entertainment by caged animals. Meanwhile, surveys fail to find that zoogoers are much educated by their visits.

A few zoos have highly visible reintroduction programs, but most do little or nothing of this kind. Most of the seemingly successful programs (lion tamarins, whooping cranes, red wolves, the Arabian oryx), when looked at more carefully, reveal the zoo as relatively unimportant in the process. The zoo is not really a suitable facility for a captive breeding program. Reintroductions are complicated and difficult procedures, which involve not simply zoology, but politics, economics, social reform, education, long-term funding stability, restoration and protection of wild habitats, and zoos are not equipped to undertake much of such activity.

If zoos were to accept that their first priority is to return animals to the wild, then many of their animals are not genetically suitable for such return, often because of inbreeding, depression, or hybridization. All the Siberian tigers in zoos in North America are descendants of seven animals; they have been through a genetic bottleneck. Neither they nor their descendants could ever be released. Zoos would have to do much culling—killing the animals with undesirable genes to make space for animals with desirable genes for reintroduction. Zoos are unwilling to do this, nor would their public support it, especially with the primates or charismatic megafauna, and thus zoos are forced to keep animals for years, even decades, that have no contribution to make to any reintroduction program.

Zoos have made increasing efforts to place their animals in naturalistic settings, though most improvements have been only cosmetic and restricted to areas viewed by the public; and there have been valiant but scattered attempts at behavioral enrichment. The zoo advocates are persistent. The catchphrases of the new zoos sound good: "Strengthening the bond between people and the living earth" (Minnesota Zoo). "Bettering the bond between people and the planet" (Louisville Zoo). Maryland's Baltimore Aquarium seeks to "create an understanding of the environment and the ecological balance of life" (Norton et al., 1995, pp. 25–26).

William Conway, as director of the Bronx Zoo in New York, claims: "Except for zoos and zoolike institutions, no other conservation or animal welfare organizations actually provide ongoing animal-by-animal care for wild creatures, sustaining them generation after generation" (Conway, in Norton et al., 1995, p. 7). Conway hardly seems to register that with animal-by-animal care generation after generation, one no longer has wildlife, nor wildlife conservation. Wildlife in a zoo is a contradiction in terms, which becomes the more evident the longer it is there. The ethics of keeping animals in zoos remains confused, and there seem to be no satisfactory solutions on the horizon (Jensen and Tweedy-Holmes, 2007). Safari Parks are really just big open zoos. Much the same can be said for animals in aquariums, for example, with dolphins.

6. Research Animals: Experimenting for Animal/Human Good

The U.S. federal government mandates an animal ethic. The Animal Welfare Act, first passed by the U.S. Congress in 1966 and variously updated (7 U.S.C Chapter 54, Sections 2131-2159; Public Law 89-544), requires humane treatment of animals. The Act applies to the treatment of animals in laboratories, to dealers who sell animals to laboratories, dog and cat breeders, zoos, circuses, roadside menageries and transporters of animals. The care of animals used in research is stipulated in considerable detail in a series of Animal Welfare Regulations released by the U.S. Department of Agriculture (see http://awic.nal. usda.gov). A university, for example, must have an Institutional Animal Care and Use Committee that reviews research projects (Silverman, Suckow, and Murthy, 2000). Private research facilities that receive any federal funding must also have such committees. The National Institutes of Health also requires animal ethics review, often with more stringent standards. Federal agencies, although technically under different regulations, are expected to operate in parallel. The Canadian Council on Animal Care has produced a *Guide to the Care and Use of Experimental Animals* (Offert, Cross, and McWilliam, 1993).

Predictably many groups have managed to lobby to get excluded from legislation: retail pet stores, state and county fairs, livestock shows, rodeos, purebred dog and cat shows. The Act does not apply to factory farming. The Act exempts mice and rats (largely for pharmaceutical companies), birds, and fish, although many such ethics committees do extend their review to research involving rodents and birds. Enforcement of the Act is the responsibility of a division of the United States Department of Agriculture known as APHIS (Animal and Plant Health Inspection Service), which periodically sends unannounced inspectors to examine ongoing animal care. (Among animal activists, we might add, APHIS has a bad reputation. Under USDA Wildlife Services, it was formerly the Animal Damage Control service, known for killing thousands of animals deemed to be pests to agriculture or human health, including coyotes, prairie dogs, foxes, beavers, possums, ravens.)

Universities and colleges that conduct research using animals, including medical research, must have such animal care and use committees. They review all research involving animals, as required under the Animal Welfare Act, subsequent amendments, and related laws and regulations. This includes both research with human benefit as a first priority, typically the case in medical research, and research with animal benefit (often with simultaneous human benefit, as with research on diseases or better nutrition in livestock (brucellosis) and poultry (West Nile disease). Research has to be meaningful, likely to produce new results, and cannot duplicate what has already been done. Alternatives to the use of animals must be considered, if animal pain is to be inflicted. Such issues are extensively examined both in veterinary medical and research ethics (Rollin, 2006) and in bioethics (Sideris, McCarthy, and Smith, 1999; DeGrazia, 1991).

There are concerns about the extent of animal pain involved in the research, as well as before and after experiments. There is concern about animal stress, about how animals die. For example, if the experiment requires infecting animals with a terminal disease, researchers may be required to euthanize animals in late stages of the disease, rather than continuing the suffering. Some experiments have involved performing brain surgery experiments using dogs, testing novel procedures that might be useful to humans, and these might be rejected if such dogs were judged to be left in long-term pain.

Use of animals in research intended to benefit human health, although it must be justified, is typically thought to be more acceptable than causing animal suffering in the course of teaching. The University of Washington Medical School has been using ferrets to train medical students how to insert breathing tubes in emergency procedures used on premature infants. A ferret, anaesthetized, might be used six or eight times in practice intubation, and then used again two weeks later. A group of physicians concerned for animal welfare filed a complaint, alleging that this violates the Animal Welfare Act, arguing that simulators, plastic models with realistic anatomical features, should be used instead. University of Washington medical personnel claimed that such simulators were inadequate for teaching how to insert such tubes in infants that were quite premature (Ostrom, 2011; Physicians Committee for Responsible Medicine, 2011)

Invasive experimenting on primates, once widespread, has been almost entirely stopped. One of the most celebrated discoveries in modern medicine, the Salk and Sabin polio vaccines used thousands of monkeys in the research that led to the discovery of these vaccines, as well as test animals in its continued production. This would not now be permitted. In a famous case, at the Head Injury Clinic, University of Pennsylvania, monkeys and baboons were deliberately injured in order to practice experimental surgery, simulating the sorts of "whiplash" injuries received by humans in automobile crashes and sports. Laboratory videotapes were stolen by animal liberation agents who infiltrated the laboratory and gave the tapes to PETA, People for the Ethical Treatment of Animals. When a video made from the tapes (PETA, 1984) was shown to the Congressional Committee that funded the laboratory, funding was withdrawn. The chief veterinarian was fired (Sideris et al., 1999).

Hugh LaFollette and Niall Shanks (1996) argue that medical research using animals is misplaced. Their main argument is that, since animals are not humans, they are not good medical models for human diseases. Taken alone, that is merely a pragmatic consideration. If animals are good medical models, as they sometimes may be, then use them. But LaFollette and Shanks' larger agenda is moral. It is morally wrong to use animals in medical experiments, if there are unlikely to be important results curing human diseases. With that many, perhaps most, researchers would agree. The two sides disagree, however, about whether animals are good research models. Both appeal alike to evolutionary origins and to clinical practice.

One side claims that humans evolved into something with such a different physiology that animal studies are not helpful. Chemicals may be toxic to humans and not to animals, and vice versa. Thalidomide was tested in animals (although not pregnant ones), with no adverse results; in humans it tragically deformed the fetus in wombs (about 8,000 children). AIDS is disastrous in humans, but little affects green monkeys, from which it originated. Many medical trials in animals do not reliably predict what will happen in humans (van der Worp et al., 2010).

The other side claims that the whole idea of evolution is that humans physiologically are remarkably similar to animals, especially in many basic metabolisms and structures, such as the genes making protein molecules (95% similar with chimps, though less in the brain, 88% with rodents, 60% with chickens) (Gunter and Dhand, 2005). In fact, researchers constantly use animal models with great success, while remaining alert to possibly different responses. Animal experimentation has led to effective treatments for high blood pressure, asthma, transplant rejection, diphtheria and whooping cough vaccines, as well as to the polio vaccine. Hardly a new drug is ever used on humans without prior testing on animals. And today hardly anyone does such testing without some concern for whether the animal pain is justified, often because they have compassion for animals, perhaps also fearing adverse publicity or loss of institutional permission.

State divisions of wildlife review research proposals, both laboratory animals and field studies. Some concerns, for example, have been insuring that procedures for capturing animals (by netting, trapping, darting) cause minimal animal harm. Is it permissible to use live birds or animals as bait to capture predators? There are concerns about handing animals when injured and how euthanasia is to be performed. There is consideration of statistically significant animal size. No more animals may be used than necessary to validate the results. If enough animals cannot be involved—too expensive putting radio collars on them—the experiment may be rejected.

One Colorado wildlife veterinarian, Michael Miller, no longer does challenge studies in bighorn sheep. This requires infecting a number of sheep with a bacterial pneumonia to test new vaccines. If the vaccine fails, the sheep will die. But this also means that all of the infected control group will die. In a restoration project, Colorado wildlife biologists re-located Canada lynx in Southern Colorado, to discover that, if simply released, most of them died, especially any females that were pregnant. This was judged to inflict too much suffering on the animals to justify the restoration. Thereafter the biologists were careful to acclimate the lynx and to release them with ample supplies of body fat, with much more success.

————

Humans have moral responsibilities to animals. Almost no one in the world today would deny that. But philosophers will want to rephrase that: Some humans have some moral responsibilities to some animals. In the decades since the environmental turn, that has increasingly become: All humans have more serious moral responsibilities to animals than we classically thought. Hunting, killing, eating, raising, keeping, watching, petting, preserving, displacing, racing, breeding, researching animals—almost nothing that we do to them is without an ethical dimension. Ethics is for people, but is ethics only about people? The answer is: No! Moral agents cannot make man the only measure of things. People on their landscapes can and ought to respect animal life—the beasts in flesh and blood.

References

Abbott, Alison, and Helen Pearson. 2004. "Fear of Human Pandemic Grows as Bird Flu Sweeps through Asia," *Nature* 427(5 February):472–473.

Armstrong, Susan, and Richard G. Botzler, eds. 2008. *The Animal Ethics Reader*, 2nd ed. New York: Routledge.

Beck, A. M., and A. H. Katcher. 1996. *Between Pets and People: The Importance of Animal Companionship*, rev. ed. West Lafayette, IN: Purdue University Press.

Bekoff, Marc, with Carron A. Meaney. 1998. *Encyclopedia of Animal Rights and Animal Welfare.* Westport, CT: Greenwood Press.

Black Entertainment Television (BET). 2010. Online at: http://www1.bet.com/OnTV/BET-Shows/michaelvick/default.htm

Bostock, Stephen St. C. 1993. *Zoos and Animal Rights: The Ethics of Keeping Animals.* London: Routledge.

Brooman, Simon, and Debbie Legge. 1997. *Law Relating to Animals.* London: Cavendish.

Callicott, J. Baird. 1980. "Animal Liberation: A Triangular Affair." *Environmental Ethics* 11:311–338.

———. 1989. "Animal Liberation and Environmental Ethics: Back Together Again." Pages 49–59 in Callicott, *In Defense of the Land Ethic: Essays in Environmental Philosophy.* Albany: State University of New York Press.

Carey, John. 1999. "Where Have All the Animals Gone?" *International Wildlife* 29(no. 6, Nov./Dec.):12–20.

Cartmill, Matt. 1993. *A View to a Death in the Morning: Hunting and Nature Through History.* Cambridge, MA: Harvard University Press.

Causey, Ann S. 1989. "On the Morality of Hunting," *Environmental Ethics* 11:327–343.

Clayton, Patti H. 1998. *Connection on the Ice: Environmental Ethics in Theory and Practice.* Philadelphia: Temple University Press.

Connor, Steve. 2000. "BSE Report: The Main Findings: Portrait of a Nation Fed a Diet of Reassurances," *The Independent (London)*, 27 October, p. 4.

DeGrazia, David. 1991. "The Moral Status of Animals and their Use in Research: A Philosophical Review," *Kennedy Institute of Ethics Journal* 1:48–70.

de Leeuw, A. Dionys. 1996. "Contemplating the Interests of Fish: The Angler's Challenge." *Environmental Ethics* 18:373–390.

Evans, J. Claude. 2005. *With Respect for Nature: Living as Part of the Natural World*. Albany: State University of New York Press.

Fisher, John A. 1987. "Taking Sympathy Seriously: A Defense of Our Moral Psychology Toward Animals," *Environmental Ethics* 9:197–215.

Goodpaster, Kenneth E. 1978. "On Being Morally Considerable," *Journal of Philosophy* 75:308–325.

Gunn, Alastair S. 2001. "Environmental Ethics and Trophy Hunting," *Ethics and the Environment* 6(no. 1):68–95.

Gunter, Chris, and Ritu Dhand, 2005. "The Chimpanzee Genome." *Nature* 437(1 September):47.

Hancocks, David. 2001. *A Different Nature: The Paradoxical World of Zoos and their Uncertain Nature*. Berkeley: University of California Press.

Hargrove, Eugene C., ed. 1992. *The Animal Rights/Environmental Ethics Debate: The Environmental Perspective*. Albany: State University of New York Press.

Hawkins, Ronnie. 2001. "Cultural Whaling, Commodification, and Culture Change," *Environmental Ethics* 23:287–306.

Hungry Horse News, 1989. "Nature Plays Cruel with Lame Deer," April 5, p. 1.

Hutchins, Michael, Brandie Smith, and Ruth Allard. 2003. "In Defense of Zoos and Aquariums: The Ethical Basis for Keeping Wild Animals in Captivity," *Journal of the American Veterinary Medical Association* 223:958–966.

Jamieson, Dale. 1985. "Against Zoos." Pages 108–117 in Peter Singer, ed., *In Defense of Animals*. New York: Harper and Row.

———. 1995. "Animal Liberation Is an Environmental Ethic," *Environmental Values* 7:41–57.

———. 2008. *Ethics and the Environment: An Introduction*. Cambridge, UK: Cambridge University Press.

Jensen, Derrick, and Karen Tweedy-Holmes. 2007. *Thought to Exist in the Wild: Awakening from the Nightmare of Zoos*. Santa Cruz, CA: No Voice Unheard.

Kaloff, Linda, and Amy Fitzgerald, eds. 2007. *The Animals Reader: The Essential Classic and Contemporary Writings*. Oxford, UK: Berg Publishers.

Kowalsky, Nathan, ed. 2010. *Hunting — Philosophy for Everyone: In Search of the Wild Life*. Hoboken, NJ: Wiley-Blackwell.

LaFollette, Hugh, and Niall Shanks. 1996. *Brute Science: Dilemmas of Animal Experimentation*. London: Routledge.

List, Charles. 2004. "On the Moral Distinctiveness of Sport Hunting," *Environmental Ethics* 26:155–169.

Loftin, Robert W. 1984. "The Morality of Hunting," *Environmental Ethics* 6:241–250.

Magnuson, Jon. 1991. "Reflections of an Oregon Bow Hunter," *Christian Century*, March 13.

McMahan, Jeff. 2010. "The Meat Eaters." *New York Times*, September 19. Opinionator forum, online: http://opinionator.blogs.nytimes.com/2010/09/19/the-meat-eaters/?emc=eta1

McNeil, Donald G. 1999. "The Great Ape Massacre," *New York Times Magazine*, May 9, Section 6, pp. 54–57.

———. 2005. "To Prevent Mad Cow Disease, F.D.A. Proposes New Restrictions on Food for Animals," *New York Times*, October 5, p. A18.

Miller, Michael W., N. Thompson Hobbs, William H. Rutherford, and Lisa W. Miller, 1987. "Efficacy of Injectable Ivermectin for Treating Lungworm Infections in Mountain Sheep," *Wildlife Society Bulletin* 15:260–263.

Nierenberg, Danielle, 2005. *Happier Meals: Rethinking the Global Meat Industry*. Worldwatch Paper 171. Danvers, MA: Worldwatch Institute.

Nordheimer, Jon. 1990. "High-Tech Medicine at High Rise Costs is Keeping Pets Fit," *New York Times*, September 17, p. A1.

Norton, Bryan G., Michael Hutchins, Elizabeth F. Stevens, and Terry L. Maple. 1995. *Ethics on the Ark: Zoos, Animal Welfare, and Wildlife Conservation*. Washington, D.C.: Smithsonian Institution Press.

Offert, Ernest D., Brenda M. Cross, and A. Ann McWilliam. 1993. *Guide to the Care and Use of Experimental Animals*, 2nd ed. Ottawa: Canadian Council on Animal Care.

Ostrom, Carol M. "Group Faults UW's Use of Ferrets at Med School," *Seattle Times*, February 10, 2011, A1, A6.

Palmer, Clare. 2010. *Animal Ethics in Context*. New York: Columbia University Press.

Pauley, John A. 2003. "The Value of Hunting," *Journal of Value Inquiry* 27:233–244.

PETA (People for the Ethical Treatment of Animals). 1984. *Unnecessary Fuss*, video. Online at: http://www.animalliberationfront.com/MediaCenter/UnnFuss01.wmv

Phillips, Nicholas, June Bridgman, and Malcolm Ferguson-Smith. 2000. *The BSE Inquiry: Return to an Order of the Honourable the House of Commons*, 16 vols. London: The Stationery Office.

Physicians Committee for Responsible Medicine. 2011. "PCRM Action Alert (University of Washington)." Online at: http://www.pcrm.org/email/uw_alert.html

Posewitz, Jim. 1994. *Beyond Fair Chase: The Ethic and Tradition of Hunting*. Helena, MT: Falcon Press.

Post, Stephen G., ed. 2004. *Animal Welfare and Rights*, set of six articles: ethical perspectives, vegetarianism, wildlife conservation and management, pets, zoos, agriculture and factory farming. Pages 183–215 in Post, ed., *Encyclopedia of Bioethics*, 3rd ed. New York: Macmillan Reference/Thomson Gale.

Raterman, Tyler. 2008. "An Environmentalist's Lament of Predation," *Environmental Ethics* 30:417–434.

Rawles, Kate. 1997. "Conservation and Animal Welfare." Pages 135–155 in T. D. J. Chappell, ed., *The Philosophy of the Environment* .Edinburgh: University of Edinburgh Press.

Regan, Tom. 2004. *The Case for Animal Rights*. Berkeley: University of California Press.

Ritvo, Harriet. 1987. *The Animal Estate: The English and Other Creatures in the Victoria Age*. Cambridge, MA: Harvard University Press.

Robbins, Jim. 1984. "Do Not Feed the Bears? *Natural History* 93 (no. 1, January):12–21.

Rollin, Bernard E. 2006. *An Introduction to Veterinary Medical Ethics: Theory and Cases*. Ames, IA: Blackwell.

Sagoff, Mark. 1984. "Animal Liberation and Environmental Ethics: Bad Marriage, Quick Divorce," *Osgoode Hall Law Journal* 22:297–307.

Schmidt, Robert L., Charles P. Hibler, Terry R. Spraker, and William H. Rutherford. 1979. "An Evaluation of Drug Treatment for Lungworm in Bighorn Sheep," *Journal of Wildlife Management* 43:461–467.

Scully, Matthew. 2002. *Dominion: The Power of Man, the Suffering of Animals and the Call to Mercy*. New York: St. Martin's Griffin.

Shabecoff, Philip. 1988. "What 3 Whales Did to the Human Heart," *New York Times*, November 6, p. E11.

Sideris, Lisa, Charles McCarthy, and David H. Smith. 1999. "Roots of Concern with Nonhuman Animals in Biomedical Ethics," *ILAR Journal* (Institute for Laboratory Animal Research) 40(1):3–14.

Silverman, Jerald, Mark A. Suckow, and Sreekant Murthy, eds. 2000. *The IACUC Handbook* (Institutional Animal Care and Use Committee). Boca Raton, FL: CRC Press.

Simon, Stephanie. 2011. "Rethinking Horse Slaughterhouses," *Wall Street Journal*, January 5, 2011, p. A3.

Singer, Peter. 1990. *Animal Liberation*, 2nd ed. New York: New York Review Book.

Stanford, Craig B. 1999, *The Hunting Apes: Meat Eating and the Origins of Human Behavior*. Princeton, NJ: Princeton University Press.

Stange, Mary Zeiss. 1997. *Woman the Hunter.* Boston: Beacon Press.

Spencer, Stuart, Eddy Decuypere, Stefan Aerts, and Johan De Tavernier. 2006. "History and Ethics of Keeping Pets: Comparison with Farm Animals," *Journal of Agricultural and Environmental Ethics* 19:17–25.

Sunstein, Cass R., and Martha C. Nussbaum. 2004. *Animal Rights: Current Debates and New Directions.* New York: Oxford University Press.

Thomas, V. G. 1997. "The Ethical and Environmental Implications of Lead Shot Contamination of Rural Lands in North America," *Journal of Agricultural and Environmental Ethics* 10:41–54.

Thorne, Tom. 1987. "Born Looking for a Place to Die," *Wyoming Wildlife* 51 (no. 3, March):10–19.

van der Worp, H. Bart, David W. Howells, Emily S. Sena, et al., 2010. "Can Animal Models of Disease Reliably Inform Human Studies?" *PLoS Medicine* 7(3): e1000245. doi:10.1371/journal.pmed.1000245

Varner, Gary E. 1995. "Can Animal Rights Activists Be Environmentalists?" Pages 169–201 in Don E. Marietta and Lester Embree, eds., *Environmental Philosophy and Environmental Activism.* Lanham, MD: Rowman and Littlefield.

———. 1998. *In Nature's Interests? Interests, Animal Rights, and Environmental Ethics.* New York: Oxford University Press.

Wells, Martin J. 1978. *Octopus.* London: Chapman and Hall.

Wood, Forrest, Jr. 1997. *The Delights and Dilemmas of Hunting.* Lanham, MD: University Press of America.

4

ORGANISMS

Respect for Life

A more inclusive ethics asks about appropriate respect toward all living things, not only the wildlife and farm animals, but now the butterflies and the sequoia trees. Otherwise, most of the biological world has yet to be taken into account: lower animals, insects, microbes, plants. If one really seeks a biologically based ethic, a sentient animal welfare ethic still leaves most of the world valueless. We already started to worry about this in the last chapter. The sentient animals form only a minuscule fraction of the living organisms on Earth. Over 96% of species are invertebrates or plants. A deeper respect for life must value more directly all living things and the generative processes that sustain life at all its levels, from the genetic to the global.

To get the big picture, look at a cartoon of life on Earth, where each group is sized according to the number of described species (see Figure 4.1). Find the tiny elephant (representing all mammals) near the gigantic beetle (representing insects). Compare the tiny elephant with the trees (representing plants) or the eight-legged arthropod (crustaceans, spiders, mites). And remember that humans, among the mammals, would hardly amount to the minuscule tail on the tiny elephant. But this is a cartoon with truth in it—putting mammals, putting humans in their place. Get the picture. Get an ethic for all of life. Perhaps

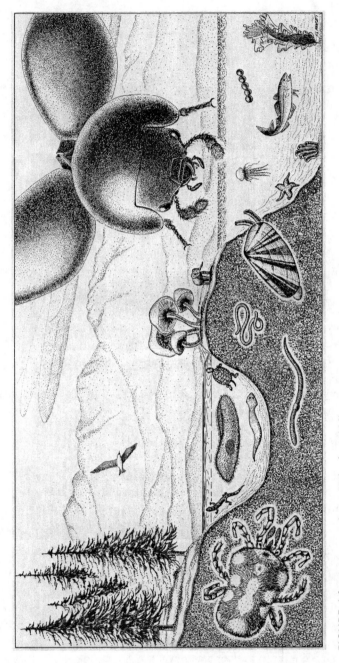

FIGURE 4.1 The buggy planet (Wheeler, 1990)

man is the only deliberative measurer of things, but man does not have to make himself the only measure he uses. Nor do we just measure sentient animals. Life is a better measure.

1. The Buggy Planet: The Little Things that Run the World

We need a little perspective. Looking around the landscape humans have a search image for large animals. We put ourselves out front. We think that we run the world, and, in Chapter 2, we looked at some of that evidence—the Anthropocene Epoch, with human-dominated landscapes widespread on Earth. But if we are trying to understand the landscape, we need to be much more inclusive, from plants to creepy crawlies. If we are marine, we need to appreciate the whales and dolphins, but just as much the coral reefs. Some 43,000 vertebrate species have been described by zoologists, of which a tenth, 4,000, are mammals. Over 990,000 species of invertebrates have been described, but, since invertebrates are less studied in detail, all the systematists believe that there are there are many more—so many more that we are unsure whether this means 3 million or 30 million. If you count numbers of individuals, a couple acres of Amazon rainforest may have a few dozen birds and mammals, but well over a billion invertebrates: insects, spiders, termites, other arthropods, nematodes. Coral reefs are built out of the bodies of coelenerates (brainless organisms that sweep food into their mouth with tentacles, such as hydras, jellyfish, sea anemones). The most abundant animals of the open sea are copepods, tiny crustaceans forming part of the plankton. In terms of living body mass, over ninety percent of living mass is invertebrates. These are "the little things that run the world" (Wilson, 1987).

These "lower organisms" can do without us, but we "higher humans" cannot do without them. Invertebrates have been around a ten times as long as mammals. They are in the food webs, of course; all the big animals eat little animals, or eat what eats little animals, or eat plants or eat what eats plants. These little things do the brunt of the recycling; those that feast on dead wood may depend on even more tiny organisms in their gut for digestion. Fungi also break down wood and other biomass, permitting recycling. Insects recycle dung. Insects pollinate many plants, including our food sources—so much so that, where these pollination process are degraded, agribusiness has to create a commercial pollination industry, breeding billions of bees.

We also get a comprehensive account if we turn to the Bible. The apex of the creation is man and woman, made of mud, made in the image of God, incarnate and set in their garden earth. Humans prove to be the great challenge to God, the contentious creature, but the world is habitat not only for humans but for the myriads of creatures—from "great sea monsters" to "birds," "beasts," and "creeping things"—which, repeatedly, God finds "good," bidding them to "be fruitful and multiply and fill" the waters, the earth, the skies (Genesis 1.20-22).

God enjoys biodiversity. That includes the creepy things, and here we might recall the biologist J.B.S. Haldane's famous remark, when asked by theologians what he had learned about the Creator from studying creation in biology, that God had "an inordinate fondness for beetles" (quoted in Hutchinson, 1959).

Haldane's remark is cute, but not profound, the anthropocentrists (including many theologians) will reply. Yes, there are myriads of beetles, but often beetle species are not that different from one another—a few spots or bristles here or there. Humans differentiate within their *Homo sapiens* species (Einstein and Mother Teresa); beetles of a species do nothing of that kind, and even related species hardly differ. The personal differences between Susan and Sally, both members of *Homo sapiens*, are much more exciting.

There are more microbes in Susan's body, Sally's body than there are persons on Earth. We kill millions of yeast cells every time we bake bread. But none of this has any ethical importance. An ant is only about a millionth the size of a human, and even less important. Lewis Thomas, an astute biologist, concludes: "A solitary ant, afield, cannot be considered to have much of anything on his mind; indeed, with only a few neurons strung together by fibers, he can't be imagined to have a mind at all, much less a thought. He is more like a ganglion on legs" (1975, p. 12). All the plants and the vast number of these simple organisms don't have a mind at all. So, dealing with them is no moral matter.

2. Plants: Nothing Matters! Never Mind?

Maybe the problem is that we have let ourselves get imprisoned in our own felt experiences. We might have blinders on, psychological and philosophical blinders that leave us unable to detect anything but experientially based valuers and their felt values. Over-instructed in philosophy, we are under-instructed in biology, unable to accept a biologically-based value account, that is otherwise staring us in the face. Organisms post a defended, semipermeable boundary between themselves and the outside world; they assimilate environmental materials to their own needs. They can be healthy or diseased. Some accounts claim that the minimal form of autonomy necessary and sufficient for characterizing biological life is what is termed *autopoiesis*, literally self-making. Some defense of a "self" (a somatic, bodily self, not a sentient, psychological self) is thus required.

Let's focus on plants, to make sure we are not biased by our preference for minimal neural experience. Considering plants makes clear the differences between a life ethic and an animal rights ethic. A plant is not an experiencing subject, but neither is it an inanimate object, like a stone. Nor is it a geomorphological process, like a river. Plants are quite alive. They resist dying. Plants, like all other organisms, are self-actualizing. Plants are unified entities of the botanical though not of the zoological kind; that is, they are not unitary organisms with highly integrated centered neural control, but they are modular organisms, with a meristem that can repeatedly and indefinitely produce new vegetative modules, additional stem nodes and leaves when there is available space and resources, as well as new reproductive modules, fruits and seeds.

Plants repair injuries and move water, nutrients, and photosynthate from cell to cell; they store sugars; they make tannin and other toxins and regulate their levels in defense against grazers, they make nectars and emit pheromones to influence the behavior of pollinating insects and the responses of other plants, they emit allelopathic agents to suppress invaders, they make thorns, trap insects. They can reject genetically incompatible grafts. A plant is a spontaneous, self-maintaining system, sustaining and reproducing itself, executing its program, making a way through the world, checking against performance by means of responsive capacities with which to measure success.

Something more than merely physical causes, even when less than sentient experience, is operating within every organism. There is *information* superintending the causes; without it the organism would collapse into a sand heap. The information is used to preserve the plant identity. This information is recorded in the genes, and such information, unlike matter and energy, can be created and destroyed. That is what worries environmentalists about extinction, for example. In such information lies the secret of life.

Plants do not have ends-in-view, and in that familiar sense they do not have goals. Yet the plant grows, reproduces, repairs its wounds, and resists death, maintaining a botanical identity. All this, from one perspective, is just biochemistry—the whir and buzz of organic molecules, enzymes, proteins—as humans are, too, from one perspective. But from an equally valid—and objective—perspective, the morphology and metabolism that the organism projects is a valued state. *Vital* is a more ample word now than *biological*. We could even argue that the genetic set is a *normative set*; it distinguishes between what *is* and what *ought to be*—not of course in any moral or conscious sense—but in the sense that the organism is an axiological system. The genome is a set of conservation molecules. A life is spontaneously defended for what it is itself.

For classical ethicists, all this seems odd. Plants are not valuers with preferences that can be satisfied or frustrated. It seems curious to say that wildflowers have rights, or moral standing, or need our sympathy, or that we should consider their point of view. We would not say that the needless destruction of a plant species was cruel, but we might say that it was callous. We would not be concerned about what the plants did feel, but about what the destroyers did not feel. We would not be valuing sensitivity in plants, but censuring insensitivity in persons.

These biologically-centered ethicists are now claiming, however, that environmental ethics is not merely an affair of psychology, but of biology. The concentric circles keep expanding. Every organism has a *good-of-its-kind*; it defends its own kind as a *good kind*. True, virtuous persons ought not to be callous. But that does not end the question; we at once ask what are the properties in plants to which a virtuous person should be sensitive. Judgments of disgust are derived from an admiration for something of value in the organisms.

An objector can say, "The plants don't care, so why should I?" But plants do care—using botanical standards, the only form of caring available to them. The plant life per se is defended—an intrinsic value. Though things do not matter *to* trees, a great deal matters *for* them. We ask, What's the matter *with* that tree? If it is lacking sunshine and soil nutrients, we arrange for these, and the tree goes to work and recovers its health. Such organisms do "take account" of themselves; and we should take account of them.

The tree is benefiting from the water and fertilizer; and *benefit* is—everywhere else we encounter it—a value word. Biologists regularly speak of the "selective value" or "adaptive value" of genetic variations. Plant activities have "survival value," such as the seeds they disperse or the thorns they make. Natural selection picks out whatever traits an organism has that are valuable to it, relative to its survival. When natural selection has been at work gathering these traits into an organism, that organism is able to value on the basis of those traits. It is a valuing organism, even if the organism is not a sentient valuer, much less a conscious evaluator. And those traits, though picked out by natural section, are innate in the organism; that is, stored in its genes. It is difficult to dissociate the idea of value from natural selection.

Any sentigenic, psychogenic, vertebragenic, or anthropogenic theory of value has got to argue away all such natural selection as not dealing with "real" value at all, but mere function. Those arguments are, in the end, more likely to be stipulations than real arguments. If you stipulate that valuing must be felt valuing, that there must be somebody there, some subject of a life, then plants are not able to value, and that is so by your definition. But what we wish to examine is whether that definition, faced with the facts of biology, is plausible. Perhaps the sentientist definition covers correctly but narrowly certain kinds of higher animal valuing, namely that done by sentient animals, and omits all the rest. To say that the plant has a good of its own seems the plain fact of the matter.

Let's look over the shoulders of some scientists and their discoveries. Studies of dragonflies in the Carboniferous show that their wings "are proving to be spectacular examples of microengineering" giving them "the agile, versatile flight necessary to catch prey in flight." They are "adapted for high-performance flight" (Wootton et al., 1998, p. 749). "To execute these aerobatic maneuvers, the insects come equipped with highly engineered wings that automatically change their flight shape in response to airflow, putting the designers of the latest jet fighters to shame" (Vogel, 1998, p. 598).

Dragonflies have to change their wing shape in flight without benefit of muscles (as in birds and bats), so they use a flexible aerofoil with veins that enable the wing surface to twist in direct response to aerodynamic loading, when suddenly changing directions or shifting from upstroke to downstroke.

A hind-wing base mechanism is especially impressive in the way it mixes flexibility and rigidity. "The 'smart' wing-base mechanism is best interpreted as an elegant means of maintaining downstroke efficiency in the presence of these adaptations to improve upstroke usefulness" (Wootton et al., 1998, p. 751). The flexible wings did "matter" to the Carboniferous dragonflies.

The social behavior of honeybees is, in a way, rather stereotyped. But biologists who study bees also find that such behavior is also labile in different environments, evidenced by their waggle and other dances conveying information to other bees about the location of food or suitable nest sites. The bees integrate multiple sources of environmental information in "deciding" the appropriate behavior in dynamically changing circumstances. Thomas D. Seeley, neurobiologist and world authority on communication in honeybees, describes the bee as "a sophisticated decision maker, one capable of integrating numerous pieces of information (both current perceptions and stored representations) as she chooses the general type and specific form of signal that is appropriate for a particular situation" (2003, p. 22; 2010; see also Hölldobler and Wilson, 2009). Critics may insist that, impressive though this is, it is nonreflective. Still bees seem rather smart at what they do.

Botanists report studies in what they call "a plant's dilemma." Plants need to photosynthesize to gain energy from the sun, which requires access to carbon dioxide in the atmosphere. They also need to conserve water, vital to their metabolism, and access to atmosphere evaporates water. This forces a tradeoff in leaves between too much and too little exposure to atmosphere. The problem is solved by stomata on the undersides of leaves, which can open and close letting in or shutting out the air. "The stomatal aperture is controlled by osmotic adjustment in the surrounding cells. In a sophisticated regulatory mechanism, light, the carbon dioxide required for photosynthesis, and the water status of the plant are integrated to regulate stomatal aperture for optimization of the plant's growth and performance" (Grill and Ziegler, 1998, p. 252). The details of such "plant strategies" vary in different species, but are quite complex, integrating multiple environmental and metabolic variables—water availability, drought, heat, cold, sunlight, water stress, and energy needs in the plant—for sophisticated solutions to the plant's dilemma (Craine, 2009).

Even the cyanobacteria, blue-green algae, which are relatively primitive single-celled organisms, can track day and night with molecular clocks built with a genetic oscillator rather similar to those in more advanced organisms. Discovering this, Marcia Barinaga says, "Keeping track of day-night cycles is apparently so essential, perhaps because it helps organisms prepare for the special physiological needs they will have at various times during the daily cycle, that clocks seem to have arisen multiple times, recreating the same design each time" (Barinaga, 1998, p. 1429).

One has to use language with care; we should guard against overly cognitive language. But scientists do have to describe what is going on. Why is the organism not valuing what it knows how to do—keep a molecular clock or make resources of food it gathers at night? Not consciously, but we do not want to presume that there is only conscious value or valuing. That is what we are debating, not assuming. And what we are claiming is that life is organized vitality, which may or may not have an experiential psychology. A value-er is an entity able to feel value? Yes, and more. A value-er is an entity able to defend value. On the second meaning, plants too defend their lives. In an objective gestalt some value is already present in nonsentient organisms, normative evaluative systems, prior to the emergence of further dimensions of value with sentience. There is no feeling in the organism, but it does not follow that humans cannot or ought not to develop, as Barbara McClintock put it, "a feeling for the organism" (Keller, 1983).

There is praise for those dragonfly wings in the Carboniferous, coming from the scientists who study them. What is a philosopher to say? "Well, those are interesting wings to the scientists who study them, but they were of no value to the dragonflies." That seems implausible. Perhaps one can go part-way and say: "Well, those wings did have value to the individual dragonflies who owned them. Instrumentally, the dragonflies found them useful. But a dragonfly is incapable of intrinsically valuing anything. Much less do these wings represent anything of value to the species line. Similar engineering features persist, Wootton and his associates (1998) add, in present-day dragonflies, living 320 million years later than the fossil dragonflies they studied in Argentina. That does sound like something that has been useful for quite a long time. Could that be of value to the species line?

The repeated discovery of molecular clocks in those cyanobacteria is important in fulfilling the organisms' "needs," and that seems pretty much fact of the matter. After that, do we want to insist that nevertheless this has no "value" to these organisms or their species lines, who have several times discovered how these internal clocks, similarly "designed," increase their adapted fit?

In Yosemite National Park, there are giant sequoia trees, some of the largest trees on Earth. In 1881 a tunnel was cut through one of them, named the Wawona Tree, large enough to drive a horse-and-buggy through, and later automobiles. The tree was world famous, a highlight of trips West for nearly a century. Impressed by the tree, amused tourists (including, once, this author) took photos of themselves driving their cars through a tree. In 1969, with a heavy snow load, the tree blew over in a winter storm, perhaps weakened by the tunnel cut, although it had stood for many winters. Soon people asked the Park Service to cut another "drive-through sequoia," but the rangers refused. A new ethic found it inappropriate to mutilate a giant sequoia for amusement.

There are two ways to interpret this refusal. One is that driving an automobile through a tree is just tacky, not the sort of thing becoming to park visitors—maybe they could amuse themselves in Disneyland. But the deeper ethic is that a sequoia has age, size, persistence resisting fire, insects, disease, an integrity, a good of its own, intrinsic value. A tunnel fails to respect this intrinsic good. Of course, the two perspectives can combine—human virtue respecting plant good of its own—but philosophical analysis will recognize differences. The Wawona Tree, often visited in summer, was seldom visited in winter; deep snows made it a challenge to get there. When the seasonal humans left, no longer virtuously respecting the giant, the sequoia good of its own remained, all four seasons, continuing across millennia, whether or not tacky tourists or, before them, native Americans (probably more respectful) were in the woods.

You may be thinking: Well, okay, no more-drive-through sequoias, but we use trees all the time, some redwoods included. True, but we still need to consider whether the use is justified, and whether we overuse them. Some years back, campers would cut boughs from trees to make a springy mattress for the night; they had been taught to do this in their Boy Scout handbook. But no responsible backpacker would do this today. Trees are not to be used trivially.

Americans consume about a half a million trees each week to have their Sunday paper. Newspapers are a good thing, up to a point; but, since the Sunday paper is mostly ads and much of it is only glanced at, one might argue that Americans having their Sunday papers does not warrant sacrificing half a million trees a week. The sellers might, for example, impose a return tax so that half the papers are recycled, and that would save a quarter of a million trees a week.

At Christmas time, a National Christmas tree is put up on the White House lawn. Once a year, American foresters go to some national forest, find a fine spruce tree, or other conifer, in the prime of its life, cut it down, ship it far across the country on a railroad flatcar, put it up on a lawn in downtown Washington, and place lights on it. There is a ceremony, the president wishes Americans "Merry Christmas," photographers take pictures, which are printed in those newspapers. The cut tree stands ten days, withering, and is then tossed. Can this be justified?

Or is this teaching the wrong thing about trees? Why not locate such a tree in a national forest, a different tree each year. Then light it up where it grows, let the president go there, with photographers traipsing along. Ten days later, take the lights off and put up a sign that this was the national Christmas tree in that year. A decade or later, touring the country, daddy can take little Jimmie on a hike to see the national Christmas tree the year Jimmie was born. Maybe Jimmie grows up, gets to be a dad, and takes little Suzie to see another Christmas tree. Dad, Jimmie, Susie all get exercise and a greater appreciation for what trees are in themselves—added on to whatever is the holiday significance of the tree.

Where plant species are endangered, we may save the plants, even if this kills animals—thousands of animals to save a few plants. San Clemente Island is far enough off the coast of California for endemic species to have evolved in the isolation there; some species of plants and animals are found there and nowhere else on Earth. The island also has a population of feral goats, introduced by the Spanish in the 1500s as a source of meat for sailors. After the passage of the Endangered Species Act, botanists resurveyed the island and found some additional populations of endangered plants. But goats do not much care whether they are eating endangered species. They had probably already eradicated several never-known species. So, the U.S. Fish and Wildlife Service and the U.S. Navy, which owns the island, planned to shoot thousands of feral goats to save three endangered plant species, *Malacothamnus clementinus*, *Castilleja grisea*, *Delphinium kinkiense*, of which the surviving individuals numbered only a few dozens.

Some goats were shot. Then the Fund for Animals took the case to court to stop the shooting, and the court allowed the Fund to live trap and relocate what animals they could. Relocated animals survive poorly, however; most die within six months. Trapping was difficult; the goats reproduced about as fast as trapped. So, the shooting continued during the 1980s. The remaining goats were wary and in inaccessible canyons, which required their being shot by helicopter. Altogether about 29,000 live goats were removed from the island and 15,000 shot. At the end, there were only six feral goats on the island, five females and one billy, called a Judas goat, because, radio-collared, he was used to lure the females to where they could be shot. These last were killed in 1991 (Keegan, Coblentz, and Winchell, 1994; and personal communication, Jan Larson and Clark Winchell, Natural Resources Office, Naval Air Station, North Island, San Diego, California).

Despite the Fund's objections, the Park Service killed hundreds of rabbits on Santa Barbara Island to protect a few plants of *Dudleya traskiae*, once thought extinct and curiously called the Santa Barbara Live-Forever. This island endemic was once common. But New Zealand red rabbits were introduced about 1900, fed on it, and by 1970 no *Dudleya* could be found. With the discovery in 1975 of five plants, a decision was made to eradicate the rabbits (Mohlenbrock, 1983, pp. 180–182).

Does protecting endangered plant species justify causing animal suffering and death? Does the fact that the animals were brought in from South America make a difference? An ethic based on animal rights will say, "No", but a more broadly based environmental ethic will prefer plant species, especially species in their ecosystems, over sentient animals that are introduced misfits. We might say that, one on one, a goat does have more intrinsic value than a plant. So, if the trade off were merely a thousand goats for a hundred plants, oblivious to instrumental, ecosystem, and species considerations, the goats would override the plants. But the picture is more complex. Out of place from their original ecosystems, goats are degrading the ecosystems in which they presently exist, producing extinctions of plant species that are otherwise well adapted to those ecosystems. The prevailing ethic here found that the well-being of plant species outweighed the welfare of the goats.

The question, notice, is not: Does subjective life count more than objective life? Rather: Does only subjective life count? To say that the threshold of our moral sensitivity is just the same as the threshold of felt sensitivity is to say that moral concern is directed only toward inwardness; its scope does not include outwardness, except relationally. That is, in a sense, to make morality *subjective*, to attach it to subjects and deny it to objects. Only subjects—indeed on Earth only human subjects—can be moral *agents*. But who are their moral *patients*?

3. Genetic Value: Smart (Cybernetic) Genes

All these organisms are found in species lines. There is historical evolutionary and ongoing genetic creativity that makes life possible. Contemporary geneticists are insisting that thinking of this process as being entirely "blind" misperceives it. Genes have substantial solution-generating capacities. Though not deliberated in the conscious sense, the process is cognitive, or cybernetic. A genome has an array of sophisticated enzymes to cut, splice, digest, rearrange, mutate, reiterate, edit, correct, translocate, invert, and truncate particular gene sequences. There is much redundancy (multiple and variant copies of a gene in multigene families) that shields the species from accidental loss of a beneficial gene and provides flexibility on which these enzymes can work.

John H. Campbell, a molecular geneticist, writes, "Cells are richly provided with special enzymes to tamper with DNA structure," enzymes that biologists are extracting and using for genetic engineering. But this "engineering" is already going on in spontaneous nature:

> Gene-processing enzymes also engineer comparable changes in genes in vivo.... We have discovered enzymes and enzyme pathways for almost every conceivable change in the structure of genes. The scope for self-engineering of multigene families seems to be limited only by the ingenuity of control systems for regulating these pathways.
>
> (1983, pp. 408–409)

These pathways may have "governors" that are "extraordinarily sophisticated." "Self-governed genes are 'smart' machines in the current vernacular sense. Smart genes suggests smart cells and smart evolution" (Campbell, 1983, pp. 410, 414).

In a study of whether species as historical lines can be considered "intelligent," Jonathan Schull concludes:

> Plant and animal species are information-processing entities of such complexity, integration, and adaptive competence that it may be scientifically fruitful to consider them intelligent.... Plant and animal species process information via multiple nested levels of variation and selection

in a manner that is surprisingly similar to what must go on in intelligent animals. As biological entities, and as processors of information, plant and animal species are no less complicated than, say, monkeys. Their adaptive achievements (the brilliant design and exquisite production of biological organisms) are no less impressive, and certainly rival those of the animal and electronic systems to which the term "intelligence" is routinely (and perhaps validly) applied today.

(1990, p. 63)

The result, according to David S. Thaler (1994), is "the evolution of genetic intelligence."

Leslie E. Orgel, summarizing the origin of life on Earth, says "Life emerged only after self-reproducing molecules appeared.... Such molecules yielded a biology based on ribonucleic acids. The RNA system then invented proteins. As the RNA system evolved, proteins became the main workers in cells, and DNA became the prime repository of genetic information." "The emergence of catalytic RNA was a crucial early step" (1994, p. 4). If there was "a crucial early step," that certainly sounds like something of value was at stake.

Not only does such problem solving take place early on, and continuously thereafter, but the genes, over the millennia, get better at it. Past achievements are recapitulated in the present, with variations, and these results get tested today and then folded into the future. Christopher Wills concludes, "There is an accumulated wisdom of the genes that actually makes them better at evolving (and sometimes makes them better at not evolving) than were the genes of our distant ancestors.... This wisdom consists both of the ways that genes have become organized in the course of evolution and the ways in which the factors that change the genes have actually become better at their task" (1989, pp. 6–8).

Donald J. Cram, accepting the Nobel prize for his work deciphering how complex and unique biological molecules recognize each other and interlock, concludes: "Few scientists acquainted with the chemistry of biological systems at the molecular level can avoid being inspired. Evolution has produced chemical compounds that are exquisitely organized to accomplish the most complicated and delicate of tasks." Organic chemists can hardly "dream of designing and synthesizing" such "marvels" (1988, p. 760).

Reporting "Molecular Strategies in Evolution," geneticists have found so many examples of "how the genome readies itself for evolution" that they are making a "paradigm shift." Abandoning the idea that genetic mutation is entirely blind and random, and that genetic errors are suppressed to minimize change, geneticists are impressed with the innovative, creative capacities in the genome. These "new findings are persuading them that the most successful genomes may be those that have evolved to be able to change quickly and substantially if necessary" (Pennisi, 1998, p. 1131).

Genes do this by using transposons, gene segments, mobile elements that they can use rapidly to alter DNA and the resulting protein structures and metabolisms in time of stress. "Chance favors the prepared genome," says Lynn Caporale, a biotechnology geneticist. James Shapiro, a bacterial geneticist at the University of Chicago, comments: "The capability of cells has gone far beyond what we had imagined." "Cells engineer their own genomes" (quoted in Pennisi, 1998, p. 1134). Shapiro continues: "Thus, just as the genome has come to be seen as a highly sophisticated information storage system, its evolution has become a matter of highly sophisticated information processing" (2002, p. 10; see also Shapiro, 2005).

The process of genes unzipping and transcribing their sequences is, so to speak, "headed" somewhere. A genetic sequence has a potential for being an ancestor in an indefinitely long line of descendant genotype/phenotype re-incarnations. The gene does not contain simply descriptive information "about" but prescriptive "for." The gene will be a gene "for" a trait because there has been natural selection "for" what it does contributing to adaptive fit. The preposition "for" saturates both natural selection and genetics. Genes act directed toward a future, under construction. Wherever it shows up in genetics, there is a "telos" lurking in that "for." Ernst Mayr coined the term "teleonomic" for biological functions, contrasted with simple causation in physics and chemistry; also contrasted with "teleological," which, he thought, had objectionable overtones of conscious intent. What genes have is a "telos," an "end." Magmas crystallizing into rocks, and rivers flowing downhill have results, but no such "end."

Rather than wishing to filter out the intentional elements in biology, some theoretical biologists and philosophers have, interestingly, begun using the term "intentional" as descriptive of biological information in genes. John Maynard Smith insists: "In biology, the use of informational terms implies intentionality" (2000, p. 177). That word may have too much of a "deliberative" component for most users, but what is intended by "intentional" is this directed process, going back to the Latin: *intendo*, with the sense of "stretch toward," or "aim at." Genes have both descriptive and prescriptive "aboutness"; they do stretch toward what they are about.

Intentional or semantic information is for the purpose of ("about") producing a functional unit that does not yet exist. It is *teleosemantic*. Where there is information being transmitted, there arises the possibility of mistakes, of error. The DNA, which "intends" to make a certain amino acid sequence that will later fold into a protein segment, can be misread. If the reading frame gets shifted off the "correct" triplet sequence, then the "wrong" amino acids get specified and the assembling fails. There is "mismatch." Often there is machinery for "error-correction." None of these ideas make any sense in chemistry or physics, geology or meteorology. Atoms, crystals, rocks, weather fronts do not "intend" anything and therefore cannot "err."

A mere "cause" is pushy but not forward looking. A developing crystal has the form, shape, location it has because of preceding factors. A genetic code is a "code for" something. The code is set for "control" of the upcoming molecules that it will participate in forming. If we use the word "control" with crystal formation (the size of the crystals is controlled by the temperature at formation), this "control" refers to the past. By contrast, genetic "control" faces forward. There is proactive "intention" about the future.

Perhaps the central metaphor in genetic theory is "information." Nevertheless, many philosophers of biology have reservations about the concept of "information" as applied to genes (Sterelny and Griffiths, 1999, p. 105). A common complaint is that the term is "only" "analogical." Molecules can't literally "know" any "code." What could "information" mean in a molecule? A deeper problem is that the term is difficult to make operational. Darwin famously introduced the metaphor of natural "selection" and made it powerfully descriptive of what is going on in evolutionary history. "Selection" is first something we experience in ordinary life, including the activity of breeders, and by extended meaning evolutionary processes "select" the fittest. Biologists can filter out the intentional element; the remainder does describe differential survival processes. Population geneticists have found ways to operationalize, to quantify, selective pressures. Can geneticists do the same thing for "information," "coding," "reading"?

Humans first know the meaning of the word "information" in our own experience. To speak of "information" in DNA is, at least initially, metaphorical. Are we to say the same of terms such as "translation"? The term "translate" usually means to move from one language system to another; the DNA is a symbol system, but the resulting protein molecule is not another symbol system, so perhaps "transcription" is a less metaphorical term? "Synonym" is a term first learned in human language, then applied to differing codons that result in the same amino acid. It will be difficult to strip out all the terms that start as metaphors from ordinary life: "adapt," "function," "correct," "mistake," "start," "stop," "develop," "regulate," "change," "evolve."

Genes make "copies" of their DNA chains. That word too, one can insist is metaphorical, but it does not follow that "copy" is not an authentically descriptive term. Various words, such as "replicate," "regenerate," "reproduce," "activate," "inhibit, "start," "stop," "cut," "splice," "error," "correct," enable scientists to recognize qualitative, substantive similarities, with insight into how processes work, using comparisons between familiar and unfamiliar systems. So also with "information." Strip all this dimension out of genetics, and you will not understand what is going on. Strip talk of "value" entirely out of genetics, and you are left mumbling.

To put this genetic activity—genotypes, with know-how, producing phenotypes adapted for survival—in the language of conservation biology, a plant is already engaged in the biological conservation of its identity and kind, long before conservation biologists come on the scene. What conservation biologists ought to do is respect plants for what they are in themselves—projects in conservation biology. That aligns human ethics with objective biology. The point of such thinking about plant information, about genetic information is that we should value life. Life matters, not just mind.

4. Invasive Exotics: Plants Way Out of Place

Widespread on our landscapes, rural and wild, there are exotic plants (Kudzu, see Chapter 1), also birds (starlings) and other animals (zebra mussels). Exotics are non-native species living on landscapes where they did not come to be present by natural selection, either having evolved there or moving there on their own. Nearly all of them are brought by humans, intentionally or unintentionally. Of the 150,000 plant species growing on the American landscapes, 7,000 are alien and about 10% of these are considered invasive, that is, aggressively crowding out native species. True, 90% are more or less inconspicuous, perhaps we could say that they are more or less naturalized. But the 10% are trouble-makers. Billions of dollars are spent each year to destroy the invasive non-native organisms and prevent their spread (Mooney et al., 2005; Cox, 1999; McKnight, 1993). What do advocates of environmental ethics say about these introduced exotics? There are differing points of view (Eser, 1998).

Although most find that exotics are bad, some have said that, if we welcome natural abundance, we should also welcome unnatural abundance. The root meaning of "exotic" is "from the outside." "Exotic" is an interesting word, with alternative meanings. On the one hand, a common meaning is: "intriguing," "charming," "beautiful" because unfamiliar. When one visits botanical gardens, one searches out the exotics. If one leaves the garden and finds novel flowers growing across the countryside, why not welcome the increase in biodiversity?

Really, it is a mistake to call them unnatural, since, once they have gotten into place, they do their own thing naturally, now on their own. If the original locals cannot compete with them, that's the way natural selection works. The preference for original natives is an unjustified bias. Forget about the foreign origins, enjoy these plants now. Humans too are quite exotic, non-native, and invasive. On every continent except Africa, humans are foreigners out of place; and everywhere, Africa included, they have long since transformed the native vegetation with what they brought along (corn and cows). So, if some plants and animals tag along with the human migrations, they too are "ours," no more misplaced than we are (Burdick, 2005). Isn't human ethics supposed to be inclusive of foreigners? Why cannot environmental ethics be inclusive of non-natives?

Mark Sagoff (2005), a well-known environmental philosopher, has defended exotics. Conservation biologists and other environmentalists confront serious obstacles when they seek to exclude or remove introduced plants and other non-native species, on grounds that they threaten the natural environment. Whether most of these non-natives harm the environment is debatable; apparently some 90% do not. Nor can ecologists predict how specific introduced species will behave, so they must target all non-native species as potentially harmful, an impossibly large task. Further, introduced organisms generally and sometimes significantly add to species richness in ecosystems. There is little evidence that non-native plants have caused any extinctions of natives, except in a few small island-like environments. Honeybees are not native to the New World, but they are fully naturalized and quite useful (Schlaepfer, Sax, and Olden, 2011).

Daniel Simberloff (2005), a well-known ecologist, vigorously replied to Sagoff on both empirical and philosophical grounds. Major ecosystem-wide impacts of non-native species, including extinctions of both island and continental species, have been scientifically demonstrated, the kinds of impacts that are judged by the public to be harmful (as with Japanese brome-grass, which degrades range). Further, biologists have recently developed methods that greatly aid prediction of which introduced species will harm the environment. Although introduced species may increase local biodiversity in certain instances, this does not result in any desired changes in ecosystem function. In most localities, exotics decrease biodiversity. More importantly, globally homogenized faunas and floras tends to continental biodiversity decrease (McKinney, 2002; Hepinstall, 2008; Cronk and Fuller, 1995).

Exotics are sometimes "escapes" from plants first deliberately planted (Japanese honeysuckle, multiflora rose. More often these are weedy species (dandelions, Russian thistle). Purple loosestrife invades a pond. Such exotics often displace native vegetation. Such invasives in their new locations are not adapted fits, having evolved on other landscapes and been transported to their new locations anomalously. These plants and animals have not entered these ecosystems by any of the lawlike natural processes that, in the wild, govern community structure. Exotics do not contribute to what Aldo Leopold called the "integrity, stability, and beauty of the biotic community" (1968, pp. 224–225). Charles Elton recognized this, half a century ago: "We are living in a period of the world's history when the mingling of thousands of kinds of organisms from different parts of the world is setting up terrific dislocations in nature" (1958, p. 18). These exotics are "weeds," misplaced on landscapes.

Invasive plant species often flourish because they land on disturbed sites, similar to those from which they came, but with more resources (such as fertilizer and water). They have a life-history strategy of making many seeds rather than protecting themselves for long-lives; they are released from their natural enemies (which are left back where they came from), meanwhile, the natives still have their natural enemies to compete with. These factors compound to make invasives especially disruptive to natural systems (Blumenthal, 2005).

Exotic seeds have often been carried by jet planes to different continents. Once hemmed in by oceans, these plants play hopscotch because of human travel. These exotics are spillovers from civilization. They are like the foreign viruses that land in New York or Los Angeles and upset human health in cities, except that, instead, these upset the health of the land. Humans disturb enormous amounts of soil and make it easy for them. Exotics are waifs of culture.

One might expect, however, that exotics might make inroads where land is tilled, but that they will fail in wild ecosystems, since they are not good adapted fits. And that is often so. The invasives often linger around culture, on the roadsides, in the fence rows. One does not find them deep in the wildlands—at least not at first. But there is disturbed soil in nature as well as in culture, and these plants can gradually invade the native places. Say if you like that they did so competitively; it is equally true that they did so by assistance of ship (in the ballast), plane (dirt on passenger's shoes), and plow (turning the soil, destroying natives).

Plants do move around on their own. They invade new areas, as when climates change; and one can, if one wishes, speak of naturally invasive species (Botkin, 2001). In prehistoric times, with melting ice, species moved north perhaps 200 to 1,000 meters per year, as revealed by fossil pollen analysis. Spruce invaded what previously was tundra. Today, introduced exotic species, once they arrive, move fifty times that fast, typically 50 kilometers a year (Whitlock and Millspaugh, 2001). Most of these introductions crossed oceans by boat or by air, thousands of times faster than any natural plant movements. Most are rapidly propagating species that arrived in North America within the last two centuries.

Invasion by exotics is an ongoing global event. Look forward a century. Michael Soulé says:

> In 2100, entire biotas will have been assembled from (1) remnant and reintroduced natives, (2) partly or completely engineered species, and (3) introduced (exotic) species. The term *natural* will disappear from our working vocabulary. The term is already meaningless in most parts of the world because anthropogenic [activities] have been changing the physical and biological environment for centuries, if not millennia.
>
> (1989, p. 301)

That forces us to ask whether we want an entirely managed nature, where humans engineer and assemble the biotas, or disassemble them by ignorance and accident: a landscape where nature has come to an end. Did we not say, in Chapter 2, we now live in the Anthropocene Epoch, with human-dominated landscapes widespread on Earth? Whatever wild nature was present in the Americas before the native Americans arrived 15,000 years ago, even if it could be known, was Pleistocene nature. Climates have since changed; and nature today, had it been left on its own, might be vastly different from any Pleistocene nature. So, the quest for pristine natural landscapes, museum pieces out of the past, is a hopeless quest—so another argument goes. All we have, or have ever had, is a dynamically changing nature occupied by humans. Humans are the creatures who rule on their landscapes, and, in that sense, we have rebuilt, or, by pristine criteria, contaminated every landscape we observe.

Still, perhaps there can remain on wild and rural landscapes some remnants of what was once native. But now a new protest arises. This is backward looking, because such museum-piece landscapes are vanishing. Bits and pieces of our landscape can be preserved, and there, looking backward, we can be nostalgic about a past that we really no longer have. National parks are grand, but quaint: corners of a continental landscape mostly managed for multiple use, these parks being intentionally managed to create an illusion of wild nature.

Environmentalists do want to respect continuity with the past, but they are not that comfortable with thinking of conservation as preserving museum-pieces. They prefer to think of dynamic ongoing landscapes, and they do not find weedy ecosystems, filled with invasives, to provide that continuity past, present, and ongoing into the future. Yes, respect life, but respect life in place, not life misplaced. Environmental ethics is about individuals, but individuals included in appropriate places. That is a more genuinely inclusive ethic; not an inclusive smorgasbord of species. We must respect ecosystems (as we see in the next chapter); we have to consider niches and adapted fits.

We can take "weed" as a metaphor for the whole story. In gardens, a weed is a plant out of place. Now-invasive plants once and elsewhere did have a niche, an adapted fit in places where they evolved. But scattered all over myriads of landscapes, they are weedy. One does not want a weedy landscape. Initially this means a landscape where fields and pastures are full of weeds that we dislike. Later it means a landscape where wild nature has been invaded with exotics. One does not want a garden with weeds. One does not want a home landscape with weeds. One does not want a national park, a natural park, with weeds. On a larger scale, garden Earth, with tens of thousands of species misplaced and far from home, becomes a weedy planet, with less biological richness and less ecological integrity.

5. Respect for Life: Biocentrism

Biocentrism is a worldview claiming respect for all living organisms. Biocentrism is sometimes used as a general synonym for any naturalistic or non-anthropocentric ethics. More specifically, biocentrism refers to an ethics of respect for life, now with the focus on any and all living beings—plants, microbes, lower animals—not just an ethic centered on humans (anthropocentrism), nor one directed only to the higher animals, who can suffer pains and pleasures. The question is not, "Can it suffer?" but "Is it alive?"

This view has philosophical precedents. Albert Schweitzer was a famous advocate of such an ethics, for which he was awarded the 1953 Nobel Peace Prize. "A man is truly ethical only when he obeys the compulsion to help all life which he is able to assist, and shrinks from injuring anything that lives.... Life as such is sacred to him. He tears no leaf from a tree, plucks no flower, and takes care to crush no insect," not at least unnecessarily, or without appropriate justification (Schweitzer, 1949, p. 310). Schweitzer's ethic was deeply grounded in his Christian faith. There are parallels in many religions, for example the non-injury ethic (*ahimsa*) of Buddhism or Jainism. In the book of Genesis (as we recalled at the beginning of this chapter), God commands the earth to bring forth vegetation, plants, trees, and swarms of living creatures and finds them to be very good (Genesis 1).

In more recent philosophical analysis, biocentrism is set forth with rigorous argument by Paul Taylor: "The relevant characteristic for having the status of a moral patient is not the capacity for pleasure or suffering but the fact that the being has a good of its own which can be furthered or damaged by moral agents" (1981a, p. 314). Taylor develops this at length in his *Respect for Nature* (1986). Humans are non-privileged members of the Earth's community of life. We have an evolutionary kinship and common origin with other species. Humans are absolutely dependent on other forms of life, but they do not depend on us. Each species of life, exemplified in its member organisms, has its own excellences. Plants can photosynthesize, as animals cannot; and all animals, humans included, depend on this photosynthesis.

A bristlecone pine tree, surviving for several thousand years, makes human life seem quite transient. Earth was teeming with life long before humans arrived, entering a world where others had resided for hundreds of millions of years. Nor are humans the only or final evolutionary goal. The community of life continues to be interdependent. All organisms are teleological centers of life (plants seek light and water, defending their lives), as we found above, looking at genetics. They have a welfare, a good of their own.

More controversially, Taylor called for "biocentric egalitarianism." The belief in human superiority is an unjustified bias; we should be species impartial and egalitarian. Biocentrism "regards all living things as possessing inherent worth—the same inherent worth" (Taylor, 1981b, p. 217). Humans do mathematics better than monkeys; monkeys climb trees better than humans. Sequoia trees do what they do quite well. Ants do what they do quite well. These other species are equally good at doing what is appropriate for them to do. We should respect them all. "The killing of a wildflower, then, when taken in and of itself, is just as much a wrong, other-things-being-equal, as the killing of a human" (Taylor, 1983 p. 242).

Critics have replied that this is incredible. Although sequoia trees, wildflowers, and ants do their thing quite well, this overlooks the richness of experience which is present at differing levels in differing species. That differential richness of experience also produces in moral agents differential responsibilities.

Perhaps all living organisms are equally to be considered, for what they are, but this does not imply equal moral significance for them all. Thinking of humans on their landscapes, we found ways in which humans are a part of nature, but also found humans radically different from any other species, unique in their dignity (see Chapter 2).

James Sterba is a biocentrist who attempts reconciliation between anthropocentrism and biocentrism (1995, 2001). Biocentrism may seem to claim that there is no sound reason for thinking that any species is special or superior, including humans, with the apparent implication that there are no good grounds for treating either individuals of different species, or living things collectively, differently. So it seems that human interests count for no more than the interests of any other living thing or system. But, according to Sterba, this implication need not follow.

It is morally permissible to act preferring human interests on self-defense grounds (as Taylor also sometimes argues). This includes showing preference for human interests for the sake of preservation of human basic needs. Sacrificing nature is justified when this gets people feed, clothed, sheltered. Sterba formulates this as "a principle of human preservation" (2001, p. 34). "Actions that are necessary for meeting one's basic needs or the basic needs of other human beings are permissible even when they require aggressing against the basic needs of individual animals and plants or even of whole species or ecosystems" (Sterba, 1995, p. 196).

Even though this shows a preference for humans, Sterba thinks that this is not a problem because it is the way all species behave; they all show preference to their own species. But the good obtained must be proportionate to the harm caused. There will be tension here whether a human is becoming too "aggressive" about "necessary" and "basic" needs. At this point, Sterba's critics reply that one can expect (and fear) that "necessary" and "basic" will prove elastic enough that various advocates can shrink and stretch them to their liking. Do humans satisfy legitimate basic needs when, showing preference for their own species, they continue to increase their population and displace other species?

Lawrence Johnson defends the idea that all living organisms are to be respected morally because they have "interests," not just those with considered preferences, but all those that have vital, biological interests, something "at stake" (Johnson, 1991, 2011). Robin Attfield argues that "all individual animals and plants have interests. For all have … a direction of growth, and all can flourish after their natural kind," and so trees, for example, can count morally, though their significance in practice is frequently rather small (1981, pp. 40–41). In practice, of course, though the life of one tree or grass plant may not count much, since such organisms are very numerous, in the aggregate they may count a great deal.

Kenneth Goodpaster argues for a "'life principle' of moral considerability." Every living organism is self-sustaining in its organized defending of its living state against the disorganization that would otherwise proceed through entropy, or the natural tendencies for things to rot and decay.

> The typifying mark of a living system ... appears to be its persistent state of low entropy [high organization], sustained by metabolic processes for accumulating energy, and maintained in equilibrium with its environment by homeostatic feed back processes.... The core of moral concern lies in respect for self-sustaining organization and integration in the face of pressures toward high entropy [disorganization].
>
> (Goodpaster, 1978, p. 323)

Biocentrists hope to defend an *objective* morality, one with a focus on objective life. Animal welfare ethics holds a hedonist theory of value, as though pain is nature's only disvalue and pleasure its only value. In a biocentric ethic, pains and pleasures will be part of a larger picture, derivative from and instrumental to further values at the ecosystemic level, where nature evolves a flourishing community in some indifference to the pains and pleasures of individuals, even though pain and pleasure in the higher forms is a major evolutionary achievement.

Humans must and ought to use plants in many ways, for food, for timber, for cellulose—as the "basic needs" justification allows. Still, biocentrists argue forcefully that there are occasions when humans encounter plants—sequoia trees, or the rare Chapman's rhododendron—in ways that require the organisms to be taken into account for what they are in themselves. Given their adapted fitness in their ecosystems, there is at least a presumption that these are good kinds, right where they are, and therefore that it is right for humans to let them be, to let them evolve. That leaves plants, along with all kinds of living things, and their species, and the processes that support them all in place. Humans should use this life with respect, restraint, and gratitude.

6. Respect for Life: Naturalizing Values/Virtues

Indeed humans can and ought to respect life, and when they do this they locate intrinsic value in nature. But what account should we give of this? Such locating seems to be some sort of human activity, some relation taken up by persons who become concerned for what these living things are in themselves. But is this *discovering* values already there? Or is it *placing* such value there—choosing (virtuously?) to value some non-human life intrinsically, rather than instrumentally?

By the placing account, values in nature are always "anthropocentric," or at least "anthropogenic" (generated by humans). Bryan G. Norton concludes: "Moralists among environmental ethicists have erred in looking for a value in living things that is *independent* of human valuing. They have therefore forgotten a most elementary point about valuing anything. Valuing always occurs from the viewpoint of a conscious valuer.... Only the humans are valuing agents" (1991, p. 251). Anthony Giddens, a distinguished social theorist, following Robert Goodin, a philosopher, agrees: "Objects in nature can only have value through us—when we speak of value there is inescapably a human element involved, since there must be someone to hold these values" (2009, p. 54).

Humans have, says Ernest Partridge, "the Midas touch," recalling the mythical Midas gifted with the capacity to turn to gold whatever he touched (1998, p. 86). Humans bring value into the world when they point at something and choose to value it. We humans carry the lamp that lights up value, although we require the fuel that nature provides. Actual value is an event in our consciousness, though natural items while still in the dark of value have potential intrinsic value.

Life is worth valuing, but there is a value ignition when humans arrive—something like the way wood is always flammable, but not on fire until actually burning. Or, to change the metaphor, something like the way the light comes on in the refrigerator when we open the door; before that everything is in the dark. Intrinsic value in the realized sense emerges relationally with the appearance of the human-generator. The *attributes* under consideration are objectively there before humans come, but the *attribution* of value is subjective. The object causally affects the subject, who is excited by the incoming data and translates this as value, after which the object, such as a sequoia tree appears as having value, rather like it appears to have green color. Some speak of a "dispositional" account of intrinsic value.

J. Baird Callicott defends such a view. All intrinsic value is "grounded in human feelings" but is "projected" onto the natural object that "excites" the value. "Intrinsic value ultimately depends upon human valuers." "Value depends upon human sentiments" (1984, p. 305). We humans can and ought to *place* such value on natural things, at times, but there is no value already *in place* before we come. Intrinsic value is our construct, interactively with nature, but not something discovered which was there before we came. "There can be no value apart from an evaluator,... all value is as it were in the eye of the beholder [and],... therefore, is humanly dependent" (Callicott, 1980, p. 325). Such value is "anthropogenic." (Callicott, 1992, p. 132).

This, Callicott says, is a "truncated" sense of value where "'intrinsic value' retains only half its traditional meaning. An intrinsically valuable thing on this reading is valuable *for* its own sake, *for* itself, but is not valuable *in* itself, i.e. completely independently of any consciousness" (Callicott, 1986, pp. 142–143). Some critics complain that the term *intrinsic*, even when truncated, is misleading. What is meant is better specified by the term *extrinsic*, the *ex* indicating the external, anthropogenic ignition of the value, which is not *in*, *intrinsic*, internal to the nonsentient organism, even though this value, once generated, is apparently conferred on the organism.

Another way of respecting life intrinsically comes from those who advocate environmental virtue ethics (James, 2006; Sandler, 2007; Sandler and Cafaro, 2005; Cafaro, 2010). An admirable trait in many persons is their capacity to appreciate things outside themselves. An interest in natural history ennobles persons. It stretches them out into bigger persons. Humans must inevitably be consumers of nature; but they can and ought sometimes be more: admirers of nature. That redounds to their excellence. One condition of human flourishing is that humans enjoy natural things in as much diversity as possible—and enjoy them, at times, because such creatures flourish in themselves.

The Americans, the British, the Australians, or any people should be ashamed if they destroy the biodiversity on their landscape; they will be more excellent people if they conserve this biodiversity, all creatures great and small. Humans of decent character will refrain from needless destruction of all kinds, including destruction of even unimportant species. We can always gain excellence of character from acts of conservation. We have a duty to our higher selves to respect life. There is generated a human virtue, actualizing a uniquely human capacity and possibility for excellence, when a person respects a wild animal's life for what that life is in itself, a different and yet related form of life. "In an environmental virtue ethics, human excellence and nature's excellence are necessarily entwined" (Cafaro, 2002, p. 43). To be truly virtuous one must respect values in nature for their own sake, and this is inevitably tributary to human flourishing.

By Robert L. Chapman's account: "Virtue ethics is more interested in character development, and while we can attribute intrinsic value to the 'integrity, stability and beauty' (harmony) of the biotic community, it remains a human activity that will be evaluated from a human-in-nature perspective.... You cannot properly value one without the other.... Cooperation exemplified by virtuous actions preserves a place for human participation and ultimately a placed-based identity befitting human development" (2002, p. 136). If we want a healthy society, then we need to preserve nature so that we still have something natural with which to have such encounters.

Critics of environmental virtue ethics still worry whether the focus is in the right place. If this excellence really comes from appreciating otherness, then such human virtue is tributary to value in other forms of life. Excellence is intrinsically a good state for the self, but there are various intrinsic goods that the self desires and pursues in its relation to others that are not self-states of the person who is desiring and pursuing. An enriched humanity results, with values in biodiversity and values in persons compounded—but only if the loci of value are not confounded. Otherwise the focus of the ethic is misplaced. These species have been around for millions of years. Yes. And why save them? It makes *me* a better person. My quality of life is entwined with theirs. But that confuses the by-product with the located focus of value. The wild other does not become valuable if and when it results in something valuable for me. It is valuable for what it is, whether I am around or not, and recognizing that value does valuable things to me. Such an ethic is best called a value-based ethic, not a virtue-based ethic.

Still, the environmental virtue ethicists are right to remind us that we need to cultivate our human excellences, if we are to succeed in protecting life. We need benevolence and compassion toward other animals. We need respect for other life forms. We need gratitude for their presence on landscapes along with ourselves. We need humility to accept a limited share of Earth's resources—rather than trying to exploit as much as possible. We need wisdom—a capstone human virtue (the "sophia" found in "philo-sophy," "the love of wisdom")—if we are to know who we are, where we are, and what we ought to do.

The *discovered-in-place* account finds *autonomous intrinsic value* in nature, already there and recognized when humans arrive (Rolston, 1983; 1994; Agar 1997, 2001; Lee, 1996; Naess, 1989; McShane, 2007). Less formally, but perhaps more plainly: organisms have a good of their own. This account may not object to humans placing intrinsic value on natural things—Americans may choose the bald eagle as a national symbol and place a special value on these eagles in result. But a truncated sense of intrinsic value is not good enough. Organisms have value for themselves and on their own.

In fact, biology is value-laden. Biologists talk about values all the time. "An ability to ascribe value to events in the world, a product of evolutionary selective processes, is evident across phylogeny. Value in this sense refers to an organism's facility to sense whether events in its environment are more or less desirable" (Dolan, 2002, p. 1191). Remember those aerobatic dragonflies with their high-performance flight back in Carboniferous times, or the plants solving their photosynthetic/water dilemma with complex stomata. Adaptive value, survival value, is the basic matrix of the governing Darwinian theory. An organism is the loci of values defended; life is otherwise unthinkable.

As we found when looking at "smart genes," this defense of value is coded into the behavior programmed by DNA; but, in organisms with the capacity to acquire information during their lifetimes, it may also involve learned behavior. "Evolution has endowed certain organisms with several means to sense the adaptive value of their behavior" and these "value systems themselves can be modified and extended by experience." So both "innate and acquired value" are involved (Friston et al., 1991, pp. 229, 238).

Organisms gain and maintain internal order against the disordering tendencies of external nature. They keep recomposing themselves, while inanimate things run down, erode, and decompose. Organisms pump out disorder. Life is a local counter-current to entropy, an energetic fight uphill in a world that overall moves thermodynamically downhill (recalling Erwin Schrödinger in *What Is Life?*). An organism is thus a spontaneous cybernetic system, self-maintaining, sustaining and reproducing itself on the basis of information about how to make a way through the world. There is some internal representation that is symbolically mediated in the coded "program" and metabolism executing this goal, a checking against performance in the world, using some sentient, perceptive, or other responsive capacities by which to compare match and mismatch. On the basis of information received, the cybernetic system can reckon with vicissitudes, opportunities, and adversities that the world presents. In the "dynamics of emergent processes," says Brian Goodwin, a biologist, "organisms cease to be mere survival machines and assume intrinsic value, having worth in and of themselves" (1994, p. xvi).

The tree is value-able ("able-to-value") itself. If we cannot say this, then we will have to ask, as an open question, "Well, the tree has a good of its own, but is there anything of value to it?" "This tree was injured when the elk rubbed its velvet off its antlers, and the tannin secreted there is killing the invading bacteria. But is this valuable to the tree?" Botanists say that the tree is irritable in the biological sense; it responds with the repair of injury. Such capacities can be "vital." These are observations of value in nature with just as much certainty as they are biological facts; that is what they are: facts about value relationships in nature.

Values are like color, the humanists say. Both arise in interaction. Trees are no more valuable than they are green on their own. This account seems plausible, if one is asking about certain kinds of values, such as the fall colors we enjoy. But consider rather the information that makes photosynthesis possible. Photosynthesis is rather more objective than greenness. What is good for a tree (nitrogen, carbon dioxide, water) is observer-independent. But is not the good of the tree (whether it is injured or healthy) equally observer-independent? The tree's coping based on DNA coding is quite objective.

The sequoia tree has, after all, been there two thousand years, whether or not any green-experiencing humans were around. *Sequoia sempervirens*, the species line, has been around several million years, with each of its individual sequoia trees defending a good of their kind. Why is the tree not defending its own life just as much fact of the matter as its use of nitrogen and photosynthesis to do so? Organisms have their own standards, fit into their niche though they must. They promote their own realization, at the same time that they track an environment. In that sense, as soon as one knows what a sequoia tree is, one knows what a good sequoia is. One knows the biological identity that is sought and conserved.

One must not be confused here by comparing such organisms with human beings, who have career choices, as nonhumans do not. Jack the Ripper was a good murderer in the sense that he was clever and was never caught, but being a murderer is reprehensible. Jack had a good of his own; as a normative system he sought to kill. But his career choice, his norm, was morally wrong. Among moral agents one has to ask not merely whether x is a normative system, but to judge the norm. But organisms, sentient or not, are amoral normative systems, there are no career choices, and there are no cases where an organism seeks a good of its own that is morally reprehensible. Neither wolves nor nettles are bad because they defend their kinds of good. In organisms, the distinction between having a good of its kind and being a good kind vanishes, so far as any faulting of the organism is concerned.

Yes, but biology is not enough, the philosopher-critics will reply. True, plants seek life and avoid death and this comprises a good of their own, biologically. But we need some further reason why this is a good thing, really, philosophically. John O'Neill puts it this way:

> That Y is a good of X does not entail that Y should be realised unless we have a prior reason for believing that X is the sort of thing whose good ought to be promoted. While there is not a logical gap between facts and values, in that some value statements are factual, there is a logical gap between facts and oughts. "Y is a good" does not entail "Y ought to be realized."
>
> (1992, p. 132)

Robin Attfield wonders: "Even if trees have needs and a good of their own, they may still have no value of their own" (1981, p. 35).

Now the idea is that some natural things might have a good of their own and still not be good—such as germs (*Plasdmodium* causing malaria), weeds, greenflies, mosquitoes, skunks, rattlesnakes, weasels. They do not have stand-alone good, real value, though they may have a good for themselves. True, each has a *good-of-its-kind*, but that does not make it a *good kind*. They might be bad in relation. In relation to whom? In relation to some valuer who knows better what real value is. Agreed, nonhumans are not to be judged for their moral goodness. But still we might find that some organism, during the course of pressing its normative expression, upset the ecosystem or caused widespread disease; we find that it is a bad organism. In this sense *Choristoneura fumiferana*, the spruce budworm that is ravaging northeastern boreal forests, or *Plasmodium vivax*, the malaria parasite, might be judged bad kinds, though each has a good of its kind. They are bad kinds instrumentally in the roles they play.

Remember though, that an organism cannot be a good kind without situated environmental fitness. With rare exceptions, organisms are well adapted to the niches they fill. By natural selection their ecosystemic roles must mesh with the kind of goods to which they are genetically programmed. An ecosystem is a perpetual contest of goods in dialectic and exchange (as we develop in the next chapter), and it is difficult to say that any organism is a bad kind in this instrumental sense either. The misfits are extinct, or soon will be. In spontaneous nature any species that preys upon, parasitizes, competes with, or crowds another will be a bad kind from the narrow perspective of its victim or competitor. But if we enlarge that perspective it typically becomes difficult to say that any species is a bad kind overall in the ecosystem.

Such an "enemy" may even be good for the "victimized" species, though harmful to individual members of it, as when predation keeps the deer herd healthy, and drives the species toward increased fleetness over evolutionary time. Beyond this, the "bad kinds" typically play useful roles in population control, in symbiotic relationships, or in providing opportunities for other species. Cape May warblers, usually, rare, thrive during budworm outbreaks; other birds that eat the worms can nest twice in a season when normally they would be hard-pressed to complete one nesting.

Still, one might find examples of organisms with a situated environmental fitness that seem bad arrangements. In the communities that evolve, there is constant struggle. There are upsets. There are false starts, trials and errors, but there is much fitting together of smart genes discovering positive value. The life adventure on Earth requires some wandering around, exploring paths that fail, or at least lose out to others who explore better paths. There are deformed organisms in nature, bad organisms of their kind, and even monstrosities: things that have no natural kind, unfitted for any habitat. Such individuals are immediately eliminated, although in the course of experimental mutation they are required, if life is to continue. So even mutants and monsters play their roles in the trial and error by which the evolutionary ecosystem tracks changing environments and achieves new life forms.

True value, real goodness, must be relational—so we are told. But these relations are seldom judgments about bad arrangements in ecosystems. Philosophers usually do not have enough empirical knowledge to make such judgments. In relation to whom? The common answer is "in relation to humans"-who dislike weeds, skunks, and weasels in the chicken coop, though not weasels (ermine) as coats on their backs. A better, because more objective and less selfish answer, is "in relation to life in all its rich natural history."

Where we find living things valuing their lives, have we reason to count this morally? The question is essentially: Ought we to respect this ongoing life? Is a philosopher still going to insist: Well, all this inventiveness, strategy, remarkable efficiency, wisdom of the genes, exquisite organization to accomplish delicate tasks, all these marvels to the contrary, there is nothing of value here? True, these cell biologists have been finding something "wonderful" in genome strategies, but philosophers are wise about the use of language and know that this is only "wonderful" when cell biologists get there to wonder about those dragonflies, beetles, cyanobacteria, corals, sequoia trees. Or at least nothing was "astounding" until a human being came around to be astounded. We do not think that the genomes have a sense of wonder or are astounded. Still, the biological achievements are there long before we get let in on them. Facing up to these facts, which are quite as certain as that we humans are valuers in the world, it can seem "astounding" arrogance to say that, in our ignorance of these events, before we arrived there was nothing of value there.

Traditionalist philosophers insist there is not—no real independent value in the leaf stomata, genome evolution, dragonfly wings, or bacterial clocks. These wised-up philosophers will insist that environmentalists who find value out there in plants and insects, certainly those who find it in genetic information, have not yet faced up their epistemological naivete. They persist in ontological realism, unaware of how contemporary analytic or postmodern philosophy has made any scientific knowing of any objective nature out there impossible, much less any realism about natural values. Scientists are exporting their human experiences and overlaying nature with them when they set up these frameworks of understanding. Though unsophisticated biologists have used "value" regarding plants, careful analysis will put that kind of "value" in scare quotes. This so-called value is not a value, really, not one of interest to philosophers. because it is not a value with interest in itself. Even if we found such interest-taking value, as we do in the higher animals, we humans would still have to evaluate any such animal values before we knew whether any "real" value were present.

The biologists may say that whatever survives is "better" adapted than what it has replaced. But this, philosophers will reply, is only a biological sense of "better." There is nothing moral about it. In wild nature, organisms are not moral agents at all. The new survival tricks may be meaner and more cruel than before, causing other individuals in that same species to lose out, or other species to go extinct. Even though an organism evolves to have a situated environmental fitness, not all such situations are good arrangements; some can be clumsy or bad. Some might even be evil. Nature is "red in tooth and claw," and the last thing philosophers want to do is to imitate nature.

Philosophers know *better* what is really "*better*." But when we press these philosophers to specify what is this overall-filtering-super-value that legitimates or de-legitimates the diverse survival-goods of their own in these myriads of species on Earth, the philosophers start to stutter. Challenged to name the good ones (elk, impala, sequoia trees, baobab trees) and name the bad ones (those rattlesnakes and greenflies), and maybe some in-between ones (wolves and weasels), the answers look mostly like anthropocentric biases. Philosophers may say that the overall good is pleasure, or utility (whose utility?), or what is right, or some Platonic ideal (perfect deer?), or what keeps the community flourishing, or what humans find wonderful, or something like that. The deeper problem is that, despite the excellence of our increasingly scientific accounts in biology, nature has been mapped philosophically as a moral blank space, as value-free in and of itself. But in doing this, we make a fallacy of mislocated value, a humanistic mistake taking value to lie exclusively in the satisfaction of our human preferences.

Can we not say that in general that the evolution and ongoing continuing of life on Earth is a good thing? Generally perhaps yes, the reply comes; but this is not enough to let us conclude in any particular case that the achievement of a some particular organism's goals is a good thing. We celebrate life collectively, value it as a whole, but particularly we are picky about what we find of value—leave out those mosquitoes and rattlesnakes. We cannot always back down from universals to particulars. Life as a whole is good, but nothing follows about specific lives.

Or maybe we need to think of it both as a whole (collectively) and as particular species (distributively). "Ought mosquitoes and rattlesnakes to exist?" is a distributive increment, one small part, in the global collective question, "Ought life on Earth to exist?" If the answer to the particular question is not always the same as the answer to the collective question, we can still say, at least, since life on Earth is an aggregate of many species, that the two are sufficiently related that the burden of proof lies with those who wish deliberately to disvalue some species and simultaneously to care overall for life on Earth. The whole idea of the value of biodiversity, as biologists say, or "plenitude of being," as philosophers used to say, presumes that life collectively is a good thing and ought to be respected. If you say, "Biodiversity of life is good, but mosquitoes are bad," it's up to you to explain why.

No. No! The skeptical philosophers will say: Have you never heard of the naturalistic fallacy? Life *is*. One *ought* to respect it. If philosophers have ever settled on anything, they unanimously forbid moving from what *is* the case (a description of biological facts) to what *ought to be* (a prescription of duty). Any who do so commit the naturalistic fallacy. Philosophers may not know much biology, but they do know logic. If x has a good of its own, then x is good. If x is good, then you ought to protect it. One counterexample will defeat such premises, and the counterexamples are legion—those germs, weeds, skunks, greenflies, weasels (Nolt, 2006, 2009).

Well, even if there are some counterexamples, surely we regularly use this form of argument: Sally has a good of her own. Sally is good. One ought to respect Sally. Humans have a good of their own. Humans are good. You ought to protect human life. We may argue for an instrumental good; Sally is a good cook. We need our neighbors—as store clerks and friends. But we just as often argue that there is some good inherent in the these others. Those who disagree with such argument, and harm Sally, or murder other humans, will soon find themselves in jail. Why not be more inclusive, and extend such consideration to nonhumans—at least often if not always? Does that not seem logical, as well as biological? Even the virtue ethicists claimed that humans realize an excellence otherwise unachievable when they value others for what they are in themselves. Presumptively, if spontaneous natural lives are of value in themselves, and if humans encounter and jeopardize such value, it would seem that humans ought not to destroy values in nature, not at least without overriding justification producing greater value.

No, the reply may come, this is an unjustified extrapolation, from humans who are complex rational, self-conscious, emotional agents to those beetles or sequoia trees who have no such capacities. True, they have a life that they defend, call it a good of their own, but the kind of life that they have, their kind of good, lays no moral on us humans—as is proved by the germs and greenflies counterexamples. Yes, environmental ethicists insist, a comprehensive ethic is quite rational; the humans-as-better-valuers ethic is not so much rational as myopic. Environmental ethics calls humans to a genuine self-transcendence, to a larger respect for life on Earth.

This may not be the best possible world, but Earth is the only one we know that has produced any life at all, and the life it has produced is, on the whole, a good thing. These claims about good kinds do not say that organisms are perfect kinds, nor that there can be no better ones, only that natural kinds are good kinds until proven otherwise. At least the burden of proof is on a human evaluator to say why any natural kind is a bad kind and ought not to call forth admiring respect.

Humans are not so much lighting up value in a merely potentially valuable world, as they are psychologically joining ongoing planetary natural history in which there is value wherever there is positive creativity. While such creativity can be present in subjects with their interests and preferences, it can also be present objectively in living organisms with their lives defended, and in species that defend an identity over time, and generate the storied achievements of natural history. The valuing human subject in an otherwise valueless world is an insufficient premise for the experienced conclusions of those deep into biology. Nature has added up all this defending of individuals into wonderful life on the planet. What's going on is life persisting in the midst of its perpetual perishing. Humans ought to respect such life.

References

Agar, Nicholas. 1997. "Biocentrism and the Concept of Life," *Ethics* 108:147–168.

———. 2001. *Life's Intrinsic Value: Science, Ethics, and Nature.* New York: Columbia University Press.

Attfield, Robin. 1981. "The Good of Trees," *Journal of Value Inquiry* 15:35–54.

Barinaga, Marcia. 1998. "New Timepiece Has a Familiar Ring," *Science* 281(4 September): 1429–1431.

Blumenthal, Dana. 2005. "Interrelated Causes of Plant Invasion," *Science* 310:243–244.

Botkin, Daniel. B. 2001. "The Naturalness of Biological Invasions," *Western North American Naturalist* 61:261–266.

Burdick, Alan. 2005. "The Truth about Invasive Species," *Discover* 25(no. 5, May):35–41.

Cafaro, Philip. 2002. "Thoreau's Environmental Ethics in *Walden,*" *The Concord Saunterer,* 10(2002):17–63.

Cafaro, Philip, ed. 2010. *Environmental Virtue Ethics,* theme issue of *Journal of Agricultural and Environmental Ethics* 23(nos. 1-2):1–206.

Callicott, J. Baird. 1980. "Animal Liberation: A Triangular Affair," *Environmental Ethics* 2:311–338.

———. 1984. "Non-anthropocentric Value Theory and Environmental Ethics," *American Philosophical Quarterly* 21:299–309.

———. 1986. "On the Intrinsic Value of Nonhuman Species." Pages 138–172 in Bryan G. Norton, ed., *The Preservation of Species.* Princeton, NJ: Princeton University Press.

———. 1992. "Rolston on Intrinsic Value: A Deconstruction," *Environmental Ethics* 14:129–143.

Campbell, John H. 1983. "Evolving Concepts of Multigene Families," *Isozymes: Current Topics in Biological and Medical Research, Volume 10: Genetics and Evolution,* 401–417.

Chapman, Robert L. 2002. "The Goat-stag and the Sphinx: The *Place* of the Virtues in Environmental Ethics," *Environmental Values* 11:129–144.

Cox, George W. 1999. *Alien Species in North America and Hawaii: Impacts on Natural Ecosystems.* Washington, D.C.: Island Press.

Craine, Joseph M. 2009. *Resource Strategies of Wild Plants.* Princeton, NJ: Princeton University Press.

Cram, Donald J. 1988. "The Design of Molecular Hosts, Guests, and Their Complexes," *Science* 240:760–767.

Cronk, Quentin C. B., and Janice L. Fuller. 1995. *Plant Invaders: The Threat to Natural Ecosystems.* London: Chapman and Hall.

Dolan, R. J. 2002. "Emotion, Cognition, and Behavior," *Science* 298:1191–1194.

Elton, Charles S. 1958. *The Ecology of Invasions by Animals and Plants.* London: Metheun and Co.

Eser, Uta. 1998. "Assessment of Plant Invasions: Theoretical and Philosophical Fundamentals." Pages 95–107 in Uwe Starfinger, K. Edwards, I. Kowarik, and M. Williamson, eds., *Plant Invasions: Ecological Mechanisms and Human Responses.* Leiden, The Netherlands: Backhuys.

Friston, K. J., G. Tonoi, G. N. Reeke Jr., et al. 1991. "Value-Dependent Selection in the Brain: Simulation in a Synthetic Neural Model," *Neuroscience* 59:229–243.

Giddens, Anthony. 2009. *The Politics of Global Climate Change.* Cambridge, UK: Polity Press.

Goodpaster, Kenneth E. 1978. "On Being Morally Considerable," *Journal of Philosophy* 75:308–325.

Goodwin, Brian. 1994. *How the Leopard Changed Its Spots: The Evolution of Complexity.* Princeton, NJ: Princeton University Press.

Grill, Erwin, and Ziegler, Hubert. 1998. "A Plant's Dilemma," *Science* 282 (9 October):252–254.

Hepinstall, Jeffrey A., Marina Alberti, and John M. Marzluff. 2008. "Predicting Land Cover Change and Avian Community Responses in Rapidly Urbanizing Environments," *Landscape Ecology* 23:1257–1276.

Hölldobler, Bert, and Edward O. Wilson, 2009. *The Superorganism: The Beauty, Elegance, and Strangeness of Insect Societies.* New York: W. W. Norton.

Hutchinson, G. Evelyn. 1959. "Homage to Santa Rosalia, or Why Are There so Many Kinds of Animals." *American Naturalist* 93:145–159.

James, Simon P. 2006. "Human Virtues and Natural Values," *Environmental Ethics* 28:339–353.

Johnson, Lawrence E. 1991. *A Morally Deep World.* Cambridge, UK: Cambridge University Press.

———. 2011. *A Life-Centered Approach to Bioethics: Biocentric Ethics.* Cambridge, UK: Cambridge University Press.

Keegan, Dawn R., Bruce E. Coblentz, and Clark S. Winchell. 1994. "Feral Goat Eradication on San Clemente Island, California," *Wildlife Society Bulletin* 22 (no. 1):56–61.

Keller, Evelyn Fox. 1983. *A Feeling for the Organism: The Life and Work of Barbara McClintock.* New York: W. W. Freeman.

Lee, Keekok, 1996. "The Source and Locus of Intrinsic Value: A Reexamination," *Environmental Ethics* 18:297–309.

Leopold, Aldo. 1968. *A Sand County Almanac.* New York: Oxford University Press.

Maynard Smith, John. 2000. "The Concept of Information in Biology," *Philosophy of Science* 67:177.

McKinney, Michael L. 2002. "Urbanization, Biodiversity, and Conservation," *BioScience* 52: 883–890.

McKnight, Bill N., ed.. 1993. *Biological Pollution: The Control and Impact of Invasive Exotic Species.* Indianapolis: Indiana Academy of Science.

McShane, Katie. 2007. "Why Environmental Ethics Shouldn't Give Up on Intrinsic Value," *Environmental Ethics* 29:43–61.

Mohlenbrock, Robert H. 1983. *Where Have All the Wildflowers Gone?* New York: Macmillan.

Mooney, Harold A., Richard N. Mack, Jeffrey A. McNeeley, et al., eds. 2005. *Invasive Alien Species: A New Synthesis.* Washington: Island Press.

Naess, Arne. 1989. *Ecology, Community and Lifestyle: Outline of an Ecosophy.* Cambridge, UK: Cambridge University Press.

Nolt, John. 2006. "The Move from *Good* to *Ought* in Environmental Ethics," *Environmental Ethics* 28:355–374.

———. 2009. "The Move from *Is* to *Good* in Environmental Ethics," *Environmental Ethics* 31:135–154.

Norton, Bryan G. 1991. *Toward Unity Among Environmentalists*. New York: Oxford University Press.

O'Neill, John. 1992. "The Varieties of Intrinsic Value," *The Monist* 75:119–137.

Orgel, Leslie E. 1994. "The Origin of Life on the Earth," *Scientific American* 271(no. 4, October):4, 76–83.

Partridge, Ernest. 1998. "Values in Nature: Is Anybody There?" Pages 81–88 in Louis J. Pojman, ed., *Environmental Ethics: Readings in Theory and Application*, 2nd ed. Belmont, CA: Wadsworth.

Pennisi, Elizabeth. 1998. "How the Genome Readies Itself for Evolution," *Science* 281(21 August):1131–1134.

Rolston, Holmes, III. 1983. "Values Gone Wild," *Inquiry* 26:181–207.

———. 1994. "Value in Nature and the Nature of Value." Pages 13–30 in Robin Attfield and Andrew Belsey, eds., *Philosophy and the Natural Environment*. Cambridge, UK: Cambridge University Press.

———. 2001. "Naturalizing Values: Organisms and Species." Pages 76–86 in Louis P. Pojman, ed., *Environmental Ethics: Readings in Theory and Application*, 3rd ed. Belmont, CA: Wadsworth.

Sagoff, Mark. 2005. "Do Non-Native Species Threaten The Natural Environment?" *Journal of Agricultural and Environmental Ethics* 18:215–236.

Sandler, Ronald S. 2007. *Character and Environment: A Virtue-Oriented Approach to Environmental Ethics*. New York: Columbia University Press

Sandler, Ronald, and Phillip Cafaro, eds. 2005. *Environmental Virtue Ethics* Lanham, MD: Rowman and Littlefield.

Schlaepfer, M. A., D. F. Sax, and J. D. Olden. 2011. "The Potential Conservation Value of Non-Native Species," *Conservation Biology*, no. doi: 10.1111/j.1523-1739.2010.01646.x

Schrödinger, Erwin. 1944. *What Is Life?* Cambridge, UK: Cambridge University Press.

Schull, Jonathan. 1990. "Are Species Intelligent?" *Behavioral and Brain Sciences* 13:63–75.

Schweitzer, Albert. 1949. *The Philosophy of Civilization*. New York: Macmillan.

Seeley, Thomas D. 2003. "What Studies of Communication Have Revealed about the Minds of Worker Honey Bees." Pages 21–33 in Tomonori Kikuchi, Noriko Azuma, and Seigo Higashi, eds., *Genes, Behaviors and Evolution of Social Insects*. Sapporo, Japan: Hokkaido University Press.

———. 2010. *Honeybee Democracy*. Princeton, NJ: Princeton University Press.

Shapiro, James A. 2002. "Genome System Architecture and Natural Genetic Engineering." Pages 1–14 in Laura F. Landweber and Erik Winfree, eds., *Evolution as Computation*. New York: Springer-Verlag.

———. 2005. "A 21st Century View of Evolution: Genome System Architecture, Repetitive DNA, and Natural Genetic Engineering," *Gene* 345(2005):91–100).

Simberloff, Daniel. 2005. "Non-native Species *Do* Threaten the Natural Environment!," *Journal of Agricultural and Environmental Ethics* 18(2005):595–607.

Soulé, Michael E. 1989. "Conservation Biology in the Twenty-first Century: Summary and Outlook." Pages 297–303 in David Western and Mary Pearl, eds., *Conservation for the Twenty-first Century*. New York: Oxford University Press.

Sterba, James. 1995. "From Biocentric Individualism to Biocentric Pluralism," *Environmental Ethics* 17:191–207.

———. 2001. *Three Challenges to Ethics: Environmentalism, Feminism, and Multiculturalism*. New York: Oxford University Press.

Sterelny, Kim, and Paul E. Griffiths. 1999. *Sex and Death: An Introduction to Philosophy of Biology*. Chicago: University of Chicago Press.

Taylor, Paul. 1981a. "Frankena on Environmental Ethics," *Monist* 64:313–324.

———. 1981b. "The Ethics of Respect for Nature," *Environmental Ethics* 3:197–218.

———. 1983. "In Defense of Biocentrism," *Environmental Ethics* 5:237–243.

———. 1986. *Respect for Nature: A Theory of Environmental Ethics.* Princeton, NJ: Princeton University Press.

Thaler, David S. 1994. "The Evolution of Genetic Intelligence," *Science* 264:224–225.

Thomas, Lewis. 1975. *The Lives of a Cell.* New York: Bantam Books.

Vogel, Gretchen. 1998. "Insect Wings Point to Early Sophistication," *Science* 282(23 October):599–601.

Wheeler, Quentin D. 1990. "Insect Diversity and Cladistic Constraints," *Annals of the Entomological Society of America* 83:1031–1047.

Whitlock, Cathy, and Sarah H. Millspaugh. 2001. "A Paleoecologic Perspective on Past Plant Invasions in Yellowstone," *Western North American Naturalist* 61:316–327.

Wills, Christopher. 1989. *The Wisdom of the Genes: New Pathways in Evolution.* New York: Basic Books.

Wilson, Edward O. 1987. "The Little Things that Run the World (The Importance and Conservation of Invertebrates)," *Conservation Biology* 1(4):344–346.

Wootton, R. J., J. Kuikalová, D. J. S. Newman, and J. Muzón. 1998. "Smart Engineering in the Mid-Carboniferous: How Well Could Palaeozoic Dragonflies Fly?" *Science* 282(23 October):749–751.

5

SPECIES AND BIODIVERSITY

Lifelines in Jeopardy

Individuals have a good of their own, as we developed in the last two chapters. They also are goods of their kind (species). Many of these species are also threatened with extinction. When animals, birds, and plants vanish from the landscape, this raises public concern. The *Millennium Ecosystem Assessment*, reporting a multi-national consensus of hundreds of experts, concluded: "Over the past few hundred years, humans have increased species extinction rates by as much as 1,000 times background rates that were typical over Earth's history" (2005a, p. 3; see also 2005b). The loss of species seems intuitively bad, but why? What values are attached to species? Why ought we to save them? At the species level, responsibilities seem to increase. So does the intellectual challenge of defending duties to species. What are species? The question is scientific, one to be answered by biologists. Have humans duties to them? The question is ethical, to be answered by philosophers.

1. Science—The *Is* Question: What Are Species?

There is a scientific problem to be considered first. We will later find it challenging to argue from an *is* (that a species exists) to an *ought* (that a species ought to exist). But we will first have to look over the shoulders of biologists to see if they know what a species is. At this point we find the biologists somewhat uncertain. Some say that the concept is arbitrary, conventional, a mapping device that is only theoretical. Duties to species would be as imaginary as duties to contour lines, or to lines of latitude and longitude. Ornithologists once reassessed an endangered species, the Mexican duck, *Anas diazi*, and lumped it with the common mallard, *A. platyrhynchos*, as subspecies *diazi*. U. S. Fish and Wildlife authorities took it off the endangered species list partly as a result. Did a species vanish? It would seem that this is relevant to whether we have a duty to this species.

Biologists have a systematic classifying scheme usually put as a hierarchy: *kingdom, phylum, class, order, family, genus, species*. If a species is only a category or class, boundary lines may be arbitrarily drawn, and the class is nothing more than a convenient grouping of its members. Individual organisms exist, but if species are merely classes, they are inventions that aggregate member organisms in this fashion or that. No one proposes duties to genera, families, orders, phyla; everyone concedes that these do not exist in nature.

Darwin once wrote, "I look at the term species, as one arbitrarily given for the sake of convenience to a set of individuals closely resembling each other" (1968, p. 108). Some natural properties are used to make distinctions—reproductive structures, bones, teeth. But which properties are selected and where the lines are drawn are decisions that vary with taxonomists. Indeed, biologists routinely put after a species the name of the "author" who, they say, "erected" the taxon.

Nevertheless, most biologists (Darwin included) tend to be realists about species, as they are not about families, orders, phyla. Species are natural kinds, reproducing out there in the world. *Ursus arctos* (the grizzly bear) is an ongoing dynamic bear-bear-bear sequence, a specific form of life historically maintained over generations for thousands of years. The sow devotes her life to her cubs. In the birth-death-birth-death system a series of replacements is required. Reproduction is typically assumed to be a need of individuals, but since any particular individual can flourish somatically without reproducing at all, indeed may be put through duress and risk or spend much energy reproducing, by another logic we can interpret reproduction as *the species* staying in place by its replacements, recreating itself by continuous performance.

A female animal does not have mammary glands, nor a male testicles, because the function of these is to preserve its own life; these organs are defending the line of life bigger than the somatic individual. The locus of the value that is defended over generations is as much in the *form* of life, since the individuals are genetically impelled to sacrifice themselves in the interests of reproducing their kind. The species line too is value-able, able to conserve a biological identity. Indeed it is more real, more value-able than the individual, necessary though individuals are for the continuance of this lineage (Rolston, 1988).

A biological "species" is not just a class. A species is a living historical form (Latin *species*), propagated in individual organisms, that flows dynamically over generations. G. G. Simpson concludes: "An evolutionary species is a lineage (an ancestral-descendant sequence of populations) evolving separately from others and with its own unitary evolutionary role and tendencies" (1961, p. 153). Ernst Mayr holds: "Species are groups of interbreeding natural populations that are reproductively isolated from other such groups" (1969a, p. 26). He can even emphasize that *"species are the real units of evolution,* they are the entities which specialize, which become adapted, or which shift their adaptation" (1969b, p. 318).

Some philosophers have claimed that species are integrated individuals, and that species names are really proper names, with organisms related to their species as part is to whole (Ghiselin, 1974; Hull, 1978). Niles Eldredge and Joel Cracraft find: "A species is a diagnosable cluster of individuals within which there is a parental pattern of ancestry and descent, beyond which there is not, and which exhibits a pattern of phylogenetic ancestry and descent among units of like kind." Species, they insist, with emphasis, are *"discrete entities in time as well as space"* (Eldredge and Cracraft, 1980, p. 92).

Biologists and philosophers do find it difficult to pinpoint precisely what a species is, and there may be no single proper way to define species. There are four main accounts. (1) By a morphological account, a taxonomist considers the form, including the shape, the flowers, the organs of a specimen, and groups it with others of like morphology. Such a taxonomist would need to know nothing about the history of the examined individual, nor ever to have seen one alive. (2) By a phylogenetic account, taxonomists place together organisms with identical, or nearly identical, evolutionary histories, so they will need evidence of the organism's past. If they cannot get this in the fossil record, perhaps they can examine the gene pool. (3) By a "biological" account (the term is somewhat misleading), systematists place together all individuals that do or could interbreed. So, they watch and see if they mate and if the off-spring are fertile. (4) We noticed earlier that some think species are more like proper-named individuals (Abraham Lincoln, or England), than like natural kinds (humans or islands).

It turns out, unsurprisingly in view of evolutionary natural history, that all four accounts, despite their differing principles, pick out more or less the same group of individual organisms. We have to say "more or less" because there are exceptions (some hybrids are fertile; differing phylogenetic lines arrive at the same morphological form). But this is not only unsurprising, it is unproblematic in view of the processes of speciation, where species evolve one into another and are sometimes in transition.

There may be no single, quintessential way to define species; rather there are several dimensions of similarity, rather like family resemblances. A polytypic gestalt of features may be required, variant but related ways of identifying a species. All we need to raise the issue of duty, however, is that species be objectively there as living processes in the evolutionary ecosystem; the varied criteria for defining them (descent, reproductive isolation, morphology, gene pool) come together at least in providing evidence that species are really there. In this sense, species are dynamic natural kinds, if not corporate individuals. A species is a coherent, ongoing form of life expressed in organisms, encoded in gene flow, and shaped by the environment.

The claim that there are specific forms of life historically maintained in their environments over time does not seem arbitrary or fictitious at all but, rather, as certain as anything else we believe about the empirical world, even though at times scientists revise the theories and taxa with which they map these forms. Species are not so much like lines of latitude and longitude as like mountains and rivers, phenomena objectively there to be mapped. The edges of all these natural kinds will sometimes be fuzzy, to some extent discretionary. We can expect that one species will slide into another over evolutionary time. But it does not follow from the fact that speciation is sometimes in progress that species are merely made up, instead of found, as evolutionary lines articulated into diverse forms, each with its more or less distinct integrity, breeding population, gene pool, and role in its ecosystem.

Many species are closely related to others in their genera, and the loss of a particular species is less tragic if, so to speak, 85% of that form of life continues elsewhere in the genus. Nevertheless each species has elements of uniqueness. Each brings to realization some potential in nature unreached by others. It is sometimes suggested that mammals and birds should be saved at the species level, but that for nongame and noncommercial fish and many plants (unless of special interest to humans), saving at the level of genus would be enough. Those natural kinds that do not differ much even as genera (some insects, nematodes, microbes) might be saved at the family level—at least this is all the law should require. There is increased intrinsic value as one goes up the ecosystemic pyramid, and so there is more point in saving advanced forms in more detail. Lower down, fauna and flora should be saved mostly for their instrumentality, and saved in specific detail only if this is critical for roles in ecosystems.

There are several troubles with this proposal. To begin with, species are real historical entities, interbreeding populations; families, orders, and genera are not. What ought to be saved would largely be lost—the breeding populations. Further, species are most similar where the speciation process is dynamic and fecund; there the dynamic lineages are profuse and procreative. To try to preserve representatives of families or orders in isolated fragments of habitats would preserve puzzle pieces taken out of the whole gestalt, and a species would soon no longer work as it formerly did in the biotic community, removed from the full set of interactions with its competitors and neighbors. So we conclude that species are dynamic life forms preserved in historical lines that persist genetically over millions of years, overleaping short-lived individuals. So far from being arbitrary, species are the real survival units.

2. Ethics—The *Ought* Question: Ought We to Save Species?

The International Union for Conservation of Nature (IUCN) maintains a *Red List of Threatened Species*, which documents the extinction risk of (at current numbers) 47,677 species, of which 17,291 are threatened, including 12% of birds, 21% of mammals, 30% of amphibians, 27% of reef-building corals, and 35% of conifers and cycads (2010). The Living Planet index documents that populations of wild species have declined by 30% since 1970. The U.S. Endangered Species list contains about 1,250 animal and 800 plant species, but the procedures for listing species are complicated, and all conservationists realize that the number is far higher. In the United States, the "actual number of known species threatened with extinction is ten times higher than the number protected under the Endangered Species Act" (Wilcove and Master, 2005, p. 414).

Species are, presumptively, good kinds. But we need some argument (Rolston, 1985). The first line of argument is that species are good for something. We do not yet even need to ask whether species have goods of their own, or are good kinds. How are they good for us? We ask whether they have medical, industrial, agricultural, scientific, or recreational uses (Chivian and Bernstein, 2008; Marton-Lefèvre, 2010).

To give only a few examples: Vincristine and vinblastine, extracted from a Madagascar periwinkle (*Catharanthus roseus*), are used to treat Hodgkin's disease and leukemia. A variety of wild tomato (*Lycopersicon chmielewskii*), found in Peru, has been bred into and enhanced the tomato for the U.S. industry, making a firmer tomato for machine handling, resulting in multi-million dollar profits. An obscure Yellowstone thermophilic microbe, *Thermophus aquaticus*, was discovered to contain a heat-stable enzyme, which can be used to drive the polymerase chain reaction (PCR), used in a gene-copying technique. The rights to the process sold in 1991 for $300 million, and the process is now earning $100 million a year. Norman Myers urges "conserving our global stock" (1979). "To keep every cog and wheel is the first precaution of intelligent tinkering," cautioned Aldo Leopold (1970, p. 190). Save all the parts. Who knows what might be useful?

Wild species may be indirectly important for the roles they play in ecosystems. They are "rivets" in the airplane, the Earthship in which we humans are flying (Ehrlich and Ehrlich, 1981). The loss of a few species may have no evident results now, but the loss of many species imperils the resilience and stability of the ecosystems on which humans depend. Myers' metaphor is a sinking ark, going back to the Noah story. But to worry about a sinking ark seems a strange twist from that story. Noah built the ark to preserve each species, brought on board carefully, two of each kind. In the Ehrlich/Myers account, the species-rivets are preserved to keep the ark from sinking! The reversed justification is revealing.

Critics have responded that it is difficult to argue that every species is a rivet; rare ones are unlikely to be. The metaphor is faulty; Earth is not a well-engineered machine that needs all its parts. Ecosystems are more plural and loosely structured than that. Nevertheless, there is reliable scientific evidence that the loss of many species can upset ecosystems on which humans depend (remember the bees pollinating crops in Chapter 4) (World Health Organization, 2005).

A further argument is that species, now especially the rare ones, are often clues to natural history. No sensible person would destroy the Rosetta Stone (the obelisk found at Rosetta in Egypt in 1799, which enabled the deciphering of ancient, forgotten languages). No self-respecting humans will destroy the mouse lemur, endangered in Madagascar and thought to be the nearest modern animal to the primates from which the human line evolved. Destroying species is like tearing pages out of an unread book, written in a language humans hardly know how to read, about the place where we live.

Some species are resources, rivets, or Rosetta stones, but some are not. Do these have any value that warrants saving them? A frequent argument is that here we can extend the sorts of arguments already used by the virtue ethicists and others in the previous chapter about caring for individuals. Most ethicists say that one ought not needlessly to destroy endangered species; virtuous persons are not vandals. In a more enlightened view, human well-being depends on relationships not only with other humans, but with life on Earth. David Schmidtz explains: "It would be a failure of self-interest to care only about ourselves. We must care about something beyond ourselves. Otherwise we won't have enough to care about, and will as a result be unhealthy" (2008, p. 3). If humans live on a wonderland Earth, they will be impoverished so long as they remain unappreciative of their rich surroundings—even if they never find any resource uses for these other species.

A person who re-forms his or her evaluation of wild species benefits because one is now living in a richer and more harmonious relationship with nature. Generous persons save the whales and butterflies and are the better off because of their increased virtues. *Noblesse oblige.* At a basic level, a healthy and productive life in harmony with nature is quite possible without wolves on the landscape. But still more fundamentally, Bryan Norton (1999) argues, considering wolf policy (in Norway, similarly in Montana), legislation is needed to force the sheepherders to accept the wolves; and, accompanying that, they need to be persuaded to see that the wolves are good for them. "I would argue that in this case the local people … should be pushed to change somewhat in the direction of wolf protection" (p.398).

Otherwise, those sheepherders will "have sacrificed their birthright of wildness for a few sheep." People should want wolves on the landscape lest future generations "feel profoundly the loss of wilderness experiences." "Too often, local communities have acted on the basis of short-term interests, only to learn that they have irretrievably deprived their children of something of great value" (Norton, 1999, pp. 397–398,). Keep the wolves, and other endangered species, so that we and our children can tingle in awe. This may be a human benefit, but it also seems to be recognizing some value in the awe-some wolves.

Hustai National Park, located west of Ulaanbaatar, Mongolia, was set up as a refuge to reintroduce the wild Mongolian Takhi, or Przewalski's horse, back into the wild. This horse has sixty-six chromosomes; all other horses have fewer chromosomes. This is considered the world's only living genuinely wild horse; others are feral as they have been domesticated. In 1992, sixteen horses were taken from captive stock in Holland and the Ukraine and released in the park refuge. The population has increased to about 260 horses, and is a source of great Mongolian national pride. The goal is five hundred horses (Wilford, 2005).

More pragmatically, there are debates about ownership of values associated with biodiversity. Historically, wild plant species, seeds, and germplasm have been considered in the public domain, or part of "the common heritage of mankind." But increasingly Third World nations have been claiming that species within their boundaries are their national property. The Convention on Biological Diversity begins: "States have sovereign rights over their own biological resources" (Preamble) and continues: "Recognizing the sovereign rights of States over their natural resources, the authority to determine access to genetic resources rests with the national governments and is subject to national legislation" (Article 15) (United Nations Conference on Environment and Development, 1992). These nations have been increasingly insisting that they share in the benefits of patents and other intellectual property rights based on the development of genetic resources found on their lands (Normile, 2010). This seems more plausible where such plants were in local use and perhaps bred over generations for increased production, but less plausible where the plants were simply found in the wild.

Some natural resources, such as ores and trees, can be national resources, but it is not clear that nations can or should own species, which is more like owning the structure of gold than owning a deposit of gold. Did the Peruvian government, or the people of Peru, or the local indigenous people, own the tomato species found wild in their forests from which geneticists bred a useful gene into agricultural tomatoes? The plant was wild, more like a ball nettle than a tomato; the locals never bred it for any use; they didn't even know it was a tomato. Even plants that are agriculturally useful have been moved around the world (wheat, bananas, corn, apples, potatoes, tomatoes, coffee) and are not thought to belong to country of origin, which may not even be known.

The Convention on Biological Diversity, though it insists on "sovereign rights to exploit natural resources," avoids the language of ownership. It speaks instead of "access to genetic resources." That can be interpreted as ownership, but need not be. Patent holders do own what they give access to. Nation states might similarly own the species to which they give access. But by contrast, landowners may control access to their property, even though they do not own the wildlife on it. Sovereign nations may control access to their territories, even though they do not own the wild species on their landscapes.

In 1991, Merck Pharmaceuticals signed an agreement with the National Biodiversity Institute of Costa Rica, a government agency. The Institute has been attempting to identify all wild plant species in the country, do a preliminary screening, and make agreements with pharmaceutical companies for further use of promising plants. Merck provided $1 million over several years and got, in return, the exclusive right to screen the collection for useful plant chemicals. The logic here is not that the Costa Ricans own the plants, but that they have the right to give or withhold "permission to collect" on their soil, and that they can be paid for this permission. In the Merck case, this money went to fund the collection. In other cases, it could go to fund on-the-ground conservation.

An agreement whereby profits of the industry using wild resources go to assure conservation of what remains makes perfectly good sense, oblivious to national boundaries, because these are global conservation problems and opportunities. Ownership issues and rights to exploit ought to be reconceived as a common good that we are all obligated to protect. North and South alike, as well as governments and industry, do have obligations to save the common heritage of species, if they are to share it. These species are part of the richness of biodiversity and belong to us all.

On further thought, many claim that species are good in their own right, whether or not they are good for anything. The *United Nations World Charter for Nature* states, "Every form of life is unique, warranting respect regardless of its worth to man" (United Nations General Assembly, 1982). Many will say, yes, but that document was largely aspirational, a noble ideal, and nobody expects such documents to have binding force. Perhaps. But the Convention on Biological Diversity, which at least has the status of "soft law," affirms "the intrinsic value of biological diversity" (1992, Preamble). An appraisal finding values in species as goods of their kind faces challenges, both biological and philosophical, which, from another perspective, offer opportunities for enlarging traditional frameworks of value.

A consideration of species offers a biologically based counterexample to the focus on individuals, which is characteristic in Western ethics. In an evolutionary ecosystem, it is not mere individuality that counts. The individual represents, or *re-presents* anew, a species in each subsequent generation. It is a token of a type, and the type is more important than the token. Though species are not moral agents, a biological identity—a kind of value—is here defended. The species line is the vital living system, the whole, of which individual organisms are the essential parts. The species defends a particular form of life, pursuing a pathway through the world, resisting death (extinction), by regeneration maintaining a normative identity over time. The value resides in the dynamic form; the individual inherits this, exemplifies it, and passes it on. If so, what prevents value existing at that level? Biological identity need not attach solely to the individual centered or modular organism, an animal or a plant. Having a biological identity reasserted genetically over generations is as true of the species as of the individual—persisting as a discrete, vital pattern over time. The life that the individual has is something passing through the individual as much as something it intrinsically possesses, and a comprehensive respect for life finds it appropriate to attach duty dynamically to the specific forms of life.

The species is a bigger event than the individual, although species are always exemplified in individuals. Biological conservation goes on at this level too; and, really, this level is more appropriate for moral concern, a more comprehensive survival unit than the individual organism. For example, if the predators are removed, and the carrying capacity of a landscape is exceeded, wildlife managers may have to benefit a species by culling its member individuals.

As with plants, classical ethicists will find species obscure objects of direct moral concern. Species, though they can be endangered, cannot "care"—so returns the objection we heard before. They just come and go. Even if species are biologically real, they are not valuable in a philosophically relevant sense, because they have no interests. Nicholas Rescher says, "Moral obligation is thus always interest-oriented. But only individuals can be said to have interests; one only has moral obligations to particular individuals or particular groups thereof. Accordingly, the duty to save a species is not a matter of moral duty toward it, because moral duties are only oriented to individuals. A species as such is the wrong sort of target for a moral obligation" (1980, p. 83). "The preservation of species," by the usual utilitarian account, reported by Stuart Hampshire, is "to be aimed at and commended only in so far as human beings are, or will be emotionally and sentimentally interested" (1972, pp. 3–4).

Joel Feinberg says, "We do have duties to protect threatened species, not duties to the species themselves as such, but rather duties to future human beings, duties derived from our housekeeping role as temporary inhabitants of this planet" (1974, p. 56). The relation is three-sided. Person A has a duty *to* person B which *concerns* species C, but is not *to* C. But concern for species may transcend the coordinates of classical ethical systems.

True, a species has no self defending its life. There is no analog to the nervous hookups or metabolisms that characterize individual organisms, and no sentient interests. But perhaps this singular somatic identity, the good of its own, which is respected in individual organisms, especially those with felt experiences, is not the only process that is valuable. Biology is multileveled, with processes at molecular, cellular, metabolic, organismic, species, ecosystems, and even global levels.

Rescue the sow grizzly! In the spring of 1984 a sow grizzly and her three cubs walked across the ice of Yellowstone Lake to Frank Island, two miles from shore. They stayed several days to feast on two elk carcasses, during which the ice bridge melted. Soon afterward, they were starving on an island too small to support them. The stranded bears were left to starve—if nature took its course. The mother could swim to the mainland, but she was not going to without her cubs. This time park authorities rescued the mother and her cubs (Ozment, 1984). The relevant difference was a consideration for an endangered species in an ecosystem, much interrupted by humans, who have too long persecuted the grizzlies. A breeding mother and three cubs was a significant portion of the breeding population. The bears were not saved lest they suffer, but lest the species be imperiled.

It might seem now that, inconsistently, we refuse to let nature take its course. The Yellowstone ethicists let the bison drown, callous to its suffering; they let the blinded bighorns die. But the Yellowstone ethicists were not rescuing individual bears so much as saving the species. They thought that humans had already and elsewhere imperiled the grizzly, and that they ought to save this form of life. Duties to wildlife are not simply at the level of individuals; they are also to species, and to these species in their ecosystems. Sometimes that means, as with the sow grizzly and her cubs, that we rescue individual animals in trouble, where they are the last tokens of a type.

Extinction shuts down the generative processes, a kind of superkilling. Extinction kills forms (species) beyond individuals, kills collectively, not just distributively. To kill a particular animal is to stop a life of a few years or decades, while other lives of such kind continue unabated; to superkill a particular species is to shut down a story of many millennia, and leave no future possibilities.

3. Enforcing Saving Species: The Endangered Species Act

How much concern for saving species should we write into law? Care for environmental quality will need democratic consensus, but it is also something that will require considerable enforcement. Not all duties are matters of law, but many are. If you doubt that, try stealing. Or killing. Or shooting a bald eagle. There is considerable legislation about saving biodiversity (as there was about animal welfare, chapter 3). As noted in Chapter 1, the U. S. Congress passed the Endangered Species Act (U. S. Congress, 1973). Congress also passed the Marine Mammal Protection Act of 1972. We also noted the Convention on International Trade in Endangered Species of Wild Fauna and Flora (CITES, 1973). If you are caught trying to bring a snow leopard skin into the United States, you will find yourself in prison with fines of tens of thousands of dollars.

Politically, "command and control" solutions are out of vogue; what we need instead, many cry, are "incentives." Regulations protect by restricting access, forbidding the taking of species. Better to make it worthwhile for landowners to comply (conservation easements, with reduced taxes). Even incentives, such as pollution permits, operate against a background of required compliance. They sweeten the obedience to environmental law, and introduce some voluntary choices, but the insistent command is still there. We dangle carrots up front, but at the rear we hold a stick. Law-like forms of ethics are also somewhat out of vogue; what we need instead, the ecofeminists will say, is "caring." The virtue ethicists emphasize their "virtues," observing that the virtuous behave whether or not they are commanded to do so. Caring, virtuous persons need no rules. That may be true in later stages of personal moral development; but in public life, caring in concert needs regulation, as well as incentives. The virtuous ahead, up front, may need no laws; but those at the rear, and most of us along the way, need enforcement, reinforcement—which helps us move along. Rules channel caring and discipline virtuous intentions.

The affected parties must cooperate, negotiate, and work together; there is often a tangle of complex and not always consistent regulations, dating from across decades. It takes some persistence to find workable solutions. But do not forget that it also takes an unyielding Endangered Species Act that meaningfully compels the discussion. For example, water management in the Platte River Basin, involves four listed species: whooping crane, interior least tern, the piping plover, and the pallid sturgeon, concern for which has to be blended with water law and rights that have come into place over a century of development of the U.S. Rocky Mountain West.

The environment, a public good, cannot be a private matter only; how we act must be collective, institutional, coordinated, corporate. In a community, there are things we cannot do unless we do them together. The communal good is mutual and requires broad social agreement on environmental policy. But it also requires enforcement. Few social issues have been settled the right way without enforcement—not slavery, not child labor, not women's suffrage, not workplace safety, not minimum wage, not civil rights.

Even with environmental legislation, some will be tempted to exceed the limits set by policy. This is the problem of "cheaters," persons who will in self-interest take the advantage of co-operating others. Nor is this always consciously intended; individuals may act as they have been accustomed to over many decades (taking water out of the river to water pasture), without waking up to how these customary individual goods are aggregating to bring communal evils to which we are unaccustomed (driving the pallid sturgeon into extinction). Environmental law will be needed to curb prevailing practices. The social contract must be policed. Civic law protects natural value. This is going to require nudging people along, where they do not wish to go—not yet at least, though they may, in retrospect, be quite glad when they get there. Wolves were returned to Yellowstone, with sheep ranchers muttering, "Shoot, shovel, and shut up." But these ranchers (or at least their children) are increasingly proud of the biodiversity on their landscape.

Even if 99% of citizens are glad to behave in a certain way, provided that all others do, 1% of the citizens might still freeload, and this will trigger bad faith. One rotten apple spoils a barrel. The corruption is contagious. Unless a society polices out the polluters, the rot will spread. Garrett Hardin called this, somewhat provocatively, "mutual coercion, mutually agreed upon" (Hardin, 1968,

p. 1247). Vested interests, often with much inertia, have to be divested. Habits have to be de-habituated. Self-interest is easy enough to rationalize under the old rationale. This is the way we have been doing it for decades; can what was right yesterday be wrong tomorrow? "My water rights go back to 1890? What do you mean? I can't irrigate like I used to? That's not fair!" But we cannot leave old decisions in place when new information comes on line (the effect on whooping cranes), without in effect making new and different decisions. Nudging people out of their old habits and privileges, shifting patterns of right and wrong at shifting levels of scale and scope is going to require enforcement. Public policy can and ought to take a longer view than can private market interests. Minority rights and the right to dissent have also to be considered—and enforced. But no one has the right to harm others, without justified cause. Where some destroy public goods entwined with biotic community, such as endangered species, enforcement can be justified. Law is needed to preserve those domains of value that cannot safely be left to the open marketplace.

The U.S. Congress, as we noted in Chapter 1, has had an uneasy relationship to the Endangered Species Act, authorizing a "God Committee" that can permit extinction. Some interpreters think that in the Act species have, in effect, moral standing and *de facto* legal rights (Varner, 1987; Callicott and Grove-Fanning, 2009). Somewhat anomalously, the Act has technically expired, but in fact remains in a sort of perpetual limbo, still in force, though nobody knows how to handle it politically—the values at stake are deep and run across a spectrum from respect for creation to economic development, to national character and aspirations, to the politics of the next election.

A recent issue, sparked by the listing of the polar bear, has been whether The Endangered Species Act can extend to global warming. The Environmental Protection Agency was beginning to argue that global warming, since it is putting the bear in jeopardy, could be addressed under the Endangered Species Act. But both the Bush and the Obama administrations ruled that addressing global warming was far too complex a matter to come under the appropriate range of the Act, which was never intended to be used for such purposes. Enforcement of the act is assigned to the U.S. Fish and Wildlife Service, which is not the appropriate agency to try to deal with global warming, although the fish and wildlife experts might try to figure out ways to help the climate-threatened bear adapt to the warming. In the meantime, both administrations have failed to address global warming through other means or agencies.

A further issue revolves around two legal meanings of "take," found in "taking property" and "taking species." The Fifth Amendment to the U.S. Constitution prohibits the government from "taking" private property unless it is for public use and the owner is receives just compensation. The word "take" also occurs, in a newer legal context, in the Endangered Species Act and its amendments. There are frequent prohibitions against "taking" animals and, without quite using the word, "taking" plants that belong to listed species, because by further endangering then this is tantamount to taking the species. The double question about "taking" that arises is: Do endangered species prohibitions against "taking" animals and plants on private land also involve a "taking" of property that requires just compensation?

In the 1973 Act, "the term 'take' means to harass, harm, pursue, hunt, shoot, wound, kill, trap, capture, or collect, or to attempt to engage in any such conduct" (sec. 3 (14)). This has animals in focus. The 1988 amendments regarding the protection of plants made it unlawful to "remove and reduce to possession" or to "maliciously damage or destroy" listed plants on lands under federal jurisdiction, and "to remove, cut, dig up, or damage and destroy any such species on any other area in knowing violation of any law or regulation of any State" (102 Stat. 2306, sec. 1006).

The federal government can, if it pleases and as it does in Section 7 of the Act, prohibit *its agencies* from "taking" animal or plant species wherever these occur, no matter whether these agencies operate on public or private lands. It perhaps can do this abroad as well as at home. But can the federal government prohibit a *private landowner* from taking plants on his or her own land, or prevent a citizen from taking, with a landowner's consent, plants on the private lands of others? Congress has deferred the question to state law, perhaps pragmatically, perhaps since property rights and regulations are traditionally thought to be more appropriate at state than federal levels.

State laws vary widely; some states do indeed prohibit anyone, landowner or not, from taking endangered plants on private property without state permit. Most states require of nonlandowners a permit to collect or destroy, but allow landowners to do what they please. At the same time, Congress has backed state laws that do prohibit such taking with a federal penalty, indicating that state governments can legitimately have such power, and that the federal government will support this power.

So, we are confronted with a double use of "take"—where the "taking" of life and species is set against the taking of property—and in struggling toward resolution, our moral and legal convictions about the institution of private property and its economic value are evolving in encounter with the biology and ecology of endangered species. A main line of argument is that, although landowners may own land, they do not own wildlife, as evidenced by hunting regulations. Nor do they own species, although they may own individual plants on their land. Wildlife and species are a common good, not subject to private ownership, and their "taking" can therefore be policed (Rolston, 1990).

4. Natural and Anthropogenic Extinction

It might seem that for humans to terminate species now and again is quite natural. Species go extinct all the time. Ninety-eight percent of the species that have inhabited Earth are extinct. But there are important theoretical and practical differences between natural and anthropogenic (human generated) extinctions. In natural extinction, a species dies when it has become unfit in its habitat, and other species appear in its place, a normal turnover. By contrast, artificial extinction shuts down speciation. That is not quite true, since some new microbes may evolve as a result of medical uses of antibiotics. Or when humans extinguish a species, a competitor may shift its evolutionary course. But compared to natural respeciation, re-speciation is essentially blocked on human-dominated landscapes. Natural extinction opens doors, anthropogenic extinction closes them. Humans generate and regenerate nothing; they dead-end these lines. Relevant differences make the two as morally distinct as death by natural causes is from murder.

No, the paleontological critic may reply. Although it is true that there is a steady background rate of species replacement throughout typical evolutionary history, there are in the past a few (perhaps five) rare but devastating catastrophic extinctions. The diversity of natural history was then decimated. The late Permian and late Cretaceous extinctions are the most startling. Each catastrophic extinction is succeeded by a recovery of previous diversity (Raup and Sepkoski, 1982).

Although natural events, these extinctions so deviate from the trends that many paleontologists look for causes external to evolutionary ecosystem. If caused by supernovae, collisions with asteroids, or other extraterrestrial upsets, such events are accidental to the evolutionary ecosystem. If the causes were more terrestrial—cyclic changes in climates or continental drift—the biological processes that characterize Earth are still to be admired for their powers of recovery. Uninterrupted by accident, or even interrupted, they steadily increase the numbers of species.

What does the setback of diversity do to complexity? David M. Raup, who has best documented these catastrophic extinctions, has also reflected philosophically over them. These periodic cutbacks prepare the way for more complex diversity later on. We first think that the catastrophic extinctions were quite a bad thing, an unlucky disaster. But in fact they were good luck. Indeed, were it not for them, we humans would not be here, nor perhaps would any of the other mammalian complexity. Life on Earth is so resilient that normal geological processes lack the power to cause widespread extinctions in major groups. But just such a resetting is needed—rarely but periodically. We should think twice before judging these catastrophic extinctions to be a bad thing.

Raup explains:

> Without species extinction, biodiversity would increase until some saturation level was reached, after which speciation would be forced to stop. At saturation, natural selection would continue to operate and improved adaptations would continue to develop. But many of the innovations in evolution, such as new body plans or modes of life, would probably not

appear. The result would be a slowing down of evolution and an approach to some sort of steady state condition. According to this view, the principal role of extinction in evolution is to eliminate species and thereby reduce biodiversity so that space—ecological and geographic—is available for innovation.

(1991, p. 187)

There is a big shakeup; this is, if you like, at random; it is, we must say, catastrophic, but the randomness is integrated into the creative system. The loss of diversity results in a gain in complexity. Catastrophic extinction, "has been the essential ingredient in the history of life that we see in the fossil record" (Raup, 1991, p. 189). The storied character of natural history is increased. Once "we thought that stable planetary environments would be best for evolution of advanced life," but now we think instead that "planets with enough environmental disturbance to cause extinction and thereby promote speciation" are required for such evolution (p. 188).

One might say, "Well, if catastrophic extinctions are so innovative, we need not worry about the anthropogenic ones." But that fails to understand the radical differences between natural and anthropogenic extinctions. Anthropogenic extinction has nothing to do with evolutionary speciation. Hundreds of thousands of species will perish because of culturally altered environments that are radically different from the spontaneous environments in which such species were naturally selected and in which they sometimes go extinct. In natural extinction, nature takes away life, when it has become unfit in habitat, or when the habitat alters, and supplies other life in its place. Not only do the species perish, but they perish along with their ecosystems, which are replaced with unnatural landscapes. There is little respeciation on toxic soils and none at all on Wal-Mart parking lots.

As we often find in environmental issues, circumstances get complex and lines can sometimes get blurred. Anthropogenic causes can accelerate natural causes. The Uncompahgre fritillary (*Boloria improba acrocnema*) is a butterfly that lives high in the Uncompahgre mountains in southwest Colorado. The fritillary was discovered in 1978 and described as a new species in 1984, and listed as an endangered species. It is going extinct. It can only live in the high alpine mountains, spends a first winter as an egg, becomes a larvae that lives several years eating on low willows, and hibernates in subsequent winters. Then it makes a cocoon and emerges as an adult which lives only a few days. Why is it going extinct? Most biologists think it is due to a gradual warming, preceding even global warming, but made worse by global warming.

The fritillary is caught as a relict in these high mountains, unable to migrate further north (to Wyoming) where there is more suitable habitat. Some biologists think the impending extinction is also due to sheep grazing, to hikers trampling it, and even indiscriminate collecting. Is this a species going naturally extinct? Ought we let nature take its course? Or ought conservation biologists transplant some of the fritillaries further north? Biologists have been divided about this (Britten, Brussard, Murphy, 1994).

Conservationists are at odds over the wisdom of moving species threatened by global climate change to new locations. They agree that we should do what we can to help embattled species by protecting habitat, shoring up ecosystems, assisting their survival. But what about "assisted colonization"—translocating them to new habitats further north, or likely to be wetter, or less threatened by warming? Some say that we must, at least as a last resort. Species move around naturally, and if, under the threat of global warming, they need help, why not assist them? Others say that however well intended, we are not smart enough to translocate species without upsetting ecosystems. Chances are we will do a lot more harm than good (Ricciardi and Simberloff, 2009). If it worked, would the translocated species be unnatural and of less value?

Chestnuts vanished from Eastern U.S. forests in the early decades of the last century, killed by the chestnut blight, accidentally introduced from Asia. American elms are greatly threatened by Dutch elm disease. Biologists have sought to breed chestnuts and elms resistant to these diseases, and there are efforts underway to restore both of these great American trees to their once-native forests. If successful, would these restored and genetically modified chestnuts and elms be unnatural and of less value?

Much effort has been made to save the California condor, near extinction. In the fossil record, the condor once had a much wider range (Alabama to California), and some biologists think it was going extinct naturally, and, over the last two centuries, its extinction has been delayed by the abundance of cattle carcasses, cattle brought in by European settlers. But these are atypical cases, and the main issue stands: humans threaten biodiversity extensively and globally.

Although it was once thought that much biodiversity was lost in the catastrophic extinctions, more recent studies suggest a different picture. Sean Nee and Robert M. May find, on the basis of a mathematical analysis of fossil extinctions: "A large amount of evolutionary history can survive an extinction episode ... A substantial proportion of the tree of life could survive even such a large extinction as occurred in the Late Permian." Some paleontologists have figured that up to 95 percent of marine (though not land) species perished in this extinction, though this is now thought to be an overestimate. But even if this had been so, "approximately 80 percent of the tree of life can survive even when approximately 95 percent of species are lost" (Nee and May, 1997, pp. 692–693).

This is because some species of nearly all of the main groups survive and are released to re-speciate. Think of it this way. Mass extinction cuts off more the twigs of the tree of life (the species), so to speak, than the main branches (the families, orders, classes), which persist with enough buds in species that do survive. "Much of the tree of life may survive even vigorous pruning" (Nee and May, 1997, p. 694; see also Myers, 1997).

But there is no evidence that life would similarly proliferate and elaborate as a result of the contemporary anthropogenic extinctions. Quite the contrary. We will deal more extensively with global warming in the final chapter. But here consider its effects on wild species. According to the *4th Assessment Report* of the Intergovernmental Panel on Climate Change (IPCC):

> There is medium confidence that approximately 20–30% of species assessed so far are likely to be at increased risk of extinction if increases in global average warming exceed 1.5–2.5°C (relative to 1980–1999). As global average temperature exceeds about 3.5°C, model projections suggest significant extinctions (40–70% of species assessed) around the globe.
>
> (2007, pp. 13–14)

IPPC assessments find that the eastern half of the Amazon rainforest, one of Earth's richest biodiversity locations, is vulnerable to widespread collapse and to being replaced by degraded savannas:

> Under future climate change, there is a risk of significant species extinctions in many areas of tropical Latin America (high confidence). Gradual replacement of tropical forest by savanna is expected in eastern Amazonia.... Seven out of the world's twenty-five most critical places with high endemic species concentrations are in Latin America, and these areas are undergoing habitat loss.
>
> (Parry et al., 2007, p. 54)

The U.S. Department of Interior has released a study by government and non-government conservation biologists: *State of the Birds: 2010 Report on Climate Change*. They found that nearly one-third of the nation's 800 bird species are endangered, threatened, or in significant decline, and that global warming is making much worse the stresses from loss of habitat (especially forests and wetlands), use of pesticides, hunting, migration barriers, and introduction of invasive species, which were already taking a heavy toll on native birds.

Coral reefs, which are marine biodiversity hotspots, are at risk, quite vulnerable to small increases in ocean temperatures. In Australia "significant loss of biodiversity is projected to occur by 2020 in some ecologically rich sites, including the Great Barrier Reef" (Parry et al., 2007, p. 50). Such loss may well approach the levels of what paleontologists have called catastrophic extinctions in the history of life on Earth, but, being globally anthropogenic, they are also radically different because they dramatically degrade the context of respeciation.

We can take as an icon for such tragedy the arctic fox. The fox is one of the best adapted animals on Earth to living in extreme cold. But it is smaller and cannot compete with the larger red fox, which can outcompete it for food, and also kill and eat it. Red foxes are extending their range northward as a result of global warming, and the arctic foxes are disappearing. Yes, species adapt to changing climates. But not to climate change so relatively sudden. This outpaces their ability to evolve.

5. Biodiversity: More than Species

Concern for endangered species has broadened to become concern for biodiversity. This recognizes values present at multiple biological levels: genes, organisms, species, ecosystems, regional biomes, landscapes, oceans (Wilson, 1992; Cafaro and Primack, 2001; Pereira et al., 2010). Earth's diversity includes geological and mineralogical diversity, diverse climates, myriads of different islands, mountains, bays, caves, and on and on. No two landscapes are alike; each canyon or lake has its unique features. And things are constantly changing: the seasons, the rivers, even the mountains. We value this geographical variety. But the biodiversity on Earth is particularly striking. Biodiversity spans levels of organization from genes to biomes. Environmental ethics is concerned with saving species, but also with saving habitats and ecosystems, and with having healthy and robust environments—cumulatively what we might call biological richness.

The National Forest Management Act requires the United States Forest Service to manage forests so as to "provide for diversity of plant and animal communities" (U.S. Congress, 1976, Sec. 6(g)(3)(B)). We have already noted The United Nations Convention on Biological Diversity (1992). The parties are "concerned that biological diversity is being significantly reduced by certain human activities" and are "conscious of the intrinsic value of biological diversity and of the ecological, genetic, social, economic, scientific, educational, cultural, recreational and aesthetic values of biological diversity" and "conscious also of the importance of biological diversity for evolution and for maintaining life sustaining systems of the biosphere" (United Nations, 1992, Preamble).

The Convention links conservation to using the resources of biodiversity sustainably and also to the fair and equitable sharing of benefits from these resources, especially in commercial use. Sustainable development and sustaining biodiversity are twin and entwined goals (Sachs et al., 2009). In October 2010 the Convention met in Nagoya, Japan, to evaluate progress and set future goals. It found that in some areas there is progress, but overall biodiversity is declining and goals are not being met (Global Biodiversity Outlook 3, 2010; Rands et al., 2010; Normile, 2010; Hoffman et al., 2010). The UN General Assembly, shortly before that, addressed in debate the biodiversity crisis for the first time, though without effective action (Walpole et al, 2009).

How much diversity is there? How much is at stake? We need to measure diversity—existing, threatened, or lost—in order to know what values are at issue, what conservation priorities to set. If we cannot measure diversity quantitatively, we can at least narrate diversity descriptively, and make some assessment of its quality. The extent of biodiversity is not an easy question to answer, either in the scientific or in the philosophical senses. The difficulty rises from its richness, from, so to speak, the diversity of diversity (Brooks, et al, 2006).

A first diversity index is the number of species (alpha diversity). There are between 5 and 30 million species on Earth (some say 100 million), not including bacteria and viruses. The wide gap indicates at once our certainty that the numbers are big and our uncertainty about how big (Peet, 1974; Crist, 2002). Systematists have described about 1.7 million species, and describe about 15,000 new ones each year. Generally, numbers of species become higher as one travels from poles to equator, though Earth is a more diverse planet because there are species in arctic, boreal, temperate, and tropical ecosystems. Not long ago we thought there were about 3 million species on Earth, with about half these identified—4,100 species of mammals, 8,700 birds, 6,300 reptiles, 3,000 amphibians, 23,000 fishes, 800,000 insects, over 300,000 green plants and fungi, with many thousands of protozoans. Over recent decades such estimates have been pushed steadily upward, owing to new discoveries and better taxonomy, mostly in the invertebrates (May, 2010, 1988; Myers, 1979; Wilson, 1992). In 2005 in the Foja Mountains of New Guinea, biologists found over 40 new species, including several new birds and a new echidna (Beeler, 2007).

Another diversity index is the relative abundance of species, which may be called the degree of evenness. How frequent is a species in a particular area? In wild nature, relative abundance is under ecological control; ecosystems are tropic pyramids making it typical that plant species are more numerous than animal species, and some animal species more numerous than others. Ecosystems are so structured that most species are rare. Unfortunately, the infrequent and rare species are more subject to human-introduced stress than are the common or abundant ones. The rare tend to be extinction prone.

Diversity at another level asks how much ecosystems and their species vary within a region (beta diversity). How much community diversity is there? Due to elevation and resulting climatic changes, there may be deserts, grassland plains, montane forests, and arctic tundra all within thirty miles of each other in one region, where elsewhere there is three hundred miles of nothing but grassland plains. Costa Rica, a small nation no bigger than the state of West Virginia, has more different species than all of the continental United States. This is because of its habitat diversity: there are dramatic elevation changes, the landscape is well watered, and it lies at the crossroads of two continents. Panama has as many plant species as all of Europe.

There are nearly two dozen indices of diversity of various kinds (Magurran, 1988; Pielou, 1975. Brooks et al., 2006). We need some account of whether these species are in diverse genera, families, classes, orders, phyla—hierarchical diversity. Two species in different phyla (a beetle and a chimpanzee) offer more diversity than two within the same genus. We will need some regional or global scales. If some species in a system are endemics, that will not affect local diversity indices, but such a local community, with its endemics, adds to the regional diversity (sometimes called gamma diversity). Diversity is low on remote islands, but endemism is high.

Isolation allows the few species on islands to survive and often to fill new niches under altered patterns of competition. Just this isolated survival, often producing high endemism, despite the low local diversity, adds to the global diversity. This is particularly true in Hawaii and other Pacific islands. A lighthouse keeper's cat, named Tibbles, in one year (1894) virtually exterminated the entire population of tiny, flightless Stephen's Island wrens, a relict endemic species on that oceanic island, which anciently also lived in New Zealand before the Maori exterminated it there. (A few individuals that seemed even to have survived Tibbles, died later.)

How diverse are the interconnections between species? There may be simple or quite complicated food chains, and the latter may give redundance and resiliency, or they may amplify disturbances. If the species are not equally well distributed in location, that will introduce still a further dimension to diversity. Mapping mosaics works reasonably well for areas covered with plants, but not with animals that move around—unless the animals tend to gather around certain plants. After mapping, we can measure areas, and generate some new diversity statistics. Next we will wonder what determines the mosaics, and these factors can be more or less simple or complicated (soil types, rock outcrops, fire history, species competition, competitive exclusion). For predators and prey, the variety of hiding places, nooks and crannies, is partly a matter of the geomorphology (rock ledges), partly a matter of the vegetation (hollow trees). Is the system climatically diverse (hot summers, cold winters; wet winters, dry summers) or geomorphologically diverse (mountains, plains, lakes, shorelines, desert, tundra), which may or may not be reflected in the diversity of fauna and flora (perhaps affecting the diversity of niches)?

Diversity will be largely an objective fact about ecosystems, but there will be some subjective decision calls. We may run into disagreements about lumping and splitting. We will have to make some decisions where to draw the boundary lines, or zones, or how long to watch the system. If we watch ten decades, there can be much more diversity coming and going in one of two communities, although the two communities are equally diverse if we only watch ten minutes. If the ecosystem is sizeable, we cannot census everything in it, and so we will have to sample, and worry how we sample. If the organisms are arranged in patches (and not randomly), a random sample of space will not give a reliable estimate. So, we begin to appreciate both that diversity is complex and that measuring and appreciating it, and deciding what we can and ought to save, are not simple things.

Also we might find some diversity pointless, or superfluous. Discount drug stores already offer so many kinds of shampoos that one more, no better or worse, just different, is hardly a benefit. Nor is another flavor of ice cream in a store than already sells fifty-seven flavors. One might think that nature is enormously more fecund with beetles than the American industry with shampoos, not knowing when to say "enough." But there is a relevant difference; each beetle species is an autonomous biological achievement.

We will not value finding many more parasitic disease organisms than we thought—not at least in terms of human medicine. We already lament that there are too many strains of flu virus. We have deliberately (almost) extinguished the smallpox virus (which, strictly speaking, is perhaps not alive) (Altman, 1996; Kaiser, 2011). We hope to do the same with the polio virus. We may not value two beetle species if the only difference is the location of a few spots and bristles. It is doubtful whether we should value deformed freaks of nature (such as two-headed calves), even though these are curiosities that people pay to see in sideshows, or that scientists study to understand what went wrong. We have already said that introduced exotics add diversity we do not want—dandelions in the wilderness. This subtracts from diversity on national scales, since there are dandelions practically everywhere and few areas pristine and without them. We value diversity that contributes to richness in nature at large scales.

Diversity in nature is not simply pluralism. Nature's diversity might just be chaotic. Sometimes nature can seem this way, just a blooming buzzing confusion. But ecologists know better. Diversity is complemented by integration and unity, and ecosystems are wholes, communities, that incorporate many organisms into networked pyramids. Diversity in ecosystems is not a tight, organismic unity; the integration is more open, within a complementing community. Each species has its own integrity in its niche, and each is webbed into the larger community.

Perhaps the main point to make is that species must be saved in ecosystems (the subject of Chapter 6). A species is what it is where it is. Particular species may not be essential in the sense that the ecosystem can survive the loss of individual species. But habitats are essential to species, and an endangered species often means an endangered habitat. The species and the community are complementary goods in synthesis, parallel to, but a level above, the way the species and individual organisms have distinguishable but entwined goods. It is not preservation of species that protects the relevant values, but the preservation of species in the system. It is not merely *what* they are, but *where* they are that one must value correctly.

This limits the otherwise important role that zoos and botanical gardens can play in the conservation of species. They can provide research, a refuge for species, breeding programs, aid public education, and so forth, but they cannot simulate the ongoing dynamism of gene flow over time under the selection pressures in a wild biome. They only lock up a collection of individuals; they amputate the species from its habitat. The species can only be preserved *in situ*; the species ought to be preserved *in situ*. That moves from scientific facts to ethical duties, but what ought to be has to be based on what can be (Rolston, 2004).

Neither individual nor species stands alone; both are embedded in an ecosystem. Plants, which are autotrophs, have a certain independence that animals and other heterotrophs do not have. Plants need only water, sunshine, soil, nutrients, local conditions of growth; animals, often mobile and higher up the trophic pyramid, may range more widely but in this alternate form of independence depend on the primary production of plants. Every natural form of life came to be what it is where it is, shaped as an adaptive fit, even when species acquire a fitness that enables them to track into differing environments. We noticed in Chapter 4 that invasive exotic species, introduced by humans, are often not good fits in their alien ecosystems. In wild nature, the whole population or species survives when selected by natural forces in the environment for a niche that it can occupy.

In addition to placing species in ecosystems in natural history, in environmental policy, the legislation to protect endangered species has often been used to protect as well the ecosystems of which they are part (such as the old growth forests of the Pacific Northwest, containing the spotted owl). An ecosystems approach is increasingly regarded as more efficient than a single-species approach. But there is controversy over the wisdom of using a charismatic species (the spotted owls, or wolves) as a tool for forest management, which ought to be done with a wide spectrum of values considered. This is a smaller scale issue somewhat analogous to trying to use the polar bear to stop global warming.

Philosophers sometimes do "thought experiments" to test their arguments and intuitions. One related to the value of biodiversity is called "the last man argument" (Routley and Routley, 1980). Imagine that humans have, through nuclear weapons with radiation that destroys their neurons, destroyed themselves, except for a single last man. He has only a day of life left, and sits in a control room where he can push some more buttons, releasing further nuclear weapons, that might blitz all life on the planet. Might he amuse himself in his dying hours by destroying all life on Earth? Most any person would say that he ought not to do this. This seems to reveal that life apart from humans has value, since the last man ought to respect life continuing after all humans are gone. (This has to be a last man argument because, for ecofeminists, to think of a last woman doing such a thing is absurd; only men can imagine acting with such arrogance.)

An objector can reply that the last man ought to respect sentient life, since animals that continue after human are gone can still enjoy their pleasures. One can modify the argument to suppose that the neuron-degenerating radiation will soon destroy all sentient life. Still, it seems that the last man ought not to destroy for his parting amusement the whole of non-neural life (the protozoans, for example) and the floral world. There is enormous evolutionary creativity here too; in fact, most living organisms are non-neural. They too defend and value their lives.

Philosophers are good at wiggling out of their thought experiments, and here the critics may say that what is wrong with the last person's act ought to focus on his behavior, not on the resulting barren planet millennia and eons later. He is already experiencing these blitzed states in his imagination, and that is a loss to him—even stipulating no later humans or neural animals (Elliot, 1985). But this is armchair philosophy and not very plausible—not at least for anyone who philosophizes close to the biological world. Biologists will recall that the world of evolutionary natural history was ongoing on Earth for 3.5 billion years, and that it seems arrogant of humans to suppose that nothing of value was present before *Homo sapiens* arrived. Analogously, it seems even more arrogant for this last man to suppose that nothing of value will remain after he is gone, or that the value of whatever remains is somehow forever indexed to him and his petty thoughts. True enough, the last person's character would be lamentable; but, should he destroy in a whim what took billions of years to evolve, much more of value is at stake.

6. Biodiversity vs. Humans: Win–Win? Win–Lose? Lose–Lose?

Conservationists may advocate a "win–win ecology" so that "the Earth's species can survive in the midst of human enterprise" (Rosenzweig, 2003). Here an economist who wishes to benefit the poor may say: Wildlife can be profitable to the poor. Keep some pocket reserves. Use them for eco-tourism, and the poor can benefit from the wildlife reserves on their lands. The values of species must complement human values. When persons are in harmony with nature, everyone wins, equally people, rhinos, and tigers.

Here there are likely to be skeptics on both sides. Those desiring more preservation will say that the happy assumption of win–win that there can be conservation without a price are contradicted nine times out of ten with the wildlife losing. For every one charismatic species that tourists will pay to see, there are dozens of insects, invertebrates, plants about which tourists will never care. In counterpoint, those conservationists who call themselves pragmatists will also be skeptical that anything more can be achieved. If all you can save is what tourists pay to see, do at least that. The best you can do is enlighten self-interest. That is all that is politically, economically, sociologically, biologically, feasible, or even imaginable.

But then again, we often defend our interests against other people only to learn that many of our interests are not a zero sum game, not in the human-human parliament of interests. We can learn that again in the human-nature parliament of interests. Bryan Norton claims: "In the long run, what is good for our species will also be good for other species, taken as species" (Norton et al., 1995, p. 115). David Schmitz puts this appealingly: "If we do not tend to what is good for nature, we will not be tending to what is good for people either.... We need to be human-centered to be properly nature-centered, for if we do not tend to what is good for people, we will not be tending to what is good for nature either" (2008, pp. 235–236).

Certainly this is sometimes true, part of the truth, but it may be one of those half-truths that is dangerous if taken for the whole. As we earlier noticed, biodiversity has medical, industrial, agricultural, scientific, and recreational uses. Humans and other species need air, water, soil, stable ecosystems, a healthy environment. The benefits of biodiversity in the United States are estimated to be $300 billion annually (Pimentel et al., 1997). But here we need to feature the grim consequences for humanity if humans lose biodiversity—the lose–lose side. According to a study on *The Economics of Ecosystems and Biodiversity,* half of the welfare of the world's 1.1 billion poorest people flows directly from nature, through benefits including wild harvest, crop pollination, disaster mitigation, provision of clean water, and maintenance of traditional cultures. The total annual global cost of biodiversity loss, so far as it can be estimated, is between 1.35 and 3.1 trillion dollars (depending on the discount rate) (Sukhdev, 2008).

But what if you do try to take this economic benefit to the poor (as well as to the rich) and make it the whole truth? What if we set as policy saving all and only those species that are of economic value? In Africa, says David Schmidtz, "threatened species will have to contribute to the local economy if they are to have any hope of survival" (2008, p. 231). He follows Brian Child, "wildlife will survive in Africa only where it can compete financially for space" (1993, p. 60). Likewise and more bluntly: Norman Myers says, "In emergent Africa, you either use wildlife or lose it. If it pays its own way, some of it will survive" (1981, p. 36).

Such accounts start with appeal. They advocate realistic compromise. They also can become blatantly pragmatic. They result in saving endangered species only if they are worth more alive than dead. Many would argue that even if, lamentably, such evaluations of species are inescapable in Africa and other developing nations, they ought not to be taken as morally commendable in developed nations. The Africans, who are very poor, may say "Save them only if they are worth more alive than dead," about their elephants. But what if Americans or Europeans said the same thing about their wildlife. And what if they said that about the Africans, struggling to survive. "We will help you develop, but only if you benefit us with your development. We will save you, because you are worth more to us alive than dead."

Only the charismatic megafauna bring in tourist dollars; most endangered species cannot pay their own way, and will be lost. True, the poor (and the rich) need ecosystem services, but rare species provide little or nothing in such services. Surely it is morally superior to respect more inclusively the values present and at jeopardy in endangered fauna and flora, large and small. Perhaps it is not moral at all to respect species only so far as they have cash value or provide us some service, any more than it is to respect humans only in this way.

But these matters get complex. The Convention on International Trade in Endangered Species (CITES, 1973) banned the sale of ivory to discourage poachers, and it has worked. Poorer nations would like to sell some legal ivory, taken from elephants that died naturally or were culled. They claim they can use the money for conservation of elephants; also this gives local peoples some incentive to conserve elephants. In 1997 CITES allowed three countries, Namibia, Botswana, and Zimbabwe to sell 50 tons of ivory. Conservationists worry that having some legal ivory on the market will encourage poaching; it is difficult to tell legal from illegal ivory once it is in the markets. These countries plus South Africa sold 106 tons in 2002. Opponents say such sales cannot be continued without heavy policing, and that it encourages illegal trade. What ought we to do? (Stokstad, 2010a, 2010b; Wasser et al., 2010). The same three countries wish to sell more. CITES has upheld the ivory ban, forbidding further sales. The elephants won; the poor nations lost?

Even in developed countries there are tradeoffs. The win–win account, if sometimes true, can be naive about conflicting priorities. The Delhi Sands flower-loving fly was standing in the way of building a hospital in California, and blocking an industrial development with perhaps 20,000 jobs (Booth, 1997). A California state senator exclaimed, "I'm for people, not for flies." In such a context, one might try to find some usefulness for the flies as rivet, resource, or Rosetta stone. This is likely to fail. As promising an argument as any is to urge respect for a unique species, a clever form of life defending a good of its own. The fly, along with other interesting species, inhabits only a few hundred acres of ancient inland dunes, reduced from an original habitat of forty square miles. It cannot move, but the hospital and other developments could be built elsewhere. Local developers proposed in 2007 a compromise; they would build on half the habitat and set aside half for the flies. This still might doom the fly; 97% of the original habitat is already gone. No final action has been taken.

The California gnatcatcher (*Polioptila californica*), a threatened species, inhabits some undeveloped but expensive real estate in southern California. Developers reluctantly agreed to a checkerboard pattern of development, reserving lands for the small bird and other species of concern. They found, somewhat to their surprise, that the parcels they did develop had considerably increased value, as homeowners greatly valued homes near the conservation areas punctuating the sprawl of subdivisions (Mann and Plummer, 1995).

Maybe the developers could win, to their surprise, with the gnatcatcher; but with the rare fly, maybe humans should be short-term losers. Sometimes we do have to make sacrifices, at least in terms of what we presently value, to preserve species. Also, the claim about being happier or better humans if we protect species is an empirical, statistical claim—true on average, true unless shown otherwise. There might be cases where the worth of a species, coupled with human benefits from respecting it, did not override other human benefits to be gained by sacrificing it. Then humans might be duty-bound to be losers in the sense that they sacrificed values, although they would still be winners for doing the right thing.

Peter Wenz advocates a win–win position that he calls environmental synergism. "Environmental synergists believe that synergy exists between respect for people and respect for nature. Overall and in the long run, simultaneous respect for people and nature improves outcomes for both.... Respect for nature promotes respect for people, so the best way to serve people as a group is to care about nature for itself" (2001, p. 169). So, we need a thoroughgoing caring for nature, but if we look to the deeper reason why, we still find our own enlightened self interest. Wenz concludes, with emphasis: "In sum, *people as a group get more from the environment by caring about nature for its own sake, which limits attempts to dominate nature, than by trying to manipulate it for maximal human advantage*" (2001, p. 172). This is a kind of backfire argument: you anthropocentrists should care for nature lest you get too pushy. Caring for nature is good for us; it cuts down our covetousness. If you want the most out of nature, less is more. That too sounds right—until we ask whether there is anything in nature on its "own sake" worth caring for, anything of value that justifies such care. If not, such care is just pretense, even if it keeps us healthy.

The issue whether those who do the right thing can lose is as old as Socrates, with his puzzling claim that: "No evil can come to a good man" (*Apology*, 41d). Doing the wrong thing ruins the soul, the worst result imaginable. Doing the right thing ennobles character. But can we translate this into environmental ethics? Environmental virtue ethicists think so. An inclusive moral virtue, well-rounded excellence of character, requires that we be properly sensitive to the flow of nature through us and its bearing on our habits of life. Otherwise, life lacks propriety; we do not know our place under the sun. Wallace Stegner epitomizes this memorably: "Something will have gone out of us as a people if we ever let the remaining wilderness be destroyed.... That wild country ... can be a means of reassuring ourselves of our sanity as creatures, a part of the geography of hope" (1961, pp. 97–102).

An enriched humanity results with values in persons (the anthropocentric ones) and values in nature (nonanthropocentric ones) compounded—but only if the loci of value are not confounded. It seems unexcellent—cheap and philistine—to say that better health or excellence of human character is really what we are after when we preserve endangered species. Excellence of human character does indeed result, but only when human virtue cherishes and celebrates the value found in nature.

Winning requires getting your goals right. Some of my ancestors were slave owners. They lost in the Civil War; they lost their slaves, they lost the war. But then again they didn't really lose. Without this loss, the South would not be anywhere close to the prosperous society that exists today, where whites and blacks have more genuine and more productive relationships, trade flourishes, people are autonomous, human rights are defended, and so on. The South may have lost the war, but it did not really lose, because the war defending slavery was wrong. When the right thing was done, things turned out win–win in the long term.

But I would not have said to the slave-owning whites: Free your slaves because you will get a benefit from it. That might have been true; that might have saved us a Civil War. Politics can combine multiple motives, but philosophy tries to distinguish and evaluate them. A South (or a North) from that day to this always and only driven by self-interest would never have understood either the evils of slavery or the right to freedom for all.

For men, granting equality to women has been a similar experience. Some of my friends did not get positions they wished, because women, who were well qualified, were given preferential hiring. These men lost those jobs; perhaps they took other work later, which they did not prefer. But they too won, in the larger sense, in that philosophy has been much enriched by the contributions of women philosophers. Still, I would not have thought, as a man, that I should treat women equally in order to increase my opportunities.

Apply this to environmental ethics. Consider the Pacific Northwest. There will be some losers, in the sense that some loggers will have to change jobs to save the spotted owl. They will, meanwhile, come to reside in a community that is stable in its relationship to the forests in which it is embedded, and that makes them winners. They once lived in a community with a worldview that saw the great forests of the Northwest as a resource to be taken possession of, exploited. But that is not an appropriate world view; it sees nature as commodity for human gratification, and nothing else. The idea of winning is to consume, the more the better. When the goalposts are moved, these "losers" at the exploitation game will come to live in a community with a new worldview, that of a sustainable relationship with the forested landscape, and that is a new idea of "winning." What they really lose is what it is a good thing to lose: an exploitative attitude toward forests. What they gain is a good thing to gain: a land ethic. So, should we say to them: Get a land ethic; it's good for you—somewhat like we might have said to Southern slave owners: Free your slaves; it's good for you. Or to men: Treat women more equitably; you'll be a more virtuous man.

If someone protests that this is cheating, re-defining winning by moving the goalposts, one reply is that the analogy is bad. If such a person is wrong, the goalposts, since they are misperceived, will have to be moved. That is not cheating to win, that is facing up to the truth: what was before thought to be winning is losing. But we do want to make sure we know where those goalposts are and what winning means for all concerned. This requires reconstituting an ethic where the anthropocentrists, "us humans," like "us whites" and "us men," get the focus off ourselves and focus on the inclusive conservation of values outside us, no less than inside us and our group.

Can and should humans ever lose? The world is a complicated place. There is no simple answer; the answer is first yes and later no; sometimes yes, sometimes no; in some ways and places yes, in others no; superficially yes and at depth no; yes for self-aggrandizing humans, no for communitarian humans, *if* their sense of moral community becomes inclusive of life on Earth. We have a great deal to gain by doing the right thing; and, even when it seems that we lose by doing the right thing, we typically do not: not if we get our goalposts in the right place, not if we can refocus our goals off the narrow self and enlarge them into the community we inhabit. There is always a deeper, philosophical sense in which it seems impossible to lose; that is all the more incentive to do the right thing (Rolston, 1994).

These fauna and flora have a good of their own, they are located in a good place, they are desired for their own sake; and appreciating them contributes to human flourishing. That is a win–win situation. Oppositely, losing them is losing the quality of life that comes based on them, as well as their being lost in their own right; that is a lose–lose situation. We win when we assume responsibility for heritages that are greater than we are. Some things have to be won together. Humans can and ought to inherit the Earth; we become rich with this inheritance, as and only as we oversee a richness of planetary biodiversity that embraces and transcends us. We are not choosing this inheritance for our happiness, but our happiness is bound up with it. Having moved the goalposts to where they now are, we are in significant part constituted by our earthen ecology. There are essential cultural ingredients to happiness, but repudiating the natural world in which we reside, repudiating our ecology, is itself unsatisfying. Not choosing these ecological goods in order to gain authentic happiness, therefore, is a logical, empirical, psychological impossibility.

Persisting through vicissitudes for three and a half billion years, speciation is about as long-continuing as anything on Earth can be, generating the fundamental life-values on the planet. What humans are doing, or allowing to happen through carelessness, is shutting down the life stream, the most destructive event possible. On the scale of evolutionary time, humans appear late and suddenly. Even more lately and suddenly, they increase the extinction rate dramatically. What is offensive in such conduct is not merely senseless loss of resources, but the maelstrom of killing and insensitivity to forms of life. What is required is not just prudence, but principled responsibility to the biospheric Earth. Only the human species contains moral agents, but conscience ought not be used to exempt every other form of life from consideration, with the resulting paradox that the sole moral species acts only in its collective self-interest toward all the rest.

Few past philosophers have even raised the question of duties to species, much less answered it. Now such duty is becoming clearer. If it makes any sense to claim that one ought not to kill individuals without justification, it makes more sense to claim that one ought not to extinguish species lines, without extraordinary justification. A shutdown of the life stream on Earth is the most destructive event possible. In threatening Earth's biodiversity, the wrong that humans are doing is stopping the historical vitality of life.

References

Altman, Lawrence K. 1996. "Stocks of Smallpox Virus Edge Nearer to Extinction," *New York Times*, January 25, p. A1, A9.

Beeler, Bruce M. 2007. "The Foja Mountains of Indonesia: Exploring the Lost World." Online at: http://www.actionbioscience.org/biodiversity/beehler.html

Booth, William. 1997. "Developers Wish Rare Fly Would Buzz Off," *Washington Post*, April 4, p. A01.

Britten, H. B., P. F. Brussard, and D. D. Murphy. 1994. "The Pending Extinction of the Uncompahgre Fritillary Butterfly," *Conservation Biology* 8:86–94.

Brooks, T. M., R. A. Mittermeier, G. A. B. da Fonseca, et al. 2006. "Global Conservation Priorities," *Science* 313:58–61.

Cafaro, Philip J., and Richard B. Primack. 2001. "Ethical Issues in Biodiversity Protection." Volume 2, pages 593–607 in Simon Asher Levin, ed., *Encyclopedia of Biodiversity*. San Diego, CA: Academic Press.

Callicott, J. Baird, and William Grove-Fanning. 2009. "Should Endangered Species Have Standing? Toward Legal Rights for Listed Species," *Social Philosophy and Policy* 26(no. 2):317–352.

Child, Brian. 1993. "The Elephant as a Natural Resource," *Wildlife Conservation* 96(no. 2):60–61.

Chivian, Eric, and Aaron Bernstein, eds. 2008. *Sustaining Life: How Human Health Depends on Biodiversity*. New York: Oxford University Press.

CITES, Convention on International Trade in Endangered Species of Wild Fauna and Flora. 1973. Prepared and adopted by the Plenipotentiary Conference to Conclude an International Convention on Trade in Certain Species of Wildlife, Washington, D.C., February 12–March 2, 1973, 27 U.S.T, 1088, T.I.A.S 8249.

Convention on Biological Diversity. 2010. *Global Diversity Outlook 3*. Online at: http://gbo3.cbd.int/

Crist, Eileen. 2002. "Quantifying the Biodiversity Crisis," *Wild Earth* 12(no. 1, Spring 2002):16–19.

Darwin, Charles. 1968. *The Origin of Species*. Baltimore: Penguin Books.

Ehrlich, Paul, and Anne Ehrlich. 1981. *Extinction*. New York: Random House.

Eldredge, Niles, and Joel Cracraft. 1980. *Phylogenetic Patterns and the Evolutionary Process*. New York: Columbia University Press.

Elliot, Robert. 1985. "Metaethics and Environmental Ethics," *Metaphilosophy* 16:103–117.

Feinberg, Joel, 1974. "The Rights of Animals and Unborn Generations." Pages 43–68 in W. T. Blackstone, ed., *Philosophy and Environmental Crisis*. Athens: University of Georgia Press.

Ghiselin, Michael. 1974. "A Radical Solution to the Species Problem," *Systematic Zoology* 23:536–544.

Hampshire, Stuart. 1972. *Morality and Pessimism*. New York: Cambridge University Press.

Hardin, Garrett. 1968. "The Tragedy of the Commons," *Science* 162:1243–1248.

Hoffman, Michael, Craig Hilton-Taylor, Ariadne Angulo, et al. 2010. "The Impact of Conservation on the Status of the World's Vertebrates," *Science* 330:1503–1509.

Hull, David, 1978. "A Matter of Individuality," *Philosophy of Science* 45:335–360.

Intergovernmental Panel on Climate Change (IPCC). 2007. *Summary for Policymakers of the Synthesis Report*. http://www.ipcc.ch/pdf/assessment-report/ar4/syr/ar4_syr_spm.pdf

International Union for the Conservation of Nature (IUCN). 2010. *Summary Statistics, Red List of Endangered Species.* Online at: http://www.iucnredlist.org/about/summary-statistics#How_many_threatened

Kaiser, Jocelyn. 2011. "Pressure Growing to Set a Date to Destroy Remaining Smallpox Stocks," *Science* 331:389.

Leopold, Aldo. 1970. "The Round River," in *A Sand County Almanac.* New York: Oxford University Press.

Magurran, Anne E. 1988. *Ecological Diversity and Its Measurement.* Princeton, NJ: Princeton University Press.

Mann, Charles C., and Mark L. Plummer. 1995. California vs. Gnatcatcher, *Audubon* 97(no. 1):38–48, 100–104.

Marton-Lefèvre, Julia. 2010. "Biodiversity is Our Life," *Science* 327:1179.

May, Robert M. 1988. "How Many Species Are There on Earth?" *Science* 241:1441–1449.

———. 2010. "Tropical Arthopod Species, More or Less?" *Science* 329:41–42.

Mayr, Ernst. 1969a. *Principles of Systematic Zoology.* New York: McGraw-Hill.

———. 1969b. "The Biological Meaning of Species," *Biological Journal of the Linnean Society* 1:311–320.

Millennium Ecosystem Assessment. 2005a. *Ecosystems and Human Well-being: Biodiversity Synthesis.* Washington, D.C.: World Resources Institute.

———. 2005b. *Living Beyond our Means: Natural Assets and Human Well-Being: Statement from the Board.* Washington, D.C.: World Resources Institute.

Myers, Norman. 1979. "Conserving Our Global Stock," *Environment* 21(no. 9):25–33.

———. 1981. "A Farewell to Africa," *International Wildlife* 11(no. 4):36–47.

———. 1997. "Mass Extinction and Evolution," *Science* 278:597–598.

Nee, Sean, and Robert M. May. 1997. "Extinction and the Loss of Evolutionary History," *Science* 278:692–694.

Normile, Dennis. 2010. "U.N. Biodiversity Summit Yields Welcome and Unexpected Progress," *Science* 330:742–743.

Norton, Bryan G. 1999. "Convergence Corroborated: A Comment on Arne Naess on Wolf Policies." Pages 394–401 in Nina Witoszek and Andrew Brennan, eds., *Philosophical Dialogues: Arne Naess and the Progress of Ecophilosophy.* Lanham, MD: Rowman and Littlefield.

Norton, Bryan G., Michael Hutchins, Elizabeth F. Stevens, and Terry L. Maple. 1995. *Ethics on the Ark: Zoos, Animal Welfare, and Wildlife Conservation.* Washington, D.C.: Smithsonian Institution Press.

Ozment, Pat. 1984. *Case Incident Record # 843601,* Yellowstone National Park, filed August 18. Yellowstone National Park, Wyoming, Library.

Parry, M. L., O .F. Canziani, J P. Palutikof, P. J. van der Linden, C. E. Hanson, and IPPC, eds.. 2007. "Technical Summary" in *Contribution of Working Group II to the Fourth Assessment Report of the Intergovernmental Panel on Climate Change.* Cambridge, UK: Cambridge University Press. http://www.ipcc.ch/publications_and_data/publications_ipcc_fourth_assessment_report_wg2_report_impacts_adaptation_and_vulnerability.htm

Peet, Robert K. 1974. "The Measurement of Species Diversity," *Annual Review of Ecology and Systematics* 5:285–307.

Pereira, Henrique M., Paul W. Leadley, Vânia Proença, et al. 2010. "Scenarios for Global Biodiversity in the 21st Century," *Science* 330:1496–1501.

Pielou, E. C. 1975. *Ecological Diversity.* New York: Wiley.

Pimentel, David, Christa Wilson, Christine McCullum, et al. 1997. "Economic and Environmental Benefits of Biodiversity," *BioScience* 47:747–757.

Rands, Michael R. W., William M. Adams. Leon Bennum, et al. 2010. "Biodiversity Conservation: Challenges Beyond 2010," *Science* 329:1298–1303.

Raup, David M. 1991. *Extinction: Bad Genes or Bad Luck?* New York: W. W. Norton.

Raup, David M., and J. J. Sepkoski, Jr. 1982. "Mass Extinctions in the Marine Fossil Record," *Science* 215:1501–1503.

Rescher, Nicholas. 1980. "Why Save Endangered Species." Pages 79–92 in *Unpopular Essays on Technological Progress*. Pittsburgh, PA: University of Pittsburgh Press.

Ricciardi, Anthony, and Daniel Simberloff. 2009. "Assisted Colonization Is Not a Viable Conservation Strategy," *Trends in Ecology and Evolution* 24:248–253.

Risser, Paul G., Jane Lubchenco, and Samuel A. Levin. 1991. "Biological Research Priorities—A Sustainable Biosphere," *BioScience* 47:625–627.

Rolston, Holmes, III. 1985. "Duties to Endangered Species," *BioScience* 35:718–726.

———. 1988. "Life in Jeopardy: Duties to Endangered Species," Chapter 4 in *Environmental Ethics*. Philadelphia: Temple University Press.

———. 1990. "Property Rights and Endangered Species," *University of Colorado Law Review* 61:283–306.

———. 1994. "Winning and Losing in Environmental Ethics." Pages 217–234 in Frederick Ferré and Peter G. Hartel, eds., *Ethics and Environmental Policy: Theory Meets Practice*. Athens: University of Georgia Press.

———. 2004. "In Situ and Ex Situ Conservation: Philosophical and Ethical Concerns." Pages 21–39 in Edward O. Guerrant, Jr., Kathy Havens, and Mike Maunder, eds. *Ex Situ Plant Conservtion: Supporting Species in the Wild*. Washington, D.C.: Island Press.

Rosenzweig, Michael L. 2003. *Win-Win Ecology: How the Earth's Species Can Survive in the Midst of Human Enterprise*. New York: Oxford University Press.

Routley, Richard, and Val Routley. 1980. "Human Chauvinism and Environmental Ethics." Pages 96–189 in Don Mannison, Michael McRobbie, and Richard Routley, eds., *Environmental Philosophy*. Canberra: Research School of Social Sciences, Australian National University.

Sachs, Jeffrey D., Jonathan E. M. Baillie, William J. Sutherland, et al. 2009. "Biodiversity Conservation and the Millennium Development Goals," *Science* 325:1502–1503.

Schmidtz, David. 2008. *Person, Polis, Planet: Essays in Applied Philosophy*. New York: Oxford University Press.

Simpson, George G. 1961. *Principles of Animal Taxonomy*. New York: Columbia University Press.

Stegner, Wallace. 1961. "The Wilderness Idea." Pages 97–102 in David Brower, ed., *Wilderness: America's Living Heritage*. San Francisco: Sierra Club Books.

Stokstad, Erik. 2010a. "Big Battle Brewing Over Elephants At UpComing CITES Meeting," *Science* 237 (5 February):327.

———. 2010b. "Trade Trumps Science for Marine Species at International Meeting," *Science* 328(2 April):26–27.

Sukhdev, Pavan. 2008. *The Economics of Ecosystems and Biodiversity*. Intergovernmental Panel on Biodiversity and Ecosystem Services (IPBES) http://www.eurekalert.org/pub_releases/2008-05/haog-teo052908.php#

United Nations Conference on Environment and Development. 1992. *Convention on Biological Diversity*. Online at: http://www.cbd.int/convention/convention.shtml

United Nations General Assembly. 1982. *World Charter for Nature*. New York: UN General Assembly Resolution No. 37/7 of 28 October.

U.S. Congress, 1972. Marine Mammal Protection Act. Public Law 92-522. 86 Stat. 1027.

———.1973. Endangered Species Act of 1973. Public Law 93-205. 87 Stat. 884.

———.1976. National Forest Management Act of 1976. Public Law 94-588. 90 Stat. 2949.

U.S. Department of Interior, 2010. State of the Birds: 2010 Report on Global Climate Change. Online at: http://www.fws.gov/migratorybirds/NewReportsPublications/StateoftheBirds/The%20State%20of%20the%20Birds%202010%20key%20messages.pdf

Varner, Gary E., 1987. "Do Species Have Standing," *Environmental Ethics* 9:57–72.

Walpole, Matt, Rosemunde E. A. Almond, Charles Besançon, et al. 2009. "Tracking Progress Toward the 2010 Biodiversity Target and Beyond," *Science* 325:1503–1504.

Wasser, Samuel, Joyce Poole, Phyllis Lee, et al. 2010. "Elephants, Ivory, and Trade," *Science* 327(12 March):1331–1332.

Wenz, Peter S. 2001. *Environmental Ethics Today*. New York: Oxford University Press.

Wilcove, David S., and Lawrence L. Master. 2005. "How Many Endangered Species Are There in the United States?" *Frontiers in Ecology and the Environment* 3:414–420.

Wilford, John Noble. 2005. "Foal by Foal, the Wildest of Horses is Coming Back," *New York Times*, October 11, Sec. F, p. 1.

Wilson, Edward O. 1992. *The Diversity of Life*. Boston: Harvard University Press.

World Health Organization. 2005. *Ecosystems and Human Well-Being: Health Synthesis*. Geneva, Switzerland: World Health Organization (and Millennium Ecosystem Assessment).

6
ECOSYSTEMS
The Land Ethic

Aldo Leopold, a forester-ecologist and prophet of environmental ethics, claimed, famously: "A thing is right when it tends to preserve the integrity, stability, and beauty of the biotic community. It is wrong when it tends otherwise." "That land is a community is the basic concept of ecology, but that land is to be loved and respected is an extension of ethics" (1949/1968, pp. 224–225, pp. viii–ix). We have been shifting levels: humans, animals, organisms, species lines, biodiversity. Next, we must focus on the ecosystemic level in which all organisms, humans included, are embedded. People still count, but perhaps this ecosystemic level in which people and all other organisms are embedded also counts morally.

Again, there will be *is* and *ought* questions. What are ecosystems? How ought humans to relate to them. "Ecology" is, etymologically, the logic of living creatures' homes. The word is derived from the Greek "oikos," the household, the inhabited world. In the last four decades, ecology has been thrust into the public arena. With the advent of the ecological crisis, then-Secretary of Interior Stewart Udall testified to the U.S. Congress: "We must begin to work with, not against, the laws of the planet on which we live.... This requires that we begin to obey the dictates of ecology, giving this master science a new and central position in the federal scientific establishment" (1968, p. 12, p. 14).

A land ethic might seem a naturalistic ethic, but people are living on this land, and so nature and culture soon mix. An ecological ethics mixes how the natural world is with how humans ought to behave in it, science and conscience, often with suggestions that humans ought to find a lifestyle more respectful of, or harmonious with, nature. This is likely to be combined with hopes for sustainability. Perhaps ecosystems will prove to count more than any of the component organisms, because the systemic processes have generated, continue to support, and integrate tens of thousands of member organisms. The appropriate unit for moral concern is the fundamental unit of development and survival.

Certainly, it would seem obvious that an environmental ethic is foolish not to be informed by the best ecological science available. The success of an environmental policy does not depend merely on cultural values, policy preferences, or the social institutions that drive human actors. Success depends on coupling such prescriptive values with an environmental science that is descriptively accurate and operationally competent. On the other hand, there are many pitfalls and one has to proceed cautiously.

1. Ecosystems: The *Is* Question

Biology has developed at two main levels: (1) the organismic, which is popularly described as "skin-in" biology, and (2) the evolutionary-ecosystemic, the latter is "skin-out" biology. Organismic biology, especially at cellular and molecular levels, has been on a fifty-year high, with spectacular successes in medicine, unraveling the genetic code, creating biotechnology, and so on. Evolutionary biology has profoundly redescribed the world and relocated humans within it in the century and a half since Darwin. By comparison, ecology is often thought to be a less mature science, for all its importance. Ecosystems are complicated and messy, hard to do experiments on. They are open systems that resist analysis.

The British Ecological Society asked their members for the most important ideas in ecology (Cherrett, 1989). The results, from nearly 650 ecologists, convey a sense of basic concepts, as well as a diversity of ideas, even to those unfamiliar with the detail. They ranked some fifty concepts, finding the top dozen to be:

1. The ecosystem
2. Succession
3. Energy flow
4. Conservation of resources
5. Competition
6. Niche

Early ecologists, at least within the time frames of their analysis, usually a few years or decades, favored ideas such as stability, homeostasis, equilibrium. Ecosystems had various feed-back and feed-forward loops; When rabbits have a good year, plenty of food, more fox pups survive; the extra foxes trim the rabbit population back. Such checks and balances tend to be self-regulating. Population densities are controlled by rainfall (producing food for rabbits), or parasites (worms or mange spread in the foxes dens). Predator-prey relations are statistically analyzable. Different animals and plants have their niches, roles they play in ecosystems, These are superimposed on succession, stages in ecosystem development, repeated after fires or windstorms.

Perhaps this can be ecosystem-specific. Some ecosystems can be *constant*, that is, little changing in some dimensions. Temperatures change rather little in some tropical forests; species richness or evenness may remain about the same. Some ecosystems may be *persistent*, that is, last long periods of time with little changes in species and their interrelationships. Ecosystems may have *inertia*, that is, resist external perturbations; this will probably be because of negative feed-back loops that dampen changes, such as density-dependent reproduction regulated by food supply or competition or parasites and diseases.

Ecosystems may be *elastic*; if so, they return rapidly to their former state after perturbation. This may depend on the *amplitude* of the perturbation, both the area disturbed and the degree of displacement. Ecosystems sometimes have *cyclic stability*, that is, oscillate periodically about some central mean, or they may have *trajectory stability*, that is, move steadily along routes of succession or, more vector-like, have historical tendencies (Orians, 1975). Ecosystems may be cycles on cycles at close hand but, over longer times, spirals that stretch out directionally, or search systems that select for organisms that can explore new niches. The stability of ecosystems is a dynamic stability, not a frozen sameness, though there are some perennial givens—wind and rain, soil and photosynthesis, competition, predation, symbiosis, trophic pyramids and networks.

Ecosystems can undergo successions, and be periodically rejuvenated. Ecosystemic succession—disturbance, early succession, mid-succession, late succession, and climax—is a widely embraced theory. But, depending on how frequent and extensive these interruptions are, succession can be more ideal than real. Ecosystems have their tendencies of development, after disturbance; but, if often enough interrupted, they wander though contingencies as much as they steadily develop. Such ecosystems may wander within bounds. Or, they may be stable within bounds, but, when unusual disturbances come, with enough amplitude to knock them out of bounds, they are displaced beyond recovery of their former patterns. Then they wander until they settle into some new equilibrium. There is no one and only stable state that an ecosystem should always have. Ecosystems are always on historical trajectory.

Later ecologists, perhaps because of longer time frames, have interpreted ecosystems as much more open and unstable. Steward Pickett, Thomas Parker, and Peggy Fiedler claim: "The classical paradigm in ecology, with its emphasis on the stable state, its suggestion of natural systems as closed and self-regulating, and its resonance with the nonscientific idea of the balance of nature, can no longer serve as an adequate foundation for conservation. The new paradigm, with its recognition of episodic events, openness of ecological systems and multiplicity of locus and kind of regulation, is in fact a more realistic basis" (1992, p. 84). Michael Soulé, although ardent in his conservation biology, says, "Certainly the idea that species live in integrated communities is a myth.... Living nature is not equilibrial.... Nature at the level of local biotic assemblages has never been homeostatic." "So-called biotic communities" is "a misleading term" (1995, p. 143).

If so, perhaps the land ethic preserving biotic communities is also a myth. Natural history is fractured into undefinable and indefinite assemblages that defy generalization, the loose associations feared above, in a messy, chaotic flux. Much less are such random, chaotic collections worth preserving for any beauty, integrity or stability they might have. But that takes the account too far into the disordered region.

Asking about the assembly rules for ecosystems, Evan Weiher says that ecologists find some mix of competition, co-operation, predation, disturbance (as by fire, insect epidemic, tornados), random factors, predictability and unpredictability. "I think what we are going to find out is that assembly rules are vague, gentle constraints" (Weiher, quoted in Stokstad, 2009, p. 34). There is both order and disorder; the order makes ecological science possible; the disorder keeps some element of adventure.

There are ordered regularities (seasons returning, the hydrologic cycle, acorns making oak trees, squirrels feeding on the acorns) mixed with episodic irregularities (droughts, fires, lightning killing an oak, mutations in the acorns). The rains come; leaves photosynthesize; insects and birds go their way; earthworms work the soil; bacteria break down wastes that are recycled; foxes find dens, have their pups, and hunt rabbits; and on and on. The half-life, on average, of many species is something like five million years. Lions have lived on the Serengeti plains for a long time, as have the zebras they eat. Over longer-scales there are climate changes, respeciation, new niches generated and occupied. This dynamic stability does not preclude but rather includes variation and change. There is variation, but selection requires relative stability in environments. A rabbit with a lucky genetic mutation that enables it to run a little faster has no survival advantage to be selected for, unless there are foxes reliably present to remove the slower rabbits.

Some events are more infrequent: extreme droughts or windstorms, producing big fires. Former Yellowstone Park Superintendent Bob Barbee reflected: "To this day I believe the Yellowstone fires of 1988 were unpredictable, unpreventable, uncontrollable and, finally, unimaginable" (2009, p. 10). But it is a mistake to conclude that ecosystem histories are nothing but random walk, forgetting that they also have stable dynamisms. There is also no doubt that ecosystems are full of cybernetic subsystems: for example, the species lineages that transmit information over time, generation after generation. Coded in the genetics and expressed in the coping behaviors of its member species, ecosystems will have the capacity to adjust to interruptions that come often enough to be remembered in the genetic memory. Coping with fires that come infrequently, lodgepole pines in Yellowstone can make serotinous cones, for example, and the forest replaces itself. Some species become adapted for rapid reproduction in disturbed habitats (r-selected), some adapted for sustained replacement in settled habitats (k-selected), because suitable habitats for such species recur. Provided that climatic changes, or novel species, are not too overwhelming, ecosystems that have long persisted will probably persist longer. Yellowstone forests have been there for millions of years, even if Bob Barbee's fires were unpredictable.

Natural systems were often sustained in the past for long periods of time, even while they gradually modified. Equilibrium theory and non-equilibrium theory represent two ends of a spectrum with real ecosystems somewhere in between, and whether one sees equilibrium or non-equilibrium can depend on the level and scale of analysis. If density or community structure as a whole is studied, equilibrium may appear never to be reached. However, at population levels, species diversity, or community compositions, ecosystems can show more predictable patterns, and even approach steady states on restricted ranges (Koetsier et al., 1990). R. V. O'Neill summarizes the conclusions of his research team: those who see stability and those who see change are looking at two sides of one coin: "In fact, both impressions are correct, depending on the purpose and time-space scale of our observations" (O'Neill et al., 1986, p. 3). "The dynamic nature of ecosystems," concludes Claudia Pahl-Wostl, is "chaos and order entwined" (Pahl-Wostl, 1995).

Perhaps no equilibria are permanently kept, but ecosystems are equilibrating systems composed of co-evolving organisms, with checks and balances pulsing over time. Population growth is constantly checked by food supply, predation, disease, or habitat availability, for example. There are autotrophs, heterotrophs, predators and prey, herbivores, omnivores, carnivores, trophic pyramids. There are successions (often interrupted), competition, symbiosis, energy flow, carrying capacity, niches, co-evolution, and often density-dependent regulation, as well as density independent factors. Many general characteristics are repeated;

many local details vary. Patterns of growth and development are orderly and predictable enough to make ecological science possible—and also to make possible an environmental ethics respecting these dynamic, creative, vital processes.

Many biologists incline to see the evolutionary nature as a self-organizing system. A word coined by Humberto R. Maturana, and Francisco J. Varela is "autopoiesis" (*autos*, self, and *poiein*, to produce) (Maturana and Varela, 1980). Stuart Kauffman concludes a long study of the origin of order: "We may have begun to understand evolution as the marriage of selection and self-organization" (Kauffman, 1991, 1993). The "auto" posits an innate principle of the origination of order, or genesis, similar to that present etymologically in "nature," from the Greek: *natans*, "giving birth."

Another term favored by many ecologists is "holism" A community is something more than a collection of individuals. "Holism" is the idea that the properties of a system as a whole determine how the parts behave. The features of the component parts do not explain all that is going on. The idea goes back to Aristotle: "The whole is different from the sum of its parts" (*Metaphysics* 1045a10). When a hiker who has seen all the trees asks next, "Show me the forest," some will reply that the forest is nothing more than the collection of trees. Only the trees are real. But this can start a slide down a slippery slope: communities are fictions, their organisms are real; organisms are fictions, their organs are real; organs are fictions, their cells are real; and so on down to atoms and quarks. But then we discover that quarks are just wave patterns and nothing seems real. Perhaps all these things are real, each at a different level. Trees seem as real as atoms.

So do forests. There seems little reason to count one pattern (the organism) as real and another (the ecosystem) as unreal. Any level is real if there is significant downward causation. Thus the atom is real because that pattern shapes the behavior of electrons; the cell because that pattern shapes the behavior of amino acids; the organism because that pattern coordinates the behavior of hearts and lungs; the community because the niche shapes the morphology and behavior of the foxes within it. Being real at the level of community does not require sharp edges, or complex centeredness, much less permanence; it only requires organization that shapes, perhaps freely so, the behavior of member/parts. The patterns (energy flow, nutrient cycles, succession, historical trends) to which an organism must "tune in" are set "upstairs," though patterns are altered by creativity arising "bottom up" from individual-level mutations and innovations.

There is a kind of order that arises spontaneously and systematically when many self-actualizing units jostle and seek their own programs, each doing its own thing and forced into informed interaction with other units. In culture, the logic of language or the integrated connections of the market are examples. Science or Christianity are community enterprises too vast to be comprehended by any one mind; many minds contribute to the building of each. No one individual orders language, markets, science, or religion. Individuals pursue their interests in all four, but none of these processes is fully to be explained merely as aggregated individual interests. Government too is at various scales: legislative, executive, and judicial checks and balances, at federal, state, county, and municipal levels.

Cultural heritages are generally like this, and we may legitimately respect Judaism or Christianity, or democracy or science, none of which are centrally controlled processes, all of which mix elements of integrity and dependability with dynamic change, even surprise and unpredictability. We might wish for beauty, integrity, and stability in democracy or science, without denying the elements of pluralism, historical development, and novel discoveries. Ecosystems too are wholes that incorporate but transcend their member components. (Two technical keywords for this debate are *nominalism* and *reductionism*.)

The incorporation of chaotic elements across evolutionary history has taken an interesting turn. A major refrain in contemporary biology is that order emerges out of chance. The claim now may be that natural selection can drive ordered systems to the edge of chaos because that is where the greatest possibility for self-organization, and survival in changing environments, occurs. "Evolution has tuned adaptive gene regulatory systems to the ordered region and perhaps to near the boundary between order and chaos." "Networks on the boundary between order and chaos may have the flexibility to adapt rapidly and successfully" (Kauffman, 1991, pp. 82, 84). In these "poised systems" creativity is entwined with chance and chaos. The construction of order is most probable at the edge of disorder. "Such order has beauty and elegance, casting an image of permanence and underlying law over biology. Evolution is not just 'chance caught on the wing.' It is not just a tinkering of the ad hoc, of bricolage, of contraption. It is emergent order honored and honed by selection" (Kauffman, 1993, p. 644).

There is dynamic change, and the dynamic changes through time yield historical development. Integrity in ecosystems includes the capacity to evolve. Stability, and nothing more, would squelch this creativity. On a big enough scale, ecology does meet evolution. Or, perhaps one should say, the evolution going on all the time becomes evident. Historical change is made possible by stability that supports variation.

Ecologists do have basic ideas about how ecosystems work. But they do not have much grand theory, laws that are always and everywhere true all over the Earth, seemingly because of this change and openness in ecosystems. Jonathan Roughgarden remarks: "It is difficult to imagine what could ever qualify as a 'law' in ecology" (1983, p. 597). Many philosophers of science think there are no hard "laws" anywhere in biology—or in social science—only useful generalizations. What grand theories ecologists have—for example, the Lotka-Volterra equations, which relate population size, the number of organisms that the environment will support, to time, growth rate, and carrying capacity—initially seem important, but turn out to be such gross simplifications that they are of little help in understanding actual landscapes.

They are true but abstract so greatly from particulars, that they leave "the devil in the details." Using any such laws of ecology to understand the Chesapeake Bay is something like trying to use the laws of gravity or survival of the fittest to explain the outcome of a presidential election. Perhaps the most ecologists can do is to have what Roughgarden calls a "collection of tools" (such as eutrophication of lakes, keystone species, nutrient recycling, niches, succession, or others of the fifty concepts) and put some of these to work in the particular circumstances at hand (Roughgarden, 1983, p. 597; see also Shrader-Frechette and McCoy, 1994; Peters, 1991).

Meanwhile, it is increasingly true that an ecosystemic nature, once flourishing independently of humans, is today under threat owing to human disruptions. For many, the immediate concern, to which we soon turn considering ecological/environmental economics, is about the threat to ecosystem services provided to humans. If one is more directly concerned with ecosystems in themselves, this threat can be described as a threat to ecosystem function, health, integrity, or quality. Biological *integrity* is the ability of an ecosystem to support and maintain "a balanced, integrated, adaptive community of organisms having a species composition, diversity, and functional organization comparable to that of the natural habitat of the region" (Karr and Dudley, 1981, p. 56).

Ecosystem *health* is a somewhat metaphorical term, extrapolated from health as found in individual organisms, but it is a term to which people relate easily with a sense of flourishing. Ecological *health* is the state in which the genetic potentials of an ecosystem's member species are being realized as organisms do well in their niches, these interrelated in such way that the systemic condition is dynamic and stable, the systemic capacity for self-repair when perturbed is present, and there is needed only minimal outside management. "An ecological system is healthy and free from 'distress syndrome' if it is stable and sustainable—that is, if it is active and maintains its organization and autonomy over time and is resilient to stress" (Costanza, Norton, and Haskell, 1992, p. 9; Mistretta, 2002; McShane, 2004). Biological *integrity* has as a baseline index the ecosystem that was originally there, the natural history, while biological *health* may, but need not always, require all the species that were originally there. There may be culturally-introduced replacements. If there is health, these replacements will thereafter function with minimal management intervention.

Without people around, ecosystems seem usually to function well, more or less stable, or flourishing, and to have their integrity. The processes and products originally in place, independently of humans, will with high probability have naturally selected species for their adaptive fits, since misfits go extinct and unstable ecosystems collapse and are replaced by more stable ones. Ecosystems get tested over thousands of years for their resilience. This is true even though from time to time in the past, natural systems were upset (when volcanoes exploded, or tsunamis destroyed them, or catastrophic epidemics broke out), and integrity of ecosystems then had to re-evolve. Natural systems are typically places of adapted fit, as evolutionary and ecology theory both teach.

2. Ecosystems: The *Ought* Question

After we get a satisfactory account of what ecosystems are, the next question is how ought we to relate to them. Donald Worster, for example, says: "The patterns of nature both do and ought to set a course for our lives—not the only course, or the only possible course, but a reasonably clear pattern that wise societies have followed in the past, foolish ones have scorned" (1990, pp. 1145–1146). The United States Congress passed the National Environmental Policy Act so as to help the nation "to create and maintain conditions under which man and nature can exist in productive harmony" (U.S. Congress, 1969, Sec 101).

No, the critics will now say. Certainly we have to pay some attention to the condition of the natural environment that supports human life, but this does not mean that we have any duties toward ecosystems, nor that there is any sense in which we ought morally to follow ecosystemic processes (Cahen, 1988). These critics will now say that ecosystems exist in too loose a way to count morally. Skeptical ethicists, sometimes encouraged by biologists, may think ecosystems are nothing but epiphenomenal aggregations of their more real members, like that forest (as we heard the hiker say above) which is nothing more than a collection of trees. An ethicist will have trouble valuing what does not really exist.

Now the ethicists will be troubled by the concerns we examined wondering what ecosystems are. Ecosystems can seem little more than stochastic processes. A seashore, a tundra is a loose collection of externally-related parts. Much of the environment is not organic at all (rain, groundwater, rocks, nonbiotic soil particles, air). Some is dead and decaying debris (fallen trees, scat, humus). An ecosystem has no brain, no genome, no skin, no self-identification, no telos, no unified program. It does not defend itself against injury or death. It is not irritable. The parts (foxes, sedges) are more centrally integrated than the wholes (forests, grasslands). So, it can seem as if an ecosystem is too low a level of organization to be the direct focus of moral concern. Ecosystems do not and cannot care; they have no interests about which they or we can care.

But now we should rather side with those holists and their claim that an ecosystem cannot be fully explained by an understanding of its components. To doubt *communities* because they are not organismic *individuals* is to look at one level for what is appropriate at another. One should look for a matrix of interconnections between centers, for creative stimulus and open-ended potential. Everything will be connected to many other things, sometimes by obligate associations, more often by partial and pliable dependencies; and, among other components, there will be no significant interactions. There will be shunts and criss-crossing pathways, cybernetic subsystems and feed-back loops. Qualities emerge that are corporate or holistic (such as trophic pyramids or tendencies to succession), not the qualities of any individual parts (such as metabolism or death). One looks for selection pressures and adaptive fit, not for irritability or repair of injury, for speciation and life support, not for resisting death. We must think more systemically, and less organismically.

Organisms defend only their own selves or kinds, but the system spins a bigger story. Organisms defend their continuing survival; ecosystems promote new arrivals. Species increase their kinds, but ecosystems increase kinds, and increase the integration of kinds. The system is a kind of field with characteristics as vital for life as any property contained within particular organisms. The organismic kind of creativity (regenerating a species, pushing to increase to a world-encompassing maximum) is used to produce, and is checked by, another kind of creativity (speciating that produces new kinds, interlocking kinds with adaptive fit, plus individuality and openness to future development). The collective order can be more complex than the behaviors of any of the individual parts. Ecosystemic order is a comprehensive, complex, fertile order just because it integrates (with some openness) the know-how of many diverse organisms and species. It is not an order built on the achievements of any one kind of thing. As a result there are diversity, unity, dynamic stability, novelty, spontaneity, a life-support system, the wonderland of natural history. Seen systemically, humans ought to respect and protect such systemic nature.

If we are concerned about what is value-able, able to sustain value on our landscapes, why not say that it is the productivity of such ecosystems? The products are valuable, able to be valued by the humans who come late in the process; but why not say that the process is what is really value-able, that is, able to produce these values in biodiversity? It would be foolish to value golden eggs and disvalue the goose that lays them. It would be a mistake to value the goose only instrumentally, and not for what it is in itself. A goose that lays golden eggs is systemically valuable (Ivanhoe, 2010). How much more so an ecosystem that generates myriads of species, or even an Earth that produces billions of species, ourselves included. Evolutionary history is past; we are not responsible for that. But the resulting life communities continue, and they have become our responsibility. Viewed in depth, these ecosystems remain today the source and support of individual and species alike. Such a perspective begins to naturalize ethics, generating an ethic for what Leopold called "the land."

Here is systemic value, as well as instrumental and intrinsic value. Value lies in processes as well as in products. How much more valuable is an ecosystem that generates myriads of species, or even, as we conclude in the next chapter, an Earth that produces billions of species, ourselves included!

Some interpreters have used the contingent elements in ecosystems to conclude that human environmental policy cannot be drawn from respecting or following nature; we humans will have to step in with our management objectives and re-shape the ecosystems we inhabit accordingly, bringing them into some new equilibrium consonant with our cultural goals. But, of course, that assumes that ecosystems have enough regularity and predictability to be managed.

Daniel Botkin finds little stability in ecosystems, but he amply finds order: "Nature undisturbed by human influence seems more like a symphony whose harmonies arise from variation and change over every interval of time. We see a landscape that is always in flux, changing over many scales of time and space." An ecosystem is "a certain kind of system composed of many individuals of different species ... and their environment, making together a network of living and nonliving parts that can maintain the flow of energy and the cycling of chemical elements that, in turn, support life" (1990, p. 62, p. 7). Botkin is often able to computer model these systems, else ecosystem management is impossible.

Even if natural ecosystems have characteristically settled into rather predictable patterns only slowly modified over evolutionary time, it seems likely that such systems, already quite complex, will be destabilized by human modifications, since these are often drastically different (bulldozers scraping off soil, synthetic pesticides, exotic weeds from another continent, acid rain). The fauna and flora have no genetic memory of such disruptions. Reliable predictions of these novel upsets will be beyond the capacities of ecosystem science with its presently available models and theories. An ecosystem might have naturally evolved certain checks and balances, feed-back loops, but little follows from this about what will happen with human-introduced innovations (when the Europeans move to Hawaii, for instance, where the flightless birds have no evolutionary experience with ground predators). On the scale of human duties in conservation, preservation, and land-use planning, we may still find that Leopold's land ethic, respecting the dynamic community stability, is still wise advice.

3. Ecological/Environmental Economics

Wondering about what we ought to do in environmental/ecological ethics, we might suppose that the economists can help us decide. Two fields that bring economics to bear on ecosystems are ecological economics and environmental economics. One might at first think these are two names for the same thing (as ecological ethics and environmental ethics might be), but it turns out that there are different emphases. Ecological economics is a multi-disciplinary academic field that seeks to address the interdependence of human economics and natural ecosystems. There is an International Society for Ecological Economics, with about 2,500 members. Environmental economics, as distinguished from ecological economics, is classical economics applied to natural systems. Ecological economics is green economics, where "green" refers to natural systems; environmental economics means by "green" the color of greenbacks, being green is being in the black, not in the red.

Classical economics, at least since the coming of the industrial age, has focused on labor and capital, and interpreted "land" and "natural resources" not as having any independent value, only as givens on which labor and capital could work. Inseparable from this is the idea of growth as good, human production for increased consumption, made more efficient by better organization of labor and larger markets. A principal technique, especially dealing with natural resources, is cost-benefit analysis, almost always in monetary units (dollars). The goal is more goods and services available to more people than ever before: more intelligent exploitation of nature. Yes, there are market failures, where resources are used inefficiently or unfairly (Cowen, 1988), but these can be fixed, for example by environmental regulation, taxes, modified property rights, shifting owner/producer incentives. The "invisible hand" does not always work. Still, people can use real common property effectively and fairly (Ostrom, 1990). Any solution of the poverty problem requires development, sustainable development.

Ecological economists find that this goal of forever giving people more and more, however humane it may seem, drives an escalating degradation of the natural environment, undermines ecosystem services, reduces biodiversity, pollutes air, water, soil, and makes the rich richer and the poor poorer. They find that the natural context is of crucial importance, and its neglect a main cause of the environmental crisis. The economy is inseparably entwined with biological process, a bioeconomics (Costanza et al., 1997; Spash, 1999; Kolstad, 2000; Daly and Farley, 2004; Common and Stagl, 2005; Millennium Ecosystem Assessment, 2005a).

Ecological economics thinks of the flow of energy and materials that enter and exit the economy as a kind of metabolism, digesting such life nutrients, but needing environmental sources and sinks, analogous to organisms in their environment. They may worry about pushing crop yields and losing the natural fertility of the soil, and replacing this with synthetic agricultural fertilizers in increasing amounts, even if this increases yields. Or they may worry about what high pesticide use is doing to the rivers and groundwater. Carrying capacity ought to govern resource use, rather than maximum exploitation. Environmental integrity and quality is as central as is production, growth, profit.

Those who celebrate our moving into the Anthropocene Epoch, will point out here that humans are creating novel ecosystems. Novel ecosystems are composed of new combinations of species under new abiotic conditions and are increasingly common; and, these critics may say, adaptive ecosystem management approaches must explicitly acknowledge the current status and predict the future conditions of these systems. Old styles of management, which focused on removing undesirable species or conditions from ecosystems to return them to a prior condition, are no longer sufficient. We need to consider, and experiment with, novel outcomes or trajectories, rather than simply taking preventative or therapeutic measures (Seastedt, Hobbs, and Suding, 2008). But ecological economists are doubtful about all this scaled up, clever management.

Economists need continually to consider what are now called "ecosystem services," contributions of natural processes without which no economy (or culture) can flourish, but which do not classically enter into the accounting of economists. These include primary productivity, nutrient dispersal and cycling, pollination, food, fuel, cleansing air and water, soil renewal, and living space that is habitable and pleasant. Wild pollinators, for example, provide free pollination; in some areas honeybee colonies must be supplied to replace lost wild pollinators, at a cost of billions of dollars. Robert Costanza led an effort by a dozen colleagues to value such ecosystem services. He found them difficult to value in dollars but came up with a value of about $33 trillion, in a range of $ 16 trillion to $54 trillion (Costanza et al., 1998; Pimm, 1988). The global GDP in 1997, the year of the study, was $ 27 trillion. So, natural ecosystem services exceed the entire output of the global human economy. As might be expected, the study was criticized, although critics agreed that such estimates had positive potential for bringing economists to realize the value of ecosystem services. (See *Ecological Economics* 25(1998), no. 1; the whole issue is devoted to the Costanza study.) Environmental "externalities" (as classical economists have called them)—benefits from Mother Nature that belong to no one in particular and so are enjoyed for free by all—are huge, and need to be figured into environmental regulations. These common benefits do indeed force us to re-think what we ought to do. This may also be called "translational ecology," connecting up what ecologists as scientists know with what people as citizen voters desire in environmental policy.

Economists think that "capital" is an essential concept. Capital is the material capacity to produce goods and services, thought of as a stock, such as money, buildings, machinery, patents, ongoing through the production process (possibly depreciating with time), differentiated from labor and land. Classical economists have various ways of thinking of capital. Ecological economists may now invite thinking of both human-made (manufactured) capital and natural capital (Pearce, Markandya, and Barbier, 1989, p. 3). Natural capital is the extension of the notion of capital to environmental goods and services.

Capital is, broadly speaking, a stock that yields a flow of valuable goods or services into the future. Natural capital is the stock of natural ecosystems that yields a flow of valuable ecosystem goods or services into the future. A forest provides a stock of trees or a river provides a stock of water or fish that can be sustainable indefinitely. Natural capital also provides services like recycling wastes or water catchment and erosion control. This flow of services from ecosystems requires that they function as whole systems, so the structure and diversity of the system are important components of natural capital. "Natural capital" added to "commercial capital" will make our moral duties more specific.

We will move from an upper-level moral concern that we ought to conserve the opportunities for development for ourselves and others, to a more operational level. Protect your capital. We take an idea with which the developers are quite familiar, capital, and modify this. Sustain natural capital too. This economic term seems to substitute well for "opportunity for development." We want to know how much we can spend without impoverishing ourselves, or our descendants. While a somewhat lower stock of natural capital may be sustainable, societies will be wise to allow no further decline in natural capital, given the large uncertainty and the dire consequences of guessing wrong. Keeping constant the total natural capital ought to be environmental policy as a prudent minimum condition for assuring sustainability, to be relaxed only when solid evidence can be offered that it is safe to do so (Costanza and Daly, 1992).

That seems intelligently precautionary about preserving ecosystems. The Millennium Ecosystem Assessment summarizes the findings of the largest group of natural and social scientists ever to research these issues. The authors are much more blunt: "At the heart of this assessment is a stark warning. Human activity is putting such strain on the natural functions of Earth that the ability of the planet's ecosystems to sustain future generations can no longer be taken for granted" (Millennium Ecosystem Assessment, 2005b, p. 5). The title of the report says it all: *Living Beyond our Means: Natural Assets and Human Well-Being* The Assessment concluded that 60% of the twenty-four essential ecosystem services examined worldwide have become degraded in the past fifty years. A major ecosystem service is adequate water. Thirty percent of the Millennium Ecosystem Assessment Development Goals depend on access to clean water. A third of the people on the planet lack readily available safe drinking water.

Ecosystem services are required for human well-being, but these connections are not always well understood, the outcomes of introduced changes not predictable, and those who suffer most likely to be poor. Consider the conclusion of some of the Assessment's principal authors, who worry particularly about nonlinear shifts. These occur when some threshold is reached and a small amount of further introduced change at a tipping point produces large and relatively rapid adverse changes in the climate system.

> We lack a robust theoretical basis for linking ecological diversity to ecosystem dynamics and, in turn, to ecosystem services underlying human well-being.... The most catastrophic changes in ecosystem services identified in the MA (*Millennium Assessment*) involved nonlinear or abrupt shifts. We lack the ability to predict thresholds for such changes, whether or not such a change may be reversible, and how individuals and societies will respond.... Relations between ecosystem services and human well-being are poorly understood. One gap relates to the consequences of changes in ecosystem services for poverty reduction. The poor are most dependent on ecosystem services and vulnerable to their degradation.
>
> (Carpenter et al., 2006)

Pushing development in ignorance of the resulting outcomes, risking abrupt shifts at unknown thresholds past which the poor will suffer much more degraded environments, escalates the rich getting richer at the expense of the poor. The moral imperative is to keep the ecosystem services needed for the poor, even more than those needed for the rich. Since ecosystem services are involved for persons living immediately in contact with nature, such conservation is as likely to focus on a sustainable biosphere as on sustainable development. For example, the Millennium Assessment found that drylands are under acute threat; and, on agricultural lands, excessive nutrient loading is upsetting and degrading ecosystem services to agriculture.

Some argue that thinking of nature as "natural capital" still is too monetary, "selling out on Nature," and is an inadequate way of thinking either of ecosystem services or of the value of nature in itself (McCauley, 2006). One problem with such a model is that "capital" is ordinarily somebody's possession: property owned. Though this may work for commercial capital, it may be misleading to think of the natural values we wish to protect in terms of ownership. We need a commons model (goods held in common), not an owned-capital model (economic wealth that belongs to individuals). Many of the sorts of values that we wish to sustain in nature (wilderness areas, whooping cranes, or the ozone layer) are poorly framed as our human or natural "capital" (O'Connor, 1993). Enlarging the property system will have some appeal to economists, but ethicists will doubt that what is right will best be decided here by adjudicating some kind of enlarged property rights to natural capital.

Most natural goods are off the market; markets figure returns on capital, growth of investments, dividends paid. What kinds of returns are there on natural capital? To what "owners" do these returns go? Many of these goods are what economists call "nonrival," since one person's use of them does not deprive others competitively. We all breathe the air (blowing around the globe), enjoy the rain (falling on your land and mine), hike in parks (escaping, for the day, our market concerns for dividends). Maybe this is common heritage, but if we convert it to natural capital, how does the analogous model work? Commodifying nature is not the answer; maybe this will only compound the problem.

Herman Daly has forcefully argued that essentially economics has yet to face the problem of growth on a finite resource base. E. F. Schumacher put this provocatively and influentially in his title: *Small is Beautiful* (1975). Although there are forms of growth that can be indefinitely sustained (such as in the arts, literature, humanities, scientific knowledge, computer technologies), endless growth of production from factories and fields is not possible (Daly, 1977, 1996; Daly and Cobb, 1994). But humans, economists and ethicists included, are reluctant to acknowledge this, much less to build it into their economics. As we saw in Chapter 2, humans want endless growth.

Perhaps, with an honest facing up to limits, the two fields, environmental and ecological economics, may mellow out into each other or at least find that each has pulled the other toward some compromise position. Kenneth Arrow led a group of distinguished economists and ecologists that used classical economic approaches enlarged to measure "inclusive wealth, that includes both natural and social (economic and cultural) capital (Arrow et al., 2004). Another approach uses the metaphor of an "ecological footprint." If we consider the area from which a city or a nation must draw resources to meet the demands of its lifestyle, far from arrogantly bragging about entering the Anthropocene Epoch, we will conclude that humans need to reduce, not enlarge, their footprint on Earth (Wackernagel and Rees, 1996; Sanderson et al., 2002).

Culture remains tethered to the biosystem and the options within built environments, however expanded, provide no release from nature, which remains as a life-support system. Humans today depend on air flow, water cycles, sunshine, nitrogen-fixation, decomposition bacteria, fungi, the ozone layer, food chains, insect pollination, soils, earthworms, climates, oceans, and genetic materials. An ecology still lies in the background of culture, natural givens that underlie everything else. In any future that we can presently envision, some sort of inclusive environmental fitness is required of even the most advanced culture.

Test yourself to see what preposition goes in the blanks: "Ecologists should not seek to understand objectively how nature works in itself; they should seek a knowledge that will help society to protect the environment _____ efficient use and _____ exploitation." Whether you insert *for* or *from* depends on no science, but on your value commitments. If you insert *for* in both blanks you are likely to be a classical economist. If you insert *for* in the first and *from* in the second, you are likely to be moving toward ecological economics. If you insert *from* in both blanks, you may be a deep ecologist.

4. Wilderness: The World that Runs Itself

The United States Congress has set aside hundreds of wilderness areas: wild, unmanaged ecosystems. The original Wilderness Act defined the lands Congress intended to conserve: "A wilderness, in contrast with those areas where man and his works dominate the landscape, is hereby recognized as an area where the earth and its community of life are untrammeled by man, where man himself is a visitor who does not remain" (U.S. Congress, 1964, sec. 2(c)). That seems straightforward. Although a diminishing part of the landscape, there are still areas that are dominantly wild, that is, undeveloped areas where humans do not manage nature but the processes are those of spontaneous wild nature. On Earth, most of the settled continents (excluding Europe) are between one-third and one-fourth wilderness (McCloskey and Spalding, 1989).

Of course, legal wilderness does have to be designated, as it has been by the U.S. Congress. A society has to decide what wilderness means and where they will have it. They will have to have managers to oversee conserving such wildlands. But legal wilderness has reference to primordial wilderness. Our "environment" may be our human natural environment, managed ecosystems. Most of the landscape we devote to "multiple use." But when we put the significant prefix "wild" before nature, this should make it abundantly clear that we are using words to refer to a world outside the human sector.

The National Park Service has, since its founding, had dual and sometimes conflicting goals: both to conserve nature as scenic resources for recreation for people and to conserve nature unimpaired for future generations (The Organic Act of 1916, Title 16, USC, sec. 1-4 et seq.). Unsurprisingly, legislation will incorporate various motives. Yellowstone Park was once described as "a pleasuring grounds for the nation and its people." By later accounts, Glen Cole says, "The primary purpose of Yellowstone National Park is to preserve natural ecosystems and opportunities for visitors to see and appreciate scenery and native plant and animal life as it occurred in primitive America" (Cole, 1969, p. 2). Yellowstone ought to be a biotic whole, a "natural community," untrammeled by humans, where nature takes its course and humans learn to take pleasure in it.

When the original Wilderness Act was passed in 1964, 54 areas (9.1 million acres) in 13 states were designated. Since then, Congress has enacted additions a hundred times and the wilderness system has grown almost every year and now includes 756 areas (109,494,508 acres) in 44 states and Puerto Rico. In 1980, the passage of the Alaska National Interest Lands Conservation Act added over 56 million acres of wilderness to the system, the largest addition in a single year. The most new wilderness areas were added in 1984. Overall, about 5% of the entire United States is protected—an area about the size of California. But because Alaska contains just over half of America's wilderness, only about 2.7% of the contiguous United States is protected—about the area of Minnesota.

Multiple reasons are given for having a wilderness system. A common one is that we need benchmark natural ecosystems, against which to compare the highly modified agricultural and urban landscapes that we inhabit. Another is the conservation of biodiversity (Mittermeier et al., 2003). Recreation is, as we just saw, a frequent reason, both as an outdoor theatre and as an outdoor gymnasium. Hikers want to be let in on nature's show, and to show what they can do. Often there is respect for wild natural ecosystems. Some of such nature ought to continue to exist, over and beyond whatever of nature we humans cultivate, enjoy as scenery, or otherwise need for ourselves.

Whatever the reasons, American are quite proud of their wilderness designations; other nations have copied the idea (with many modifications), but no other nation comes close to having a wilderness system of comparable size and importance. Most of the remaining wilderness in the world is unprotected. Americans congratulate themselves on having set aside a significant part of their landscape as a world that runs itself.

At this point critics enter to protest that, to the contrary, humans are very much mixed into the wilderness, mixed into the wild land itself (Cronon, 1995). Roderick Nash, tracing the history of *Wilderness and the American Mind*, reaches a startling conclusion: "Wilderness does not exist. It never has. It is a feeling about a place…. Wilderness is a state of mind" (Nash, 1979, pp. 39–40). "Wilderness" is a foil we constituted in contrast to late, twentieth-century, Western, technological culture, onging in the twenty-first. Nash concludes: "Civilization created wilderness" (Nash, 1982, p. xiii). David Lowenthal says, "The wilderness is not, in fact, a type of landscape at all, but a congeries of feelings about man and nature of varying import to different epochs, cultures, and individuals" (1964, p. 35).

Civilization creates wilderness? Lately yes, originally no. Civilization *designates* wilderness; more specifically, the U.S. Congress, acting for its citizens, designates wilderness, and other legislative bodies can and ought do so as well. That is a legislative meaning of "create," not the biological meaning. Wilderness *created* itself, long before civilization; everybody knows that, Nash included, and it is only setting up conundrums to exclaim, "Civilization created wilderness." "Wilderness is a state of mind." Backpackers in the wilderness do have states of mind. A frequent thought is that wilderness is what there was before there were states of mind. It ought not be that difficult for Lowenthal, a geographer, to distinguish between the wilderness idea, which has its vicissitudes in human minds, and wilderness out there: wild nature absent humans. Wilderness exists, objectively, even though our subjective ideas about wilderness may change over time. What philosophers of language call "reference" (that to which a term refers, which it denotes) can remain constant through changes in meaning (called "connotation"), as has happened with "water," or "gold," or "star," and "wilderness" (Kripke, 1980, p. 115ff).

Not so, continue the critics. They can get quite vociferous. The idea of wilderness, some allege, is "ethnocentric, androcentric, phallocentric, unscientific, unphilosophic, impolitic, outmoded, even genocidal" (Callicott and Nelson, 1998, p. 2). Such charges begin to sound more like rhetorical rant than reasoned argument. But the critics do have some arguments. Their attack is both theoretical and practical, on the idea of wilderness and on the fact of wilderness. One is, we might say, a mind problem; the other is a hand problem. We will consider the theoretical attack here, the practical attack in the next section.

Conceptually, nature seen as "wilderness," we are told, is just our Western, male, modern way of viewing nature, our state of mind, which sets wild nature in strong contrast to the cultivated landscape. Different peoples see nature in different ways, Christians one way, Buddhists another. The Druid concept of nature is *this*; Einstein's is *that*. Nature is a loaded word, as is revealed by the metaphors that have been used to describe it: the creation of God, the Great Chain of Being, a clockwork machine, chaos, an evolutionary ecosystem, Mother Nature, Gaia, a cosmic egg, *maya* (appearance, illusion) spun over *Brahman*, or *samsara* (a flow, a turning) which is also *sunyata*, the great Emptiness, or *yang* and *yin* ever recomposing the *Tao*. "Nature" is not so much anything out there as a category we have invented into which to put things; and we reinvent the category with our shifting models that describe this collection called "nature," depending on the mindset of the beholder. Wised up, "environmental philosophy ought to eschew the concept of nature entirely.… The 'end of nature' … may be something that *has always already occurred*" (Vogel, 2002, pp. 23–24, his emphasis; see also Vogel, 1996). Isn't "nature" always a social construct? (Hannigan, 1995; Zimmerman, 1994; Smith, 1995)

Contemporary Westerners are fond now of thinking of nature as "wilderness." But many peoples have not seen any wilderness at all. Those peoples too lived on their landscapes, and many of them saw themselves as being natural, with a more harmonious blending of nature and culture, perhaps with no distinction between nature and culture. They saw nature with a different set of mind. The nature-in-contrast-with-culture view is the epitome of social constructs, made in a self-consciously technological society. In reality, there is no nature-culture dualism; this is an artifact of the eyeglasses Westerners wear when they look at nature.

"Wilderness" is a myth of the urbane, mostly urban mind—so this argument continues. Wilderness is another one of those filter-words with which we color the nature we see. The truth is, say these critics, that we, being people, cannot know any such people-less world; that is only pretense. Seemingly at the risk of doublespeak, but in fact clarifying our language, we have to say that in the wilderness there is no wilderness, just as there is no date or time of day. All this defining wilderness and resolving to save it "constitutes" a wilderness-lens through which we modern Westerners see nature; "wild" is as much construct as "West", and these wised-up intellectuals see this.

The wilderness concept, Baird Callicott claims, is "inherently flawed," triply so. It metaphysically and unscientifically dichotomizes man and nature. It is ethnocentric, because it does not realize that practically all the world's ecosystems were modified by aboriginal peoples. It is static, ignoring change through time. In the flawed idea and ideal, wilderness respects wild communities where man is a visitor who does not remain. In the revised idea(l), humans, themselves entirely natural, reside in and can and ought to improve wild nature (Callicott, 1991). David Rothenberg says, "Wilderness is a consequence only of a civilization that sees itself as detached from nature.… This is a romantic, exclusive and only-human concept of a nature pure and untrammeled by human presence. It is *this* idea of nature which is reaching the end of its useful life" (Rothenberg, 1992, p. 2).

Some grammarians may notice that "wilderness" is a modern word we have made up. Aboriginal peoples typically do not have the word in their vocabulary, and even some Western languages (like Spanish and Danish) do not have such a word. Nevertheless, linguists do find that both the word and the idea can be ancient, as well as modern. The word "wild" is already present in Old Teutonic, the precursor of English, before 450 A.D., and means "not domesticated" or "not cultivated." The word "wilderness" is found in Old and Middle English and means "land not farmed or settled," "land in its natural state"

(Chipeniuk, 1991). In a twelfth century poem, *The Owl and the Nightingale*, the poet remarks, "Their land ... isn't civilized, rather it is a wilderness (*wildernisse*)" (Dickins and Wilson 1951, p. 54).

In Greece, Plato claims this as "the wisest of all doctrines": "that all things do become, have become, and will become, some by nature, some by art, and some by chance" (*Laws*, 10.888). In the Bible, the Hebrews regularly distinguish between their own activities and those of wild nature, especially in Job and the Psalms. Words translated as "wilderness" occurs over three hundred times in the Bible (Hebrew: *midbar,`arabah, horbah*). The Chinese anciently distinguished between nature and culture, a distinction found in the *Analects* of Confucius.

In an etymological study of the word "nature," C. S. Lewis concludes:

> This, as it is one of the oldest, is one of the hardiest senses of *nature* or *natural*. The nature of anything, its original, innate character, its spontaneous behaviour, can be contrasted with what it is made to be or do by some external agency. A yew-tree is *natural* before the topiatrist has carved it.... This distinction between the uninterfered with and the interfered with ... [is] very primitive.... What keeps the contrast alive ... is the daily experience of men as practical, not speculative beings, [such as] the antithesis between unreclaimed land and the cleared, drained, fenced, ploughed, sown, and weeded field.
>
> (1967, pp. 45–46)

Every culture can, to some extent, see beyond itself to a spontaneous nature, unaffected by human agency. Deep in a wilderness, looking up at night at the myriad stars, with coyotes howling, one sees at once that nature is not ended.

The very idea of culture, in any form, has the sense of cultivation, of taking oversight, direction, and control of a found natural process to re-direct it. That contrast is found wherever there are people with minds and hands who act on the world to alter it, revising the course of events that otherwise might naturally have taken place. Now it seems that the main "idea" in "nature" is that the natural is not a human construct; and analogously, with the world "wild." Intentional, ideological construction is exactly what wild natural entities do not have; if they had it, they would be artifacts. The main idea in nature is that nature is not our idea.

The trouble is that the smart intellectuals (they may call themselves postmoderns) are so focused on the language-lens that they can no longer see nature. For example, it cannot count against "wilderness" having a successful reference that earlier peoples did not have the word. Yes, "wilderness" is, in one sense, a twentieth century construct, as also is "the Krebs cycle," and "DNA," and the "Permian/Cretaceous extinction"; none of these terms were in prescientific vocabularies. Nevertheless, these constructs of the mind enable us to detect what is not in the human mind. We must not confuse what we see with how we see it, even though how we see does shape what we can see.

There are, no doubt, many things going on in the wilderness that we yet fail to see, because we do not have the constructs with which to see them. That does not mean, however, that there is no wilderness there, nor that these things are not going on independently of us, both our knowing and our doing (Rolston, 1991; Kidner, 2000).

Wilderness areas and nature reserves are part of our global environment, and yet not our human habitat. The wild is an environment that humans need and ought to respect; they may like to visit there. But the wild is not an environment in which we can reside and still be human. Ethics arises to govern conduct in the "polis," with its social contract, orienting behavior to protect the goods of human nature and culture. Hence, some say, ethics does not belong in the wild. It is for people, in urban or rural environments. But, again, a more radical environmental ethics, resolving to be quite inclusive and comprehensive, holds that humans can and ought to set aside wild areas for what they are in themselves, areas which we try to manage as little as possible, or to manage human uses of them so as to let nature takes its course, as far as we can. Virtuous persons ought to respect the integrity, the freedom of life, in all its wildness. True, humans are the dominant species on the landscape, which they must manage. But humans are also a moral species, who can and ought respect evolutionary ecosystems—at least on representative parts of the landscape.

Put it this way. We moderns have constituted the word "wilderness" as a filter with which the better to see these foundational forces, not earlier so well known, and to care appropriately for them, resolving in our high-tech cultures, that there will always be places where humans only visit and do not remain. Wilderness is, if you like, a new "idea(l)" ("myth") we have recently set up, but we did so because we discovered wilderness for "real." We want to conserve this realm for what it is in itself, naturally there. The rescue attempt is recent; the reality is primordial. Real wilderness is an option for us, although not for long; and it only confuses the cause of conservation to think that the human mind makes wilderness conservation either undesirable or impossible.

5. Nature: Found? Constructed? Re-constructed

If not the mind, what about the hand? Practically, humans have lived on landscapes for millennia, modifying and rebuilding them, more or less, so that now—the critics of wilderness preservation will continue—in fact there is no wild nature. There has been none in the Old World since humans evolved and left Africa. There has been none in the New World since the last ice age, when humans crossed the Bering Strait and entered this Western hemisphere. There is no nature to which humans have not set their hands, developing, managing, modifying, polluting it. On every continent, the main effort for thousands of years has been development seeking better to manage nature (Burke and Pomeranz, 2009).

Wild nature, out there independently of humans does not exist. Wilderness is a myth—by hand as well as mind. There is none to preserve. We can, if we like, restore wild nature here and there on our landscape, but that is what it will be: restored wild nature. Wild nature will be but a museum piece, something we imagine similarly to the way we do other things now past (such as pharaohs in Egypt). The only nature we have from here onward is a nature to which humans have put their hands. Human-tampered nature is the only nature we have had for thousands of years. We can, if we like, set aside some pockets of so-called wilderness here and there on the landscape, and try to stimulate or simulate wild nature there; but these will be more like big open zoos than pristine nature.

But not so fast. We have already seen such a claim contested by researchers who found that even the settled continents remain one-third to one-fourth wilderness. These researchers did exempt Europe, but even on long-settled landscapes there can be much natural woodland, treasured by owners over centuries. There may be native woodlands, often with quite old trees, secondary woodlands with trees fifty to a hundred years old, recently restored woodlands, wetlands, moors, hedgerows, mountains, such as the Alps or the Scottish Cairngorms (Peterken, 1996). Saving wildlands as baseline index for estimating degrees of human influence, degradation, or restoration of ecosystems makes no sense unless we can in fact successfully know in some degree what wild nature was, is, might be absent human activity.

In one survey, using three categories, researchers find the proportions of Earth's terrestrial surface altered as follows: (1) Little disturbed by humans, 51.9%. (2) Partially disturbed, 24.2%. (3) Human dominated, 23.9%. Factoring out the ice, rock, and barren land, which supports little human or other life, the percentages become: (1) Little disturbed, 27.0%. (2) Partially disturbed 36.7%. (3) Human dominated 36.3%. Most habitable terrestrial nature is dominated or partially disturbed by people (73.0%). Still, nature that is little or only partially disturbed remains 63.7% of the habitable Earth (Hannah et al., 1994).

In the Americas—so Callicott was arguing—not only have the Europeans been destroying (what they thought was) wilderness for five hundred years, but the aboriginals had already extinguished wilderness. There was no wilderness remaining even when Columbus arrived in 1492, because the Native Americans had been managing the landscape for fifteen thousand years. How much did the Native Americans modify the landscape? That is an empirical question, and philosophers have no particular competence in answering it.

When we ask experts, however, we get answers that mix fact and interpretation. Partly this is an ecological question, whether ecosystems were thrown out of balance. Partly it is an anthropological question, about the practices of the pre-Columbian peoples. Aboriginal cultures altered the locales in which they resided, more so in Central America, less so in portions of North America, variously in South America. In that respect, American Indian culture was not different in kind from the white man's culture. What we need to know is the degree. Did the Indians transform the pre-Indian wilderness (of 15,000 B.C. or whenever they arrived) on regional scales beyond the range of its spontaneous self-restoration?

Most of what has been designated as U.S. wilderness was infrequently used by the aborigines, since it is high, cold, arid, and often difficult to traverse on foot. The Native Americans too were visitors who did not remain—for the same reasons that the whites after them left those regions sparsely settled. We have little reason to think that in such areas the aboriginal modifications were irreversible. Just what did these Native Americans do to manage the Grand Canyon, or Mount Rainier? Or for that matter Yellowstone or the Great Smokies? Or regional wetlands such as the Everglades?

What about the more accessible temperate regimes? Were they modified so extensively and irreversibly that wilderness designation would be an illusion? Unlike the Europeans, Native Americans had no machinery; they had no iron, even for axes or plows, no wheels. The Native Americans on forested lands had no horses (prior to the Spanish) or cattle. What agriculture they had tended to reset succession; and, when agriculture ceases, the subsequent forest regeneration will not be particularly unnatural. There was limited agriculture in the North American Southwest, under the necessity of irrigation (Donkin, 1979). One does not greatly alter semi-arid ecosystems on regional scales by terracing here and there with primitive implements. There was virtually no agriculture otherwise in the Western United States, which includes the Great Plains, the Rocky Mountains, the Pacific Northwest, California, the interior deserts (Denevan, 1992). The most common crop there and elsewhere was maize, which does not persist wild, but disappears as soon as humans cease to plant it.

Otherwise the Native Americans were hunters and gatherers, without irreversible adverse effects. If one asks ecologists which of the designated wildernesses today have, in terms of determining ecosystem processes, a significantly different character now from what these areas would have had had there been no Native Americans, they have trouble finding one. Now and again an ecologist can cite a particular locality that might be different—balds in the Southern Appalachians (maybe), oak openings in the Midwest. But regional landscape transformation of ecosystem processes is of a vastly different scale.

The Native American technology for larger landscape modification was bow and arrow, spear, and fire. The only one of these that extensively modifies landscapes is fire (Pyne, 1982, Chapter 2). Fire is—ecologists have long been insisting—also quite natural. Forests in the Americas have been fire-adapted for at least thirteen million years, since the Miocene Epoch of the Tertiary Period, as evidenced by fossil charcoal deposits. The fire process involves fuel build-up over decades, ignition, and subsequent burning for days or weeks; any or all of the three may be natural or unnatural. Fire suppression is unnatural, and can result in unnatural fuel build-up, but no one argues that the Native Americans used that as a management tool, nor did they have much capacity for suppression.

The argument is that the Indians deliberately set fires. Does this make their fires radically different from natural fires? It does in terms of the source of ignition; the one is a result of environmental "policy deliberation," the other of a lightning bolt. But students of fire behavior realize that in dealing with forest ecosystems on regional scales the source of ignition is not a particularly critical factor. Once the fire has burned a hundred yards, the vegetation cannot tell what the source of ignition was. The question is whether the forest is ready to burn, whether there is sufficient ground fuel to sustain the fire, whether the trees are diseased, how much duff there is, and so on.

If conditions are not right, it will be difficult to get a big fire going; it will soon burn out. If conditions are right, a human can start a regional fire today. If not, lightning will start it tomorrow, or next year, or the year after that. On a typical summer day, the states of Arizona and New Mexico are each hit by several thousand bolts of lightning, mostly in the higher, forested regions. On average, the U.S. landscape is hit by fifty million bolts a year, ten strikes in each square mile (Krider, 1986). Doubtless the Native Americans started some fires too, but it is hard to think that their fires, centuries ago, so dramatically and irreversibly altered the natural fire regime that meaningful wilderness designation is today impossible. Natural ignition sources are available on an order of magnitude (a few years) that greatly exceeds the order of magnitude of fuel build-up for burning (several decades).

Grasslands differ in that fuel becomes available annually for a burn. Fires can retain grasslands that, unburnt, would revert first to shrubland and then to forests. This happens naturally in the Midwest where the forests transpose to grasslands and lightning is frequent. In some grasslands situations, the Native Americans might have augmented ignition relative to fuel availability, and burned unnaturally often. There is good reason to think that the Native Americans could sustain some grassland openings on a modest scale. This merely shifts succession toward earlier stages, and, released from Indian burning, such lands resume their natural succession. Meanwhile, there is no reason to think that the Native Americans, by deliberate fire policy, really modified the regional grasslands ecology of the vast American West. Also, of course, few grasslands have been designated as wilderness.

In short, though the Native Americans lived on the landscape, there was much of it that they too only visited and did not remain. Most of the land that they hunted over was relatively untrammeled by them. Even the lands that they did manage were not managed outside their resilient capacity to return to natural landscapes, when the Native American interventions are removed. The definition of wilderness, we recall, uses the term "untrammeled," and so effects of humans do not make wilderness impossible, provided that the land yet "retains its primeval character and influence, without permanent improvements or human habitation."

Perhaps Native Americans needed neither the concept of wilderness, nor, in practice, to designate any. Pre-Darwinian peoples had an immediacy of encounter with nature that scientists today may lack, and among them there are forgotten truths. These are worthy of preserving. But they had only groping access to the depths of historical time and change that have characterized Earth over the millennia. They had neither evolution nor ecology as sciences on the one hand (nor microbiology nor astronomy), and their cultural developments, on the other hand, did not threaten the stability and integrity of their ecosystems. Even we modern Westerners have re-educated ourselves about these matters. We have increased access to nonhuman phases of nature; we increasingly threaten such nature.

On Earth, man is not a visitor who does not remain; this is our home planet and we belong here. Humans too have an ecology, and we are permitted interference with, and rearrangement of, nature's spontaneous course; otherwise there is no culture. But there are, and should be, places on Earth where the nonhuman community of life is untrammeled by man, where we only visit. That opportunity we now have on landscapes, especially in the American West, and we both can and ought to preserve wilderness. Neither the human mind nor the human hand has made wilderness conservation impossible.

In fact humans can use their hands to restore wilderness: restoration biology. There are, as noted above, only scraps of native prairie remaining in the U.S. Midwest, so, some conservationists have said, we will re-create more (Jordan, 1991; Jordan, Gilpin, and Aber, 1987). Wetlands are often gone; the British have been "re-wetting" the South Yorkshire fens. Where forests have invasive species, we can take them out. Often if we cease the interruption, natural systems will be self-healing; but, especially if systems have been pushed far from their equilibriums, or if species have been exterminated, or soils lost, the damage may require managed repair. We may need clean up and fix up, a recovery plan so we can re-wild nature (Boyce, Narrain, and Stanton, 2007; Comin, 2010).

This is certainly commendable activity, but it poses some puzzles philosophically. The critics are always looking over the shoulders of conservationists. Suppose humans come in and deliberately repair a degraded prairie. There are work crews organized by the Society for Ecological Restoration. They sketch groundplans for what they will put where; they work at it over several years, often long and hard. Then there it is: Behold: A prairie! As good as new. Or is it? A prairie is a phenomenon of spontaneous nature, but what about this restored prairie? People built it. Perhaps it is an artifact, in which case it cannot be wild nature. A rebuilt prairie is a contradiction in terms. There it is: A faked prairie!

Lest you shake your head at how philosophers, arguing about words, can produce a quagmire anywhere they please, casting doubt on a perfectly commendable activity, we hasten to point out that this matter has considerable relevance. As soon as you accept, uncritically, this rebuilt prairie as the real thing, having all the values of the original, there will arrive a delegation from the mining company, who want to mine the coal under the last remnant of original prairie that does exist. If you object, contend that there is little prairie left, and refuse to license the mine, they will reply that they will, after mining, put the prairie back like it was. Almost every development project that disrupts natural systems, in order to get a permit, has to meet certain legal restoration criteria. Often, if one area is destroyed, a fishing stream or a wetland, there will be a requirement for mitigation, met when they create another fishing stream or wetland somewhere else. Or put nature back when they finish.

Restorations are seldom as good as the original. The diversity of species may not be there, nor the complexity of ecosystemic interrelations. In Appalachian forests, though the dominant trees may come back, the forest undercover is only about one-third as rich as it was before, even where there are considerable efforts at restoration (Duffy and Meier, 1992). So, the first point to make is that restorations, although valuable, are not as valuable as pristine nature, because they are not as rich (Westman, 1991). Reclaiming brownfields as greenfields is difficult.

But if the restoration were 100% successful, what then? Eric Katz calls restorations "The Big Lie!" (1992). Robert Elliot complains that they are "Faked nature!" (1982). This is because the historical genesis of the system has been interrupted; and, even though both Katz and Elliot approve of restorations, they insist that the value of even a perfect restoration is always in principle something else than the value of pristine nature, since it is not the handiwork of nature but of humans, who have cleverly restored it.

Standing before a Torrey pine, *Pinus torreyana*, along the coast of Southern California, the proper response is not: Wow, there is a rare species, surviving across millennia! But: Hurrah for the U.S. Forest Service! Their biologists in 1986 collected 30,000 seeds from 150 trees for storage and propagation, and reintroduced the pine, producing nearly 6,000 trees. Besides this, they had to control an outbreak of the ips beetle. One admires not so much the trees as the skills of the restoration biologists that put them there. The pines are not really wild. Once upon a time, they were; but now the truth is that they exist thanks to biologists. When it comes down to the truth of what it is: That Torrey pine is an artifact. The trees in these woods we are hiking through today are not authentic.

To work our way out of these troubles, notice that there are all kinds and degrees of restoration. At the one extreme, if a forest has been clearcut, or strip-mined, there is nothing there; the landscape is blitzed, so any new forest is a replacement, a replica. This would be like replicating the *Nina*, one of Christopher Columbus' ships. The replica is made from scratch and has no historical continuity at all with the original. This is not really restoration; it is replication. On the other end of a spectrum, if the forest has been cut by selection of a few trees here and there, and new trees replanted to substitute for these, there is restoration.

A restoration is the original, once damaged and now restored. A replica is a new creation, without continuity to the old one. Replicas can exist simultaneously with originals. Restorations cannot. Restorations continue much of the historical continuity. Restoration of a famous painting, such as Da Vinci's "The Last Supper," is not making a replica and passing it off as original. One is not pretending to have anything that one does not have. Restoration of a famous natural area, such as Thoreau's Walden Pond, ought to be a careful and respectful rehabilitating. The result is nature restored, not nature faked.

In nature we restore by rehabilitating. One does not rehabilitate paintings. But nature may, once we put the parts back in place, heal itself. If revegetating after a strip mine, one cannot rehabilitate either, because there is nothing to rehabilitate. But one can rehabilitate a prairie that has been not too badly overgrazed. Overgrazing allows many introduced weeds to outcompete the natives; perhaps all you have to do is pull the weeds, and let nature do the rest. That is undoing, as much as doing. Overgrazing allows some native plants to outcompete other natives, those that once reproduced in the shade of the taller grasses. So perhaps, after the taller grasses return, you will have to dig some holes, put in some seeds that you have gathered elsewhere, cover them up, go home, and let nature do the rest. Maybe you can just put the seeds in the weed holes (Gunn, 1991; Rolston, 1994, pp. 88–93).

The naturalness returns. The restoration ceases to be an artifact. In the days before high-tech medicine, physicians who were congratulated on their cures used to say, modestly, "Really, I just treated you, and nature healed you." When a doctor sets a broken arm, he just holds the pieces in place with a splint, and nature does the rest. He is not really to be congratulated for his skills at creating arms. He arranges for the cure to happen naturally. One does not complain, thereafter, that one has an artificial limb. Likewise with restoration. It is more like being a midwife than being an artist or engineer. You arrange to get the raw materials back on site, and place them where they can do their thing.

The point now is that restorations of this kind do not fake so much as facilitate nature, help it along, mostly by undoing the damage that humans have introduced, and then letting nature do for itself. As the restoration is completed, the wild processes take over. The sun shines, the rains fall, the forest grows. Birds arrive on their own and build their nests. Hawks and owls catch rodents. Perhaps you return some otters, locally extinct, and put them back in the rivers. But, after a few generations, the otters do not know they were once reintroduced, they behave instinctively as they are genetically programmed to do. They catch muskrats as they can; population dynamics is restored. Natural selection takes over. The adapted fits survive in their niches.

Succession resumes. In due course, lightning will strike and wildfire burn the forest again, after which it will regenerate itself. Even a new species could evolve. If such things happened decades, centuries, millennia after some thoughtful humans had once facilitated a restoration, it would seem odd to label all these events as artifacts, lies, fakes. Perhaps the best way to think of it is that the naturalness of a restored area is time bound. Any restoration is an artifact at the moment that it is deliberately arranged, but it gradually ceases to be so, and spontaneous nature returns—but if, and only if, humans back off and let nature take its course.

Nevertheless, the unbroken historical continuity in natural systems is important. That we, after restoration, back off to let nature take its course, proves that we could wish that the course of nature had never been broken on the landscape we now conserve. We are glad to have a broken arm healed; we would just as soon never have broken it. Though the spontaneity of natural systems might all return, the historical discontinuity can never be repaired. In that respect, the restored area does suffer permanent loss of natural value. If one is appreciating the present spontaneity of wild nature—the plant or animal in its *ecology*—that can be returned, and will, after complete restoration, be present undiminished. But if one is appreciating the *evolutionary history*—the plant or animal in its historical lineage—even though the genetics may be back in place, there has been interrupted wildness. The forest is not virgin, not pristine.

"Restore" contains the idea of putting something back like it was earlier. We need to be clear what this something is and what it is not. We are not resetting the forest to what it was a century ago. That suggests going backward in time, and that is impossible. We do not replace the past. We can only today put back in place in products of nature (seeds, seedlings, nutrients, species, soils, clean waters), and, with this, encourage the reappearance of what we are really putting back: natural processes. Restoration is not a backward looking activity, though, to be sure, one does have to look to noninterrupted systems to discover what was once there. Restoration is a forward looking event, it wants rehabilitation for the future.

Sometimes we will restore for pragmatic reasons, since we have often found that the degradation of ecosystems harms people as well. Sometimes this will be an altruistic restoration, putting it back for the sake of the wild others who re-reside there. Such restoration is restitution, a moral word. We make restitution where we ought not to have destroyed values. Restoration as restitution is, moreover, going to increase our human sense of identity with nature; we are going to appreciate the biotic community we have studied and helped to restore. We will be more careful elsewhere about our harmony with the natural systems that we must continue to disturb. That sense of identity and harmony is not unauthentic at all. It is the fundamental imperative of conserving wild ecosystems.

6. Environmental Policy: Ecosystem Management—Once and Future Nature

We already noticed in Chapter 2 that many are attracted to adaptive ecosystem management. This focuses on system-wide levels, presumably to manage for indefinite sustainability, alike of ecosystems and their outputs for human benefit. Such management connects with the idea of nature as "natural resources" at the same time that it has a "respect nature" dimension. There usually is the idea of fitting human uses into ongoing ecosystem health, or integrity. This is often a matter of managing human uses of their ecosystems with as much care as one is managing, or revising, wild nature. There is no "invisible hand" that guarantees an optimal harmony between a people and their landscape, or that the right things are done in encounter with fauna, flora, species, ecosystems, or regarding future generations. We have to do this in democratic concert, and for that we need an environmental policy for ecosystem management.

Again, as often before, this seems rational, but the devil is in the details. There is a long legal history of policy for land, but that needs to become more sensitive to ecosystem sustainability (Caldwell and Shrader-Frechette, 1993; Freyfogle, 2003). Assessing ecosystem-based management and "the need for institutional adaptation to change and ecological resilience," three ecologists conclude: "The degree to which stakeholders, scientists, and managers must consequently expand their worldviews, understanding, and ethics is daunting" (Chan, Gregr, and Klain, 2009, p. 1342; see also McLeod and Leslie, 2009).

Ecosystem management has been criticized as an umbrella idea under which different managers can include almost anything they wish, since what one is to manage ecosystems *for* is left unspecified. They might manage for maximum sustainable yield, or for equal opportunity in the next generation, or for maximum biodiversity, or for quick profit. True, the managers say, but we can be more precise about what the goals of management are. In fact, we already heard what the U.S. Congress has said: such management can help the nation "to create and maintain conditions under which man and nature can exist in productive harmony."

Five goals of ecosystem management are:

1. Conserve viable populations of native fauna and flora.
2. Conserve representative ecosystems.
3. Conserve ecological processes, including natural disturbance regimes.
4. Conserve the evolutionary potential of species and ecosystems.
5. Accommodate human uses within these goals.

Humans can only flourish if they live where their ecosystems are functioning well. There is cycling and re-cycling of energy and materials; the member organisms too are flourishing as interrelated fits in their niches. The system is spontaneously self-organizing in the fundamental processes of climate, hydrology, photosynthesis. There is resistance to, and resilience after, perturbation. The system does not have constantly to be doctored. Aldo Leopold put it this way: "Health is the capacity of the land for self-renewal. Conservation is our effort to understand and preserve this capacity" (1949/1968, p. 221).

Unhealthy systems will have "reduced primary productivity, loss of nutrients, loss of sensitive species, increased instability in component populations, increased disease prevalence, changes in the biotic size spectrum to favor smaller life-forms, and increased circulation of contaminants" (Rapport, 1989, p. 122). Monocultures have little health. Pushed more and more into artificiality, there is really no ecosystem left at all. A cornfield two miles square is almost like a twenty-acre parking lot full of cars. The individual corn plants might be healthy enough, but they are just parked there by humans, about like potted plants on the porch. There are hardly any ecosystemic connections at all, past the sunshine. Even the fossil water is pumped from a half mile below.

Highly modified once-natural systems, now requiring steady management, such as farmlands, which must be plowed, seeded, fertilized, harvested each year, cannot be said to have native biological integrity. They can perhaps have some kind of agricultural integrity, if they can be managed sustainably, and if their operation does not disrupt the surrounding natural systems (rivers, forests, native fauna and flora in the fencerows, edges, fallow fields, pastures, rangelands). Nevertheless, areas put into agriculture, or industry, or to urban uses, will always have to be enveloped by natural systems. Else the system will crash.

A properly managed ecosystem will protect natural values, as well as support cultural values, and continuing such ecological productivity and support is the bottom line for an environmental ethic. We don't want to foul our own nest. Here we can take ecosystem integrity and health not just as theoretical ideas; we can also use them to guide specific research and policy strategies. We set pollution standards, for instance, above which threshold there is evident deterioration of fish and waterfowl reproduction. Dissolved oxygen may not fall below 5 milligrams per liter in coldwater fisheries. We can study the food chains, measure energy cycling and materials recycling, measure population rises and falls, recovery rates, and so forth, to find out, scientifically, what interconnections constitute and preserve biological integrity. ("Preserving ecosystem integrity" sounds more politically correct than saying "Don't foul up your nest.")

The 100% natural system no longer exists anywhere on Earth, since there is some DDT in penguins in Antarctica. Perhaps 95% of a landscape will be more or less rebuilt for culture, considering lands plowed, grazed, forests managed, rivers dammed, and so on. We looked at some statistics in Chapter 2 about the extent of human influence. We live in "anthropogenic biomes." True, there are those wildlands we have been insisting are still there. But mostly we live in landscapes that we have to manage. On these we want some naturalness mixed with managed agribusiness, working national forests, irrigation and flood control dams, and so on.

How much naturalness is or ought to be present on a landscape? Consider the following criteria:

1. What is the historical genesis of processes now operating on the landscape? Were they introduced by humans, or do they continue from the evolutionary and ecological past? The more doctoring, the less likely there is health. That will take more intensive management.

2. What is the species constitution compared with the original makeup? The more the fauna and flora is depauperate, the less integrity and health. We still might have lands useful for agriculture or wood plantations for paper production. But there is always a sense of living on an impoverished landscape—those corn plants like acres of potted plants.

3. How much cultural energy is required for the upkeep of the modified system? The more such management requires large amounts of labor, petroleum, electricity, fertilizer, pesticides, the further we are from a system that has integrity or ongoing stability. Maybe we can get higher yields successfully for some years, but what happens when the cost of petroleum rises, or the genetically modified (GMO) soybeans or corn is no longer pest resistant?

4. How much self-organizing nature remains? What would happen without humans? Would the system reorganize itself, if not to the pristine integrity, then at least to a flourishing system? We cannot imagine, perhaps, removing humans from the system. But then again there are a number of regions that were once well inhabited; now however, due to shifting markets and new technologies, they are almost devoid of residents—ghost farms.

The trend of this twenty-first century, continuing from the twentieth, is an escalation of development that threatens the integrity and the health of ecosystems. Such developments in culture are likely to have less integrity just because they are misfitted to their supporting biological integrity. Hands-on planetary managers will reply that it is futile to try to maintain pristine natural areas. Nature, at least in the pristine sense, is at an end. We shall increasingly have managed nature, or none at all. Global warming proves that. There are no unmanaged systems, just varieties and degrees of management. Maybe so, but humans rebuild and manage the natural environments across a spectrum of options; and much nature can and ought to remain, producing biotic integrity and health on the landscapes we inhabit. Such health is best had by favoring ecosystem management that, so to speak, "goes with the flow," rather than by hands-on, high-tech management. We have not yet been reduced to nothing but environments that have to be constantly doctored and engineered.

Bioregionalism emphasizes living on regional landscapes. The most workable ethic is where persons identify with their geography. People are likely to be most motivated by what they have at stake on their at-home landscapes. True, one ought to have concern for endangered species, vanishing wildlife, intrinsic natural values, or wilderness conservation; but that is not what orients day-to-day behavior. What is politically possible is concern about the countryside of everyday experience. After all, ecology is about living "at home." That is where the land ethic really operates. That is where people can act, where they vote, and pay taxes. They need to be "natives," as much as "citizens." Michel Serres argues that "the old social contract ought to be joined by a natural contract" (1995, p. 20).

A bioregion, says Kirkpatrick Sale, is "a place defined by its life forms, its topography, and its biota, rather than by human dictates; a region governed by nature, not legislature" (1985, p. 43). Ecosystem management needs a focus on bioregions. Environmental ethics is as much applied geography as it is applied ecology. Such managed bioregionalism appeals to landscape architects, more enlightened developers, state legislators, county commissioners—all those charged with decisions about a quality environment. Ecofeminists may add that women are better suited for such caring than these managerial men, dominated by the "dominion" view, and overly inclined to be aggressive managers. Humans need to learn to "reinhabit" their landscapes. This is environmental ethics on a human scale. We humans are earthlings as well as citizens, and environmental ethics is about *our* sense of place.

Aldo Leopold concludes with a land ethic that he recommends universally. It is no accident, however, that the earlier pages of his *Sand County* [Wisconsin] *Almanac* (1949/1968) remember a January thaw, the spring flowering of *Draba*, the April mating dance of the woodcock. Leopold's biographical residence is the personal backing to his ethic. An environmental ethic needs roots in locality. In this sense, those critics of wilderness were right: ecology dissolves any firm boundary between humans and the natural world. Ecological thinking is a kind of vision across boundaries. Humans have such entwined destinies with the natural world that their richest quality of life involves a larger identification with these communities. Such transformation of the personal self will result in an appropriate care for the environment.

Management does require humanizing the landscapes on which we reside. The future will be, over most of the landscape, inescapably, a managed world. But let us not be too arrogant about our human dominance in this Anthropocene Epoch. Nature has not ended and never will. Humans stave off natural forces, but the natural forces can and will return, if one takes away the humans. In that sense, nature is forever lingering around. Given a chance, which will come sooner or later, natural forces will flush out human effects. Even if the original wildness does not return, nature having been irreversibly knocked into some alternative condition, wildness will return to take what course it may.

Watch what happens on a vacant lot when its former owners/managers move away. One might first think that there is no nature left, since the lot is filled with the rubble of artifacts—pop cans and broken concrete blocks. But nature comes back, and soon there are weeds sprouting up, a lush growth of them, if there is rain and the soil is not too contaminated. We could almost say that nature still knows how to value the place, or knows, as it flushes out the human disruptions, what values to put in place that can still be sustained there. In that sense, a vacant city lot, which might seem to be a place where nature has quite ended, is, if watched a little longer, a place that testifies eloquently to how nature, managed and mismanaged by humans though it may be, does not and cannot end.

Back East—Westerners may say—the abandoned buildings, empty stores, faded signs, unkempt farms with a half dozen old cars and tractors about the barn look—well—just trashy. But on Rocky Mountain prairies or mountains the old cabin with the roof fallen in, or the abandoned corral, convey something more—a sense of the forceful resistance of nature to our human enterprises. There are lichens growing on the broken bricks, and a tree now grows in a corner of what was once the kitchen. The ruined cabin is somber and picturesque, and the conflict between primordial nature and the culture that once sought to modify it brings us to a philosophical conclusion—one reinforced if there is a wilderness boundary sign a quarter mile further up the trail. In, with, and under culture, there is always this once and future nature.

References

Arrow, Kenneth, Partha Dasgupta, Lawrence Goulder, et al. 2004. "Are We Consuming Too Much?" *Journal of Economic Perspectives* 18:147–172.

Barbee, Bob. 2009. "I Was There" *Yellowstone Science* 17 (no. 2):7–10.

Botkin, Daniel B. 1990. *Discordant Harmonies*. New York: Oxford University Press.

Boyce, James K., Sunita Narrain, and Elizabeth A. Stanton, eds. 2007. *Reclaiming Nature: Environmental Justice and Ecological Restoration*. London: Anthem Press.

Burke, Edmund, III, and Kenneth Pomeranz, eds. 2009. *The Environment and World History*. Berkeley: University of California Press.

Cahen, Harley. 1988. "Against the Moral Considerability of Ecosystems," *Environmental Ethics* 10:195–216.

Caldwell, Lynton Keith, and Kristin Shrader-Frechette. 1993. *Policy for Land: Law and Ethics*. Lanham, MD: Rowman and Littlefield.

Callicott, J. Baird. 1991. "The Wilderness Idea Revisited: The Sustainable Development Alternative," *The Environmental Professional* 13:235–247.

Callicott, J. Baird, and Michael P. Nelson, eds. 1998. *The Great New Wilderness Debate*. Athens: University of Georgia Press.

Carpenter, Stephen R., Ruth DeFries, Thomas Dietz, et al., 2006. "Millennium Ecosystem Assessment: Research Needs," *Science* 314(13 October):257–258.

Chan, Kai M. A., Edward J. Gregr, and Sara Klain, 2009. "A Critical Course Change," *Science* 325(11 September):1342–1343.

Cherrett, J. M. 1989. "Key Concepts: The Results of a Survey of Our Members' Opinions." Pages 1–16 in J. M. Cherrett, ed., *Ecological Concepts*. Oxford, UK: Blackwell.

Chipeniuk, Raymond. 1991. "The Old and Middle English Origins of 'Wilderness'," *Environments* 21:22–28.

Cole, Glen F. 1969. *Elk and the Yellowstone System*. U.S. Department of the Interior, Office of Natural Science Studies, National Park Service (Yellowstone National Park Research Library).

Comin, Francisco A., ed. 2010. *Ecological Restoration: A Global Challenge*. Cambridge: Cambridge University Press.

Common, Michael S., and Sigrid Stagl. 2005. *Ecological Economics: An Introduction*. Cambridge,UK: Cambridge University Press.

Costanza, Robert, and Herman E. Daly, 1992. "Natural Capital and Sustainable Development," *Conservation Biology* 6:37–46.

Costanza, Robert, John Cumberland, Herman Daly, Robert Goodland, and Richard Norgaard. 1997. *An Introduction to Ecological Economics*. International Society for Ecological Economics. Boca Raton, FL: St. Lucie Press.

Costanza, Robert, et al., 1998. "The Value of the World's Ecosystem Services and Natural Capital," *Nature* 387:253–260.

Costanza, Robert, Bryan G. Norton, and Benjamin D. Haskell, 1992. *Ecosystem Health: New Goals for Environmental Management*. Washington, D.C.: Island Press.

Cowan, Tyler, ed. 1988. *The Theory of Market Failure: A Critical Examination*. Fairfax, VA: George Mason University Press.

Cronon, William. 1995. "The Trouble with Wilderness, or, Getting Back to the Wrong Nature." Pages 69–90 in William Cronon ed., *Uncommon Ground: Toward Reinventing Nature*. New York: W. W. Norton.

Daly, Herman E., 1977. *Steady State Economics*. San Francisco: W. H. Freeman.

———. 1996. *Beyond Growth: The Economics of Sustainable Development*. Boston: Beacon Press.

Daly, Herman E., and John Cobb, Jr. 1994. *For the Common Good: Redirecting the Economy toward Community, the Environment, and a Sustainable Future*, 2nd ed. Boston: Beacon Press.

Daly, Herman E., and Joshua C. Farley. 2004. *Ecological Economics: Principles and Applications*. Washington, D.C.: Island Press.

Denevan, William M. 1992. "The Pristine Myth: The Landscape of the Americas in 1492," *Annals of the Association of American Geographers* 82:369–385.

Dickins, Bruce, and R. M. Wilson, eds. 1951. *Early Middle English Texts*. Cambridge, UK: Bowes and Bowes.

Donkin, R. A. 1979. *Agricultural Terracing in the Aboriginal New World*. Tucson: University of Arizona Press.

Duffy, David Cameron, and Albert J. Meier. 1992. "Do Appalachian Herbaceous Understories Ever Recover from Clearcutting?" *Conservation Biology* 6:196–201.

Elliot, Robert. 1982. "Faking Nature," *Inquiry* 25:81–93.

Freyfogle, Eric T. 2003. *The Land We Share: Private Property and the Common Good*. Washington, D.C.: Island Press/Shearwater Books.

Gunn, Alastair S. 1991. "The Restoration of Species and Natural Environments," *Environmental Ethics* 13:291–310.

Hannah, Lee, David Lohse, Charles Hutchinson, John L. Carr, and Ali Lankerani. 1994. "A Preliminary Inventory of Human Disturbance of World Ecosystems," *Ambio* 23:246–250.

Hannigan, John A. 1995. *Environmental Sociology: A Social Constructionist Perspective*. London: Routledge.

Ivanhoe, Philip J. 2010. "Of Geese and Eggs: In What Sense Should We Value Nature as a System?" *Environmental Ethics* 32(2010):67–78.

Jordan, William R., III. 1991. "Ecological Restoration and the Reintegration of Ecological Systems." Pages 151–162 in D. J. Roy, B. E. Wynne, and R. W. Old, eds., *Bioscience—Society*. San Francisco: Wiley.

Jordan, William R., III, Michael E. Gilpin, and John D. Aber, eds. 1987. *Restoration Ecology: A Synthetic Approach to Ecological Research*. New York: Cambridge University Press.

Karr, James R., and D. R. Dudley. 1981. "Ecological Perspective on Water Quality Goals," *Environmental Management* 5:55–68.

Katz, Eric. 1992. "The Big Lie: Human Restoration of Nature," *Research in Philosophy and Technology* 12:231–241.

Kauffman, Stuart A. 1991. "Antichaos and Adaptation," *Scientific American* 265(no. 2):78–84.

———. 1993. *The Origins of Order: Self-Organization and Selection in Evolution*. New York: Oxford University Press.

Kidner, David W. 2000. "Fabricating Nature: A Critique of the Social Construction of Nature," *Environmental Ethics* 22:339–357.

Koetsier, P., Paul Dey, Greg Mladenka, and Jim Check. 1990. "Rejecting Equilibrium Theory: A Cautionary Note," *Bulletin of the Ecological Society of America* 71:229–230.

Kolstad, Charles D. 2000. *Ecological Economics*. New York: Oxford University Press.

Krider, E. Philip, 1986. "Lightning Damage and Lightning Protection." Pages 205–229 in Robert

H. Maybury, ed., *Violent Forces of Nature*. Mt. Airy, MD: Lomond Publications (in cooperation with UNESCO).

Kripke, Saul A. 1980. *Naming and Necessity*. Cambridge, MA: Harvard University Press.

Leopold, Aldo. 1949/1968. *A Sand County Almanac*. New York: Oxford University Press.

Lewis, C. S. 1967. *Studies in Words*, 2nd ed. Cambridge, UK: Cambridge University Press.

Lowenthal, David. 1964. "Is Wilderness 'Paradise Enow'? Images of Nature in America," *Columbia University Forum* 7(no. 2):34–40.

Maturana, Humberto R., and Francisco J. Varela. 1980. *Autopoiesis and Cognition: The Realization of the Living*. Dordrecht, The Netherlands: D. Reidel.

McCauley, Douglas J. 2006. "Selling Out on Nature," *Nature* 443:27–28..

McCloskey, J. Michael, and Heather Spalding. 1989. "A Reconnaissance-Level Inventory of the Amount of Wilderness Remaining in the World," *Ambio* 18:221–227.

McLeod, Karen, and Heather Leslie, eds. 2009. *Ecosystem-Based Management for the Oceans*. Washington, D.C.: Island Press.

McShane, Katie, 2004. "Ecosystem Health," *Environmental Ethics* 26:227–245.

Millennium Ecosystem Assessment. 2005a. *Ecosystems and Human Well-being: Synthesis*. Washington, D.C.: Island Press.

———. 2005b. *Living Beyond our Means: Natural Assets and Human Well-Being: Statement from the Board*. http://www.millenniumassessment.org/en/Products.aspx

Mistretta, Paul A. 2002. "Managing for Forest Health," *Journal of Forestry* 100(no. 7):24–27.

Mittermeier, R. A., C. G. Mittermeier, T. M. Brooks, et al. 2003. "Wilderness and Biodiversity Conservation," *Proceedings of the National Academy of Sciences (PNAS), USA* 100:10309–10313.

Nash, Roderick. 1979. "Wilderness is All in Your Mind," *Backpacker* 7(no. 1):39–41, 70–75.

———. 1982. *Wilderness and the American Mind*, 3rd. ed. New Haven, CT: Yale University Press.

O'Connor, Martin. 1993. "On the Misadventures of Capitalist Nature," *Capitalism, Nature, Socialism* 4 (no. 3, September):7–40.

O'Neill, R. V., D. L. DeAngelis, J. B. Waide, and T. F. H. Allen. 1986. *A Hierarchical Concept of Ecosystems*. Princeton, NJ: Princeton University Press.

Orians, Gordon H. 1975. "Diversity, Stability and Maturity in Natural Ecosystems." Pages 139–150 in W. H. van Dobben and R. H. Lowe-McConnell, eds., *Unifying Concepts in Ecology*. The Hague, The Netherlands: Dr. W. Junk B. V. Publishers.

Ostrom, Elinor. 1990. *Governing the Commons: The Evolution of Institutions for Collective Action*. Cambridge, UK: Cambridge University Press.

Pahl-Wostl, Claudia. 1995. *The Dynamic Nature of Ecosystems: Chaos and Order Entwined*. New York: Wiley.

Pearce, David, Anil Markandya, and Edward B. Barbier. 1989. *Blueprint for a Green Economy*. London: Earthscan, 1989.

Peterken, George F. 1996. *Natural Woodland: Ecology and Conservation in Northern Temperate Regions*. Cambridge, UK: Cambridge University Press.

Peters, R. H. 1991. *A Critique for Ecology*. New York: Cambridge University Press.

Pickett, Steward T. A., Thomas Parker, and Peggy Fiedler. 1992. "The New Paradigm in Ecology: Implications for Conservation Biology above the Species Level." Pages 65–88 in P. L Fiedler and S. K. Jain, eds., *Conservation Biology*. New York: Chapman and Hall.

Pimm, Stuart. 1997. "The Value of Everything," *Nature* 387:231–232.

Pyne, Stephen J. 1982. *Fire in America: A Cultural History of Wildland and Rural Fire*. Princeton, NJ: Princeton University Press.

Rapport, David J. 1989. "What Constitutes Ecosystem Health?" *Perspectives in Biology and Medicine* 33:120–132.

Rolston, Holmes, III. 1991. "The Wilderness Idea Reaffirmed," *The Environmental Professional* 13:370–377.

———. 1994. *Conserving Natural Value*. New York: Columbia University Press.

Rothenberg, David. 1992. "The Greenhouse from Down Deep: What Can Philosophy Do for Ecology?" *Pan Ecology* 7(no. 2, Spring):1–3.

Roughgarden, Jonathan. 1983. "Competition and Theory in Community Ecology," *American Naturalist* 122:583–601.

Sale, Kirkpatrick, 1985. *Dwellers in the Land: The Bioregional Vision.* San Francisco: The Sierra Club.

Sanderson, Eric W., Malanding Jaiteh, Marc A. Levy, et al. 2002. "The Human Footprint and the Last of the Wild," *BioScience* 52:891–904.

Schumacher, E. F. 1975. *Small is Beautiful: Economics as if People Mattered.* New York: Harper and Row.

Seastedt, Timothy R., Richard J. Hobbs, and Katharine N. Suding. 2008. "Management of Novel Ecosystems: Are Novel Approaches Required?" *Frontiers in Ecology and the Environment* 6:547–553.

Serres, Michel. 1995. *The Natural Contract.* Ann Arbor: University of Michigan Press.

Shrader-Frechette, Kristin, and Earl D. McCoy. 1994. *Method in Ecology: Strategies for Conservation.* New York: Cambridge University Press.

Smith, Mick. 1995. "A Green Thought in a Green Shade: A Critique of the Rationalization of Environmental Values." Pages 51–60 in Yvonne Guerrier, Nicholas Alexander, Jonathan Case, and Martin O'Brien, eds., *Values and the Environment: A Social Science Perspective.* Chichester, UK: Wiley.

Soulé, Michael E. 1995. "The Social Siege of Nature." Pages 137–170 in M. E. Soulé and G. Lease, eds., *Reinventing Nature? Responses to Postmodern Deconstruction.* Washington, D.C.: Island Press.

Spash, Clive. 1999. "The Development of Environmental Thinking in Economics," *Environmental Values* 8:413–435.

Stokstad, Erik, 2009. "On the Origin of Ecological Structure," *Science* 326:33–35.

Udall, Stewart. 1968. Statement to *House Committee on Science and Astronautics,* 90th U.S. Congress, 2nd session, *Colloquium to Discuss a National Policy for the Environment.* Committee Print.

U.S. Congress. 1964. The Wilderness Act of 1964. 78 Stat. 891. Public Law 88–577.

———. 1969. National Environmental Policy Act, 83 Stat. 852. Public Law 91–190.

Vogel, Steven. 1996. *Against Nature: The Concept of Nature in Critical Theory.* Albany: State University of New York Press.

Vogel, Steven. 2002. "Environmental Philosophy after the End of Nature," *Environmental Ethics* 24:23–39.

Wackernagel, Mathis, and William E. Rees. 1996. *Our Ecological Footprint: Reducing Human Impact on the Earth.* Gabriola Island, BC, Canada: New Society Publishers.

Westman, Walter E. 1991. "Ecological Restoration Projects: Measuring their Performance," *Environmental Professional* 13:207–215.

Worster, Donald. 1990. "Seeing Beyond Culture," *The Journal of American History* 76:1142–1147.

Zimmerman, Michael E. 1994. *Contesting Earth's Future: Radical Ecology and Postmodernity.* Berkeley: University of California Press.

7

EARTH

Ethics on the Home Planet

Views of Earth from space are the most impressive photographs ever taken. They are the most widely distributed ever, having been seen by well over half the persons on Earth. Few are not moved to a moment of truth, at least in their pensive moods. The whole Earth is aesthetically stimulating, philosophically challenging, and ethically disturbing. "I remember so vividly," said astronaut Michael Collins, "what I saw when I looked back at my fragile home—a glistening, inviting beacon, delicate blue and white, a tiny outpost suspended in the black infinity. Earth is to be treasured and nurtured, something precious that *must* endure" (1980, p. 6). There is a vision of an Earth ethic in what he sees. Leopold's land ethic needs to be upscaled to the planetary level. "What's the use of a house if you haven't got a tolerable planet to put it on?" asked Thoreau a century and a half ago (1860/1906, p. 360).

Environmental ethics today faces global issues: the hole in the ozone layer, acid rain, biogeochemistry, global warming; sustainable development and biodiversity in Africa or the Amazon, escalating populations, environmental refugees, migrating birds. Environmentalists have to consider the environmental policies of the World Bank, of The North American Free Trade Agreement (NAFTA), and the World Trade Organization (WTO). Concerns about environmental justice arise where the poor bear disproportionately the burdens of environmental degradation. Is it fair that developed nations, with one-fifth of the world's population consume four-fifths of its resources? We have already had to ask who owns genetic resources in tropical rainforests, who can patent their use, and whether world ivory trade should be banned in order to protect elephants. What about the rights of indigenous peoples in nature reserves? What about this new buzzword: "globalization" (Beck, 2000)?

Debate at the United Nations Conference on Environment and Development (UNCED) at Rio de Janeiro in 1992 was about how to couple in one worldview divergent opinions on two urgent issues: many nations on a single planet. "The Earth is one but the world is not" (United Nations World Commission on Environment and Development, 1987, p. 27). The main document produced, *Agenda 21*, is probably the most complex and comprehensive international document ever attempted. The results of the conference have been less effective than many hoped, but at least ethics, global and local, were always on the agenda, and environmental values were fundamental to every topic discussed.

Even where the commission failed to act, the failure indicated how much of value was at stake in the issues negotiated. The issues that coalesced there have been gathering over the last five hundred years, are with us today and tomorrow (evidenced in the Copenhagen summit, see below), and they will be with us for another five hundred. The then UN Secretary-General, Boutros Boutros-Ghali, closed the Earth Summit: "The Spirit of Rio must create a new mode of civic conduct. It is not enough for man to love his neighbour; he must also learn to love his world" (1992, p. 1).

Ethics in the modern West, has been almost entirely interhuman ethics, persons finding a way to relate morally to other persons—loving our neighbors. Ethics seeks to find a satisfactory fit for humans in their communities; and this has meant that ethics has often dwelt on justice, fairness, love, rights, or peace, settling the disputes of right and wrong that arise among us. But ethics now is anxious also about the troubled planet, its fauna, flora, species, and ecosystems. The two great marvels of our planet are life and mind, both among the rarest things in the universe. In the global picture, the late-coming, moral species, *Homo sapiens*, arising a few hundred thousand years ago, has, still more lately in this century, gained startling powers for the rebuilding and modification, including the degradation, of this home planet.

These are human concerns, yes. The interests of environmental ethics when done from perspectives of political ecology, sustainable development, bioregionalism, ecojustice, from an ethics of stewardship, or human virtuous caring, or a sense of place—all these tend to be humanistic and to recognize that nature and culture have entwined destinies. Still, more comprehensively, a perspective with yet more depth sees entwined destinies, people with other people, people with their planet, responsible caring in and for human and biotic communities. Animals, plants, species, ecosystems, land—perhaps these have seemed progressively less familiar ethical territory. Now, an ethic for Earth itself may seem the oddest of all.

On this Earth, home to several million species, humans are the only species who can reflect about their land ethic, about the future of the planet. Earth is the planet "right (suitable) for life," and ethics asks about the (moral) "right to life" on such a planet. Certainly it seems "right" that life should continue here. Life is, in the deepest sense, the most valuable phenomenon of all. Environmental ethics is the elevation to ultimacy of an urgent world vision (Rolston, 1995; Rasmussen, 1996; Attfield, 1999; Pojman, 2000; Singer, 2002).

1. Humans as Earthlings: Unique Species on a Unique Planet

We have named ourselves the wise species (*Homo sapiens*). This *Homo* that is so *sapiens* is today better placed than any generation in human history to ask these questions. We have been discovering deep space and deep time, as well as pushing "deep down" from molecular to subatomic nature. Humans can seem minuscule at astronomical levels, cosmic dwarfs; they can seem ephemeral on evolutionary scales. If the length of the river of life were proportioned to stretch around the globe, the human journey would be halfway across a county, and humans would have kept a journal for only a few hundred feet. The individual's reach would be a couple of steps. The human world stands about midway between the infinitesimal and the immense on natural scales. The mass of a human being is the geometric mean of the mass of Earth and the mass of a proton. "The human scale is, in a numerical sense, poised midway between atoms and stars" (Rees, 2001, p. 183). A person contains about 10^{28} atoms, more atoms than there are stars in the universe. In astronomical nature and micronature, at both ends of the spectrum of size, nature lacks the complexity that it demonstrates at the mesolevels, found at our native ranges on Earth. We humans do not live at the range of the infinitely small, nor at that of the infinitely large, but we may well live at the range of the infinitely complex. We considered earlier, in Chapter 2, whether humans are a part of or apart from nature; one of our conclusions was that the human brain is hyperimmensely complex. If we ask where are the "deep" thoughts about this "deep" nature, they are right here—in the minds of those reading this book.

Humans are a unique species on a unique planet. Andrew H. Knoll celebrates "Earth's immense evolutionary epic": "The scientific account of life's long history abounds in both narrative verve and mystery" (Knoll, 2003, p. xi). Steven Stanley finds: "dramatic evolutionary radiations" (2007, p. 11). What is novel on Earth is this explosive power to generate information vital to life using DNA. Nature on Earth rings the changes on these biomolecular possibilities, exploring biodiversity in adaptive fit.

There are other planets. The presence of several hundred possible planets has been detected, and these do seem to be diverse, though none suitable for life is yet known. Rather, it seems that planetary systems configured like our solar system are quite rare. If there proves to be a second (or prior) genesis of life elsewhere, that will be welcome. But Earth will not on that account cease to be remarkable, nor will its particular natural history—trilobites, dinosaurs, primates—and social history—Israel, Europe, China, global capitalism—cease to be unique in the universe.

We might yet discover life in our solar system, though discovering intelligent life seems quite unlikely. We might detect life on relatively near stars, but about life in other galaxies we are likely to remain long in ignorance; the distances are too great. The only second genesis we are likely ever to be able to detect in the vast reaches of space is the unlikeliest of all that we will find: intelligent life smart enough to transmit electronic signals across space. Peter D. Ward and Donald Brownlee make such conclusions, indicated in their title: *Rare Earth: Why Complex Life Is Uncommon in the Universe* (2000). Again, given the distances in space and time, we are unlikely to be able to communicate with such life. We may be the result of cosmic natural history generally, of earthen natural history peculiarly, the most complex event in the universe, and stuck in our solitude.

A good planet is hard to find, and Earth is something of an anomaly, so far as we yet know. Most planets, even though they contain suitable elements, will not be in a habitable temperature zone. Located at a felicitous distance from the sun, Earth has huge amounts of liquid water: seven oceans covering about three-quarters of its surface. *Aqua* would have been a better name than *Earth*. On Earth there is atmosphere, a suitable mix of elements, compounds, minerals, and an ample supply of energy. "It appears that Earth got it just right," conclude Peter Ward and Donald Brownlee (2000, p. 265). William C. Berger does call Earth a "perfect planet." "I believe we can all agree that we live on a glorious planet, and that our intellectual achievements have been quite amazing" (Berger, 2003, p. 3). An amazing species on a glorious planet: That seems to call for an environmental ethics.

One might first think that, since humans presumably evolved as good adapted fits in their environments, human nature will complement wild nature. Biologists may call this "biophilia," an innate, genetically based disposition to love animals, plants, landscapes with trees, open spaces, running water (Wilson, 1984). Critics find this a half truth because disconfirming evidence is everywhere. True, people like a house with a garden, with a view, but they do like a house, a big one. People are builders; their construction industry is what is destroying nature. People prefer culturally modified environments. "Man is the animal for whom it is natural to be artificial" (Garvin, 1953, p. 378). Neil Evernden says that *Homo sapiens* is "the natural alien" (1993).

The really natural thing for humans to do (our genetic disposition) is to build a culture differentiating (alienating) ourselves from nature. Human agriculture, business, industry, development consumes most of our lives, and the search for nature is only avocational recreation. Biophilia might be a positive genetic tendency. But other genetic legacies are problematic. Any residual biophilia is weak before our much more powerful desires for the goods of culture. We did earlier say that for humans to be three-dimensional persons, they must have urban and rural environments (as well as encounter with wild nature).

Now environmental ethicists find themselves with a new worry: Humans are the wise species (*Homo sapiens*), yes, but, alas, they still have Pleistocene appetites. Our evolutionary past did not give us many biological controls on our desires for goods that were in short supply. We love sweets and fats, of which in Pleistocene times humans could seldom get enough. But now we overeat and grow fat. We love sex, because in Pleistocene times, a couple reproducing as often as they could, in those days of infant and child morality, would hardly replace themselves with offspring who reached reproductive age.

Generally, that is a model for the whole overconsumption problem. True, we are a smart species. Our global powers prove that. No other species threatens Earth as do humans. Maybe we are, or ought to be, the wise species morally as well as technologically, but humans are not well equipped to deal with the sorts of global level problems we now face. We may have engines and gears, but we still have muscle and blood appetites. There are few biological controls on our desires to amass goods, to consume; for most people it has always been a struggle to get enough (indeed for many it still is). When we can consume, we love it, and over-consume. Consumer capitalism transmutes a once-healthy pattern of desires into gluttony and avarice. With escalating opportunities for consumption, driven by markets in search of profits, we need more self-discipline than comes naturally. We will next be worrying about global capitalism.

Are humans wise enough to act globally on long-term, environmentally responsible scales? The classical institutions—family, village, tribe, nation, agriculture, industry, law, medicine, even school and often church—have shorter horizons. Far-off descendants and distant races do not have much "biological hold" on us, yet our actions can gravely harm them. Across the era of human evolution, little in our behavior affected those remote from us in time or in space, and natural selection shaped only our conduct toward those closer. Global threats require us to act in massive concert of which we are incapable. If so, humans may bear within themselves the seeds of their own destruction. More bluntly, more scientifically put: our genes, once enabling our adaptive fit, may in the next millennium prove mal-adaptive and destroy us.

At first it seems obvious that self-deception is unwise, and could not possibly contribute to survival. Deer do not survive if self-deceived about cougars, nor do humans if self-deceived about their enemies. But matters get more complex in environments of high uncertainty, complex interactions, with multiple levels of results and with lag times for those results, especially where you must change customary perceptions, especially those to which you are genetically inclined.

You may do better facing the immediate future if you have a higher view of your powers to control future outcomes than the facts actually justify—unwarranted optimism. You win because you believe you can; if you don't, you lose. You do better still if you can convince others that you are right; you may get to be a leader in your community. Leaders want the good news; that promotes their agenda. They mute the bad news. They have a tendency to suppress or delay, or disbelieve the warning signs. There is an institutional tendency for bad news, discovered or suspected down in the shop or out in the field, to be suppressed as it rises up the institutional hierarchy. The bad seal on NASA Challenger 7 is a famous example (Vaughan, 1996). Engineers warned of the problem but upper echelons in NASA, in their enthusiasm for the mission, ignored it. That may also be happening in those who promote the good news of global capitalism.

2. Global Capitalism: Just? Fair? Enough!

Capitalism has many defenders. One is reminded of Winston Churchill's remark that democracy is the worst form of government, except for all the others. Both democracy and capitalism have increased human wealth. With the collapse of socialist communism, it is the only game in town (Norberg, 2003; Friedman, 2005). Also the best game in town, many argue, because global capitalism promises the rest of the world what it has given to America, Europe, and similarly developed nations: a widespread improvement in average incomes.

Capitalists are aggressive about promoting their capitalism, and making money doing so. If we are to offer first world lifestyles to everyone, they will have to do what the developed West did—become enterprising capitalists. The world economic order needs to be increasingly integrated with the reduction of trade barriers such as tariffs, export fees, import quotas, protectionist policies. Markets will be more efficient when driven by competition and by national specialization, as each country can produce at home and sell widely what it has resources for and makes best. Bigger markets and comparative advantage are made possible by increasing international interdependence—instant communication, swift transportation, advanced technologies. This opens up once-provincial societies. Developing nations will no longer be dependent on foreign aid—"trade not aid." The World Trade Organization (WTO) promotes globalization. Everybody wins under laissez-faire economics—at least those who are competitive.

A constant tension has been that nations with strong governments may regulate their industries and agriculture, forcing these (by permits, taxes, penalties) to be more environmentally responsible (avoiding pollution, promoting re-cycling). But this enlightened regulation disadvantages their industries in world markets, when other nations, with weaker or more corrupt governments, permit environmental degradation, in order to produce cheaper. China's recent economic advances have owed much to this willingness to trash its environment for profit. The rich lose, made less competitive. The poor may lose too. Breaking out of poverty requires an effective state to enforce workers rights and environmental health (Pogge, 2002). Otherwise, workers in such countries may themselves suffer as well, from water or air pollution, that their companies have no incentive to curtail. The World Trade Organization has opposed such environmental regulations by its member states. NAFTA is often thought to be even worse in discouraging environmental regulations. The result: an environmental race to the bottom.

Environmental issues, capitalist promoters may say, are not directly the concern of the international entrepreneurs (except perhaps as they affect public safety and health), but capital will flow to the poorer countries. Industry and competition will increase wages. Development can shift what these peoples sell in markets from low-profit raw or semiprocessed goods to high-profit manufactured goods and services. Such capitalist development in the poorer countries will soon make them rich enough so that they can afford environmental protection. (The World Bank has over a dozen indicators of poverty [World Bank, 2008].)

Maximizing profits in a free-trade world may produce many benefits. But business that is so minded has no evident concern for biodiversity, for preserving scenic beauty on landscapes, or even for local sustainability—if it can cut and run to another country at will. The United States wished to restrict imports of Mexican tuna that had been caught with nets that also killed dolphins. But NAFTA did not consider this to be a legitimate reason for restricting such imports. (That problem had to be solved outside NAFTA, with consumer boycotts.) The World Trade Organization has not allowed concerns about genetically modified agricultural products to be considered (so long as the food is safe to eat). Joseph E. Stiglitz (to whom we return below) recommends mandated labeling that would give consumers the opportunity to find out the environmental and human costs of the products they purchase, boycotting them if they wish (Stiglitz, 2006). But voluntary environmental protection is often weak environmental protection.

A central problem with contemporary global, capitalist-based development is that the rich grow richer and the poor poorer. Even where the poor grow rich, this may make others poorer. Many fear that this is neither ethical nor sustainable. Free trade moves capital and goods across national boundaries in international markets, but the labor also required for production is confined within nations, which means that capital can relocate production facilities and seek the cheapest labor. Capitalists can export ("outsource") jobs too, especially those that can be done on computers or online, there again in search of cheap labor. You may find that your phone call to your local bank, for example, is answered by someone in India. Capitalists win, labor loses (Daly, 2003; Daly and Cobb, 1994). The disproportionate distribution of wealth has coincided with increasing environmental consumption.

Global inequalities in income increased in the twentieth century by orders of magnitude, out of proportion to anything experienced before. The distance between the incomes of the richest and poorest country was about 3 to 1 in 1820, 35 to 1 in 1950, 44 to 1 in 1973, and 72 to 1 in 1992 (United Nations Development Programme [UNDP], 2000, p. 6; Atkinson and Piketty, 2010). For most of the world's poorest countries the past decade has continued a disheartening trend: not only have they failed to reduce poverty, but they are falling further behind rich countries (UNDP, 2005, p. 36). Now the disproportion is approaching 100 to 1. The world's poorest people (those living on less than $1 per day), about a billion persons, has decreased a little in recent decades. But the number of the quite poor (those living on less than about $2 per day), some two billion persons, remains more or less the same. The income gap between the richest one-third of nations and the poorest one-third has declined, but the income gap between the richest one-tenth and the poorest one-tenth has increased (Scott, 2001). For the first time in human history, since 2009, there are over a billion persons suffering from hunger, about one-sixth of the human race (FAO, 2009).

Lest we think this is only a problem for the developing countries, income inequality within the United States has also increased to the highest recorded levels. The top fifth of wage-earners get 49% of the pay; the bottom fifth get 3.4%. The United States has the greatest income disparity among Western industrialized nations. The government does have welfare programs that prevent the poor from starving; and laborers are paid more than enough to feed themselves and their families. But they are not receiving the benefits of increased efficiencies in production nearly as much as are their bosses (Noah, 2010, Kristof, 2010; Piketty and Saez, 2007).

The distribution of wealth raises complex issues of merit, luck, justice, charity, natural resources, national boundaries, global commons. The Earth is richly, but unevenly endowed with natural resources. Nations have diverse but uneven powers of extracting their resources, diverse and uneven powers of allocating and manufacturing these natural resources. Nations well endowed with natural resources may be noticeably worse off economically than many resource-poor jurisdictions—through exploitation, corruption, lack of development. Vice versa, nations with poor endowments in natural resources may be developed and wealthy—through trade, industry, technology, colonial powers (Morriss, 2009). Even if there were a more equitable distribution of resources, enforced by legislation, the citizens in such nations might press their politicians to develop unsustainably. People always want more, we were saying.

Still, by any standards this distribution seems unjustly disproportionate. The inevitable result stresses people on their landscapes, forcing environmental degradation, with instability and collapse (Homer-Dixon, 1999). The poor are forced to farm marginal lands, increasingly subject to droughts, as in Saharan Africa, or to plant further up on easily eroded hillsides, as in Nicaragua,

Honduras, and El Salvador. The rich and powerful are equally ready to exploit people and nature—animals, plants, species, ecosystems, and Earth itself. Ecofeminists have found this to be especially true where both women and nature are together exploited. Even if human ethicists are unwilling to conserve nature for what it is in itself, they do need to take full measure of the distribution of the benefits of exploiting natural resources.

The overconsumption problem with the rich in the developed nations is linked with the underconsumption problem among the poor in the developing nations, and this results in increasing environmental degradation in both sets of nations. Even in developing nations, the newly rich exploit the poor. Sustainable development must close the gap between the rich and the poor, between and also within nations (Gasper, 2004). Even if there were an equitable distribution of wealth, the human population cannot go on escalating without people becoming more and more poor, because the pie has to be constantly divided into smaller pieces. And even if there were no future population growth, consumption patterns cannot go on escalating on a finite Earth (Speth, 2008; Sachs, 2008). There are three problems: overpopulation, overconsumption, and underdistribution.

Such issues come under another inclusive term "environmental justice," a concern we already found to be pivotal in the environmental turn in Chapter 1 (Schlosberg, 2007; Attfield and Wilkins, 1992; Wenz, 1988; Lewis, MacLeod, and Brownsword, 2004–2008). That is the persisting claim that social justice is so linked with environmental conservation that a more fair distribution of the world's wealth is required for any sustainable conservation even of rural landscapes, much less of wildlife and wildlands. Not only are the wealthy faulted, but equally environmental ethicists will now be faulted for overlooking the poor (often of a different race, class, or sex) in their concern to save the elephants. Here the argument takes a new turn. The poor are kept poor because their development is not only constrained by the wealthy but by the setting aside of biodiversity reserves, forest reserves, hunting and catching limits. The livelihood of such poor people, for example, may be adversely affected by the elephants, who trash their crops.

Or it may be adversely affected because the pollution dump is located on their already degraded landscapes—and not in the backyard (or even on the national landscapes) of the rich. They may be poor because they are living on degraded landscapes, the degradation started by colonial empires, continued by global capitalists, and exacerbated by local poverty. Such peoples are likely to remain poor, even if developers arrive, because they will be too poorly paid to break out of their poverty.

Joseph Stiglitz, Nobel laureate, when he was Chief Economist for the World Bank, became increasingly ethically concerned about the effects of globalization on the poor.

While I was at the World Bank, I saw firsthand the devastating effect that globalization can have on developing countries, and especially the poor within those countries.... Especially at the International Monetary Fund ... decisions were made on the basis of what seemed a curious blend of ideology and bad economics, dogmas that sometimes seemed to be thinly veiling special interests ... The IMF's policies, in part based on the outworn presumption that markets, by themselves, lead to efficient outcomes, failed to allow for desirable government interventions in the market, measures which can guide economic growth and make *everyone* better off.

(2002, pp., ix, xiii, xii)

Nor are governments, pushed by such financial interests, always willing so to guide economic growth. Stiglitz wrote in April 2000:

I was chief economist at the World Bank from 1996 until last November, during the gravest global economic crisis in a half-century. I saw how the IMF, in tandem with the U.S. Treasury Department, responded. And I was appalled.

(2000, p. 56)

For such concerns about these effects of the distribution of wealth he was pressured into resigning and his contract with the World Bank was terminated. Alarmed by the increasing inequity of wealth, both internationally and domestically, Nicholas Kristof worries: "Huge concentrations of wealth corrode the soul of any nation (2010, p. A37). Ethicists need now and forever in the future to remember Lord Acton: "Power tends to corrupt and absolute power corrupts absolutely" (1887/1949, p. 364). Capitalism drives people, rich and poor, ever to want more, more, more. Especially if one excludes China, an anomalously socialist capitalism, the record of globalization for bettering the poor is unimpressive. The world would be much closer to meeting the promise of globalization if we could change free trade to fair trade (Stiglitz, Sen, and Fitoussi, 2009). The inequitable distribution of wealth is always coupled, as we have noted, with stress on the ecosystems that underlie human prosperity.

Interestingly, in recent research two of the places where it looks as though humans do learn a sense of global concern and fairness are in international markets and in religion. This dimension of religion might have been expected, especially the world religions which transcend individual and nations with a sense of compassion for, the worth and dignity of all humans, as reflected, for instance, in Christian or Buddhist missions. Learning fairness in markets may seem counter-intuitive, since markets are driven by self interest. Have we not just been much concerned about the rich exploiting the poor? But markets also require reciprocity, keeping one's bargain, truth-telling, putting oneself in another's frame of mind, turn-about and fair play—else the markets collapse.

In local markets, fair trading can be reinforced by punishment and ostracism, but in international markets this becomes harder because markets are more anonymous and indirectly reciprocal. Even if individual actors are still driven by their Pleistocene genes to act in their self-interest, social mores and corporate institutions arise that set fairness norms, generate a sense of solidarity, of trusting others, and educate the actors to their larger responsibilities (Henrich, Ensminger, and McElreath, 2010). This sustains markets, but establishing such enlarged sense of responsibility is likely to need all the help we can get from philosophers, with their concerns about both argument and morality. We are likely still further to need help from environmental philosophers with concerns about conserving natural value.

As we know from the previous chapter, ecological economists worry that economists have not yet really faced up to the problem of endless growth. Capitalism never teaches anyone to say: "Enough!" Perhaps the best way to make this point is graphically. Look at Figures 7.1a through 7.1f (Cohen, 1995; Steffen et al., 2004; Nordhaus 1977; World Commission on Dams 2000; International Fertilizer Industry Association, 2011; United Nations Environment Programme, 1999). Notice the year 1950 on these graphs, which is about the time global capitalism went into high gear. These graphs are primarily about escalating consumption in developed countries, but the first of the graphs, world population, reminds us that there are escalating numbers of people, who would, if they could, share this escalating consumption.

FIGURE 7.1 Escalating Consumption and Population (Cohen, 1995; Steffen et al, 2004; Nordhaus, 1977; World Commission on Dams 2000; International Fertilizer Industry Association, 2011; United Nations Environment Programme, 1999.

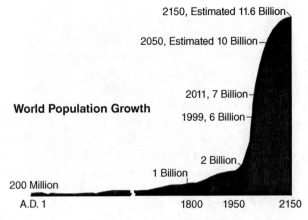

FIGURE 7.1a

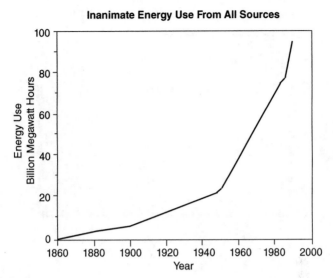

FIGURE 7.1b

The best development, according to Nobel-Prize winning economist Amartya Sen, is development that increases freedom. People want and deserve to enrich their capabilities, opportunities to choose how they want to live, and this does require political liberties, property rights, education, health care, but it does not require increasing consumption. They may ask: Where can I get the best deal? The most money? Return on investment? But they may further ask:

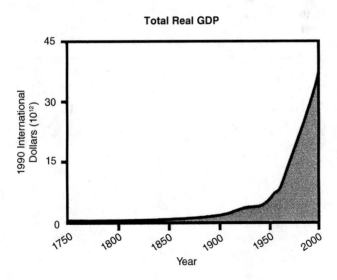

FIGURE 7.1C

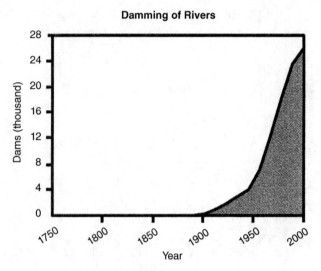

FIGURE 7.1d

How can I live the most meaningful life? The most virtuous life? The richest life? Discover the most value? Enjoy the most significant and sustained community? They may rather prefer lives more richly lived on landscapes they love, which they also protect for future generations (Sen, 1999). "Consider our sense of responsibility towards the future of other species, not merely because—nor only to the extent that—their presence enhances our own living standards" (Sen, 2004, p. 10).

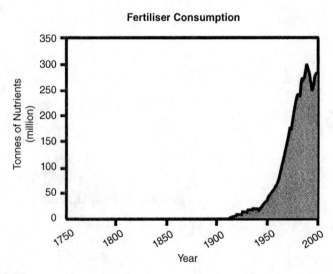

FIGURE 7.1e

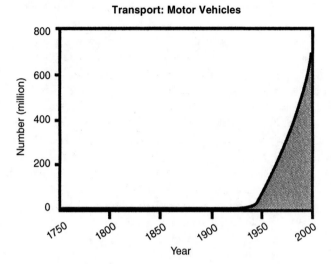

FIGURE 7.1f

Fine sounding words, the poor may reply, but it is hard to be free or conserve endangered species on $2 a day. Still, one conclusion seems inescapable. The kind of development we have seen over the past fifty years is not sustainable. Environmental ethics on global and regional scales is inextricably coupled with development ethics.

3. Global Population: Full Earth?

World population has escalated dramatically, taking almost a right angle turn in 1950 (see Figure 7.1). Population growth is concentrated in Asia, Africa, and Latin America, though it is significant even in the United States. (See details in UN Department of Economic and Social Affairs, 2008; World Bank Development Indicators, 2010.) Projections of the future vary, usually given as low, medium, and high scenarios, ranging from 8 billion to 11 billion to 14 billion by 2050. As we already noted, some 2 billion of the present 6.8 billion persons are poor, and population growth is dominantly among the poor (although population growth among the rich contributes disproportionately to escalating consumption). Currently, about 80 million persons are added to Earth's population each year. A frequent argument is that getting such persons fed is impossible without development. A frequent counter is that feeding escalating populations is impossible without environmental degradation, making feeding them increasingly more difficult (Ehrlich and Ehrlich, 1996). Either way, overpopulation is a problem (McKibben, 1998).

Population increase as such does not cause many of the concerns in the environmental crisis (acid rain, global warming, oil spills, pesticides in groundwater, DDT in eggshells). Still, ever larger numbers of humans certainly increase deforestation, soil losses, biodiversity loss, pollution; and, when these additional persons start developing, these effects will grow worse. An escalating population of impoverished people in Madagascar rely heavily on slash-and-burn agriculture, and the forest cover is down to one-third of its original (27.6 million acres to 9.4 million acres), most of the loss occurring since 1950 (Wilson, 1992, p. 267; Jolly, 1980). Madagascar is the most eroded nation on Earth. Population is expanding at 3.2% a year; remaining forest is shrinking at 3%, almost all to provide for the expanding population. This harms Madagascar's people, leads to extinctions of Madagascar's endemic species, and contributes to global warming. Limits to consumption (saying enough) must be complemented by limits to population (saying enough).

Opposition to limiting population size (often called pro-natalism) frequently has a religious basis. "Be fruitful and multiply, and fill the earth" (Genesis 1.28). Equally, it has a humanistic basis (people are a good thing; people have a right to reproduce), nationalist bases (people build nations, serve in armies, raise the crops), and commercial bases (labor in factories, customers in markets). There may be arguments about race and class bias (e.g., the whites do not want the blacks to have many children). Also, the desire to have children is built into our genes, as we recognized. There is a scientific basis. Since Pleistocene times, the human race has had to reproduce itself every generation. Natural selection favors those who can leave the most offspring in the next generation. Motherhood is a classic virtue. Environmental advocates find it hard to be "against people," so they turn to other environmental issues on which they think they can make more progress.

But too many people is indeed a serious problem. Thomas Malthus was arguing, in 1796, that population can increase exponentially (ten children, each of which a generation later has ten children), but food production, though it may increase, cannot increase exponentially, which will soon strain resources. The outcome will be starvation, postponed perhaps by farming previously wild lands, or, by one nation taking over the produce of another or by high-technology agriculture ("the green revolution").

Capitalist entrepreneurs may argue that free enterprise will promote escalating food production (Simon, 1981). Environmentalists may notice that such produced food is usually controlled by these capitalists, moving small farmers away from control over their own local food production. We have to worry not simply about producing enough food but about getting it distributed to those who need it. The poor may not be able to buy the food that is in their markets.

If a man and his wife have two surviving children, that is replacement rate. Since some have no children, the usual figure given as a statistical average replacement rate is 2.1. Above that, population will increase, surprisingly fast if even a little above. At the current growth rate of 1.11%, Earth's population will double in sixty-three years. In some nations, reproduction is below replacement; in many it is above replacement. Another way of thinking about this is that the number of deaths must equal the number of births. Environmentalists often claim that Earth, and the nations on it, need zero population growth (immigration must be figured in here); many claim that the Earth, or at least that much of the Earth, already has too many people. Studies such as the *Millennium Ecosystem Assessment* and those by the Intergovernmental Panel on Climate Change support these claims.

That the Earth is too full may be expressed as the idea that a region has a "carrying capacity" (some number of persons that can live well in that region) (Hardin, 1976). Others argue that, though this concept may make sense in ecosystems, it cannot be transferred to humans living on landscapes—because humans can get food from thousands of miles away, for example, someone living in Maine may get bananas from Central America (Aiken, 1980). The average bite of food eaten in the United States has traveled 1,200 miles. Whatever the merits of living and eating locally, humans in developed nations do not really live in a local ecology. But they do depend on ecosystems somewhere that are capable of growing their food.

Lest U.S. readers think population a problem only in developing nations, consider U.S. population growth. The United States has a total estimated resident population of nearly 312 million, the third largest in the world. The American population more than tripled during the twentieth century at a growth rate of about 1.3% a year from about 76 million in 1900 to 281 million in 2000. It reached the 200 million mark in 1967, and the 300 million mark in 2006. The total fertility rate in the United States estimated for 2010 is 2.01 children per woman, which is below the replacement threshold of 2.1. However, U.S. population growth is among the highest among industrialized countries, largely because the U.S. has higher levels of immigration. Immigrants and their U.S.-born descendants are expected to provide most of the U.S. population gains in the decades ahead. The Census Bureau projects a U.S. population of 439 million in 2050, which is a 46% increase from 2007. Such growth is unlike most European countries, especially Germany, Russia, Italy, and Greece, or Asian countries such as Japan or South Korea, whose populations are slowly declining, and whose fertility rates are below replacement (data from U.S. Census Bureau, 2010).

Fertility declines with prosperity (often called the demographic transition). By this account development will fix the problem (Hollander, 2003). Wealthy people do not want many children. But, of course, we have already noticed that developing people, though they may have fewer children, immediately escalate their consumption. Environmentalist critics may respond that, though the wealthy have fewer children, this level of wealth is reached too late. Or in many nations never reached at all, because, with the poor, a little more prosperity always brings more children, enough to eat up the prosperity, and, on the whole, people are hardly better off than before—and making more demands on their environments. The typical African nation today has over three times the population there some half century back, when these nations became independent, escaping colonialism. The population of Egypt was less than 3 million for over 5 millennia, fluctuating between 1.5 to 2.5 million, even when Napoleon went there in the early 1800s. Today, the population of Egypt is about 55 million. Egypt has to import more than half the food it needs. The effects on nature, both on land health and on wildlife on the landscape, have been adversely proportional.

Fixing population growth requires a focus on birth control, not on making the poor affluent. This is something of a chicken and egg problem. With increasing population numbers, it becomes highly problematic just to get the needy fed, to say nothing of making them rich. The main reason that planners seldom really consider the high population scenario (14 billion) is that billions of people would be starving before Earth had that many people on it.

One reply is that the focus needs to be neither development nor birth control, but education. In Africa, planners say, keep young girls in school until at least the eighth grade, and that will turn the tide. In Zimbabwe in the 1980s, with a growth rate of some 3.5%, the average married woman *desired* to have six children (Bongaarts, 1994). That growth rate has today been reduced to nearly zero (World Bank Development Indicators, 2010). When women have sufficient education, they have knowledge and power enough to make informed decisions about reproduction, less dependence on their men for support, now having workplace skills themselves, and better overall health. Mothers are more responsible than fathers for getting the children fed. With smarter mothers, population growth declines.

Whatever the complexities, whatever the solutions, it is difficult to argue that increasing population is not a serious environmental problem. The four most critical issues that humans currently face are peace, population, development, and environment. All are interrelated. Human desires for maximum development drive population increases, escalate exploitation of the environment, and fuel the forces of war. All this impoverishes life, reduces biodiversity, degrades landscapes, sacrifices wildlife and wildlands. These desires also escalate the temperature, threatening the climate.

4. Global Warming: Too Hot To Handle!

The climate is more global than the economy. Before we congratulate ourselves too much on living in the Anthropocene Epoch and being planetary managers, we ought to worry whether global warming is a global-scale issue that humans may be unable to deal with. It is, so to speak, too hot to handle. The heat is first climatological, but secondly economic and political, and in the end moral. Global warming is a threat to the global Earth and is at the same time "a perfect moral storm," that is, an utter or consummate moral quandary (Gardiner,

2011, 2006; 2004; Rock Ethics Institute, n.d.; Arnold, 2011; Posner and Weis-bach, 2010; Leichenko and O'Brien, 2008; Northcott, 2007; Jamieson, 2001; Holden, 1996). The storm is absolute, comprehensive, inclusive, ultimate; there is an unprecedented convergence of complexities, natural and technological uncertainties, global and local interactions, difficult choices scientifically, ethi-cally, politically, socially.

There are differing cross-cultural perspectives on a common heritage. There are intergenerational issues, distributional issues, concerns about merit, justice, benevolence, about voluntary and involuntary risk. There is a long lag time, from decades to hundreds of years. Surely but gradually, local *goods* cumulate into global *bads*. There are opportunities for denial, procrastination, self-decep-tion, hypocrisy, free-riding, cheating, and corruption. Individual and national self-interest is at odds with collective global interests. Garrett Hardin gave us the term "tragedy of the commons," which occurs when individuals, sharing a resource held in common, each act in self-interest and the collective result progressively degrades the collective resource. He illustrated this by shepherds placing more and more sheep on land held in common (1968). That local meta-phor has become global. Global warming is this "tragedy of the commons," now taken at the pitch.

Global warming is one human activity that might make everything on Earth unnatural. Upsetting the climate upsets everything: air, water, soils, for-ests, fauna and flora, ocean currents, shorelines, agriculture, property values, international relations, because it is a systemic upset to the elemental givens on Earth. In past history, climate changes have disrupted societies, even destroyed them (Linden, 2006). The Intergovernmental Panel on Climate Change (2007) has raised levels of alarm and left little doubt that the unprecedented warming is human caused.

Careful thinking and effective action can seem to get swamped out by the complexity of the issue. Each person's lifestyle—at home, at work, at leisure, shopping, voting—has an ever-enlarging "ecological footprint," most of all with global warming where the effects of our actions are globally dispersed—CO_2 in the air moving around the globe. If we count the oceans and poles, then nearly 75% of the Earth's surface area is international space, beyond national jurisdiction, and (if humans are to claim it at all) the common heritage of mankind. Moreover, this space is critical to sustainability—the rainfall over national lands takes up water from the oceans, the ocean is a carbon sink, polar ice determines sea levels. Climate interactions with these international regions are fundamental on a planetary scale.

All persons equally depend on this common climate, but with radically differ-ent powers to affect it. There is fragmented agency; nearly 7 billion persons dif-ferentially contribute to degrading a common resource (the atmosphere). There is serious asymmetry in power and vulnerability. Even in the powerful nations, there is a sense of powerlessness. What can only one do? Any sacrifice I make (paying more for wind power) is more likely to benefit some overuser (heating his trophy home), than it is to better the commons. That's senseless sacrifice; I don't want to be a chump. Institutional, corporate, and political structures force frameworks of environmentally disruptive behavior on individuals (such as high use of cars), and yet, at the same time, individuals support and demand these frameworks as sources of their good life (they love their SUV's).

The global character makes an effective response difficult, especially in a world without international government, where, for other reasons (such as cultural diversity, national heritages, freedom of self-determination), such government may be undesirable. Some global environmental problems can be solved by appeals to national self-interest, where international agreements serve such national interests. But the damage needs to be evident; the results in immediate prospect (such as with over-fishing agreements, whaling, the Law of the Sea, the Convention on Trade in Endangered Species, or the Montreal Protocol on ozone depleting hydrocarbons).

Global warming is too diffuse to get into such focus. Cost-benefit analyses are unreliable in the face of such uncertainties. There is something anomalous, problematic about taking the ultimate commons (the atmosphere we all breathe, the climates in which we live) and parcelling this out in private units (your right to pollute three tons of CO_2 into this atmosphere). Even the term "global warming" is misleading; better to speak of "climate change," or even "climate disruption." Atmospheric processes are quite complex; there may be more intensive droughts or more intense hurricanes. The climate extremes may be amplified; some winters colder, some summers hotter. Who wins, who loses, who can do what, with what result?

Generally, the developed nations are responsible for global warming, since they have emitted most of the carbon dioxide. Although global warming affects rich and poor, generally, the poorer nations are likely to suffer the most. These nations may have semi-arid landscapes or low shorelines. Their citizen farmers may live more directly tied to their immediate landscapes. Being poor, they are the least able to protect themselves. They are in no position to force the developed nations to make effective response. No country is immune to climate change, but the developing world will bear the brunt of the effects: some 75–80% of the costs of anticipated damages (World Bank, 2010).

Where mitigating action is possible (such as limiting emissions), the present generation may bear costs, the benefits are gained by future generations. Postponing action will push much heavier costs onto those future generations; prevention is nearly always cheaper than cleanup. The preventers live in a different generation from those who must clean-up. Classically, parents and grandparents do care about what they leave to children and grandchildren. But this intergenerational inheritance is not so local; it is rather diffuse. Americans gain today. Who pays what costs when, nobody knows. Notice, however, that by 2050, when many of these adverse effects will be taking place, 70% of all persons living on Earth today will still be alive, including most students using this book.

Here too we might worry about any planetary managers with plans for geoengineering to rebuild the planet. "Concerned scientists are now asking whether geoengineering—the intentional large-scale alteration of the climate system—might be able to limit climate change impact. Recent prominent reviews have emphasized that such schemes are fraught with uncertainties and potential negative effects" (Blackstock and Long, 2010, p. 527). The nuclear engineers will also offer plans to power the world with carbon-free nuclear energy, but that seems equally problematic (Grimes and Nuttall, 2010). There are uncertainties and potential negative effects with regard to human safety, both from power plant accidents (e.g., Three Mile Island, Chernobyl, and, most recently, Fukushima) and from waste disposal, which is hazardous for millennia, as well as the dangers of use and abuse of nuclear materials to make bombs, by rogue nations or terrorists.

These complexities and difficulties are illustrated by the Copenhagen meeting in 2009 (Brown, 2010). Copenhagen was the nineteenth meeting of governments (every year since 1990) and the fifteenth conference of the government parties to the 1992 United Nations Framework Convention on Climate Change (COP-15), which came into effect in 1994, and has been signed by almost every nation in the world, including the United States. All such negotiations have failed to achieve a global solution to the dangers resulting from climate change.

The Framework Convention sets as a standard that global emissions are to be stabilized at safe levels "on the basis of equity in accordance with their common but differentiated responsibilities and respective capacities." Developed nations "should take the lead in combating climate change and the adverse effects thereof." It also recognizes "a right to … sustainable development" (United Nations Framework Convention on Climate Change, 1992, Introduction, Article 3). The Framework Convention is a "framework," which means that it sets forth some broad principles, but little specific. These sound generally right, but the devil is in the details.

The specifics were to be worked out in "protocols" appended to the Convention in subsequent years. The first major such protocol was the Kyoto Protocol in 1997, which did set numerical emissions targets for developed nations. They agreed to set targets a little below 1990 emissions, to be met between 2008–2012, although such targets were nonbinding. This has been signed by some 190 parties; most nations in the world except the United States. Copenhagen, 2009, was to continue this effort.

Ethical concerns that became increasingly vocal surrounding Copenhagen were calls for climate justice and for increased funding for working out adaptations in the most vulnerable developing countries. These developing countries kept insisting that the developing countries were harming them (citing droughts and rising sea levels) and that increased harm was imminent and unjust. The developed countries resisted both setting any aggressive emissions targets and providing any serious funding for these developing countries. The developing countries began using the phrase "ecological debt," but no developed country was willing to accept any idea of ecological debt owed to developing countries. Vandana Shiva, outspoken among women from the developing world, insisted: "I think it is about time for the United States to stop seeing itself as a donor and recognize itself as a polluter, a polluter who must pay for its pollution and its ecological debt. This is not about charity. This is about justice" (quoted in Brown, 2010, p. 3; see also Roberts, 2009). In similar lingo favored at the People's Climate Summit (the Klimaforum, 2009), a parallel event to the official negotiations, there is "pollution on the inside" (in what people think) which is making "pollution on the outside" (in the atmosphere).

Copenhagen was a study in how powers who really wish to do little at the same time that they wish to appear to do much can find ways of positive "posturing" while dodging the issue. The United States and China managed to do nothing, and cloud their unwillingness to do anything in a dispute about whether China would permit transparent internal monitoring. U.S. President Barack Obama could not promise anything he could not get through the U.S. Congress, which did not want to do much, if anything—the Representatives and Senators always have an eye on getting re-elected. Nothing seemed to have any chance of getting through Congress that did not have China agreeing to transparent verifications, and China took this as a national affront to their integrity and dignity.

China became the world's largest polluter in total tons of emissions in the fall of 2008, which got widespread press in the United States. But the populations of the two nations are very different, and on a per capita basis the average U.S. citizen emits four times as much greenhouse gas pollution as does a Chinese person. Obama did negotiate a "Copenhagen Accord," a three-page document, eventually accepted by several dozen countries, but not an official document of the conference.

In climate change debate (carried over from other kinds of pollution), a frequent claim is that polluters should pay. The reply may be, yes, but rich polluters should pay more than poor polluters. This is partly because they are able to, partly because they have enjoyed the benefits of pollution more. But also it is because if the poor are to develop, they must be allowed some interim license to pollute in the period when they are developing but are as yet too poor to be able to afford high-cost, low-polluting technologies. Another component of the argument will be that the damages from global warming are likely to affect the poorer nations disproportionately, Their people, although developing, may still mostly be subsistence farmers, who depend immediately on their annual crops, and who live on semi-arid lands drying out or on coastal landscapes, displaced by rises in sea-level.

Polluters should pay. But what does this mean we should do with the legacy of past pollution, much of which was done before climate change was known? Are developed nations today responsible for what their grandfathers did in excusable ignorance? It is generally accepted that before 1990 not enough was known to hold those emitting CO_2 responsible. So should the polluters-pay principle only kick in after 1990?

Here some will enter the argument claiming that we ought to deal with the current situation, facing the future—and not get distracted by a past we can do nothing to change, but base current allowable emissions on equal per capita share. To meet the Kyoto goal of 5% below 1990 emission levels, that might be 1 metric ton of carbon per person per year. Current U.S. emissions are 5.4 metric tons per person per year. Nations vary widely. China is at 1.25; India is .32. But now it will be argued that what this means is that the relatively few in China and India who benefit from much development can do so because of their huge, mostly poor populations. The ethics gets swamped out by the massive population sizes of India and China.

Climate fatigue sets in. The drumbeat of dire warnings wears people out, and they quit listening (Kerr, 2009). The bad news gets old—even if it is true. Meanwhile we discount the future and shrug our shoulders: we have to look out for ourselves and the future will too. That's the way it has always been. Meanwhile too, the damage is done before we know it and is more or less irreversible.

Global warming simultaneously affects all life on Earth. Climates have changed in the past. In prehistoric times, with melting ice, species moved north variously from 200 to 1,500 meters per year, as revealed by fossil pollen analysis. Spruce invaded what previously was tundra, at a rate of about 100 meters per year. But plants cannot track climate changes of this order of magnitude. Some natural processes will remain (it still rains on whatever plants are there); but the system is more and more upset.

The plants that can survive tend to be ones that are weedy (Kudzu and Japanese honeysuckle). The five hundred wilderness areas will be something like city weedlots, with tatterdemalion scraps of nature that have managed to survive catastrophic upsets. The situation is complex again. Global warming is compounded in effects if there are toxics or pollutants on the landscape, if there are extinctions that upset the ecology, or if there is deforestation and soil loss. These multiple factors combine to drive ecosystems across thresholds beyond which they crash.

One might say: Well, obviously we should act on the best science available. But even that proves problematic. An analysis of some 1,300 climate scientists who have taken public positions on climate change finds that the scientists who are critics of climate change are far less prominent in that field, than those who believe that climate change is serious. Some 97–98% of those most actively publishing in the field hold that climate change is serious (Anderegg et al.,

2010; Giddens, 2009). Of course, the skeptics say that the scientific establishment is biased against them and their views.

We find here a mixture of the powers of reason and of rhetoric, of argument veiling self-interest, or used for denial. This is mixed into the problem of the use of technical experts in shaping democratic policy. Media coverage strives to be, they say, "fair and balanced," hearing both sides in an adversarial exchange. This sounds democratic and impartial, and it holds the attention of viewers. But the result often fails to portray the consensus of scientists competent in the field. Such media coverage also seems to presume that viewers can make up their own minds intelligently after watching several such five-minute adversarial exchanges. Scientists prominent in other fields but with scant background in climate change science and who may have vested interests in the economic fallout are able to press this "fair and balanced" mood and use it to sow doubt and postpone any climate action (Oreskes and Conway, 2010; McCright and Dunlap, 2010).

All this inability to act effectively in the political arena casts a long shadow of doubt on whether, politically or technologically, much less ethically, we humans are anywhere near being smart enough to manage the planet. Still, humans are a resilient species. We humans ought to be wise enough to deal with our oil addiction. That might require putting some price on CO_2 emissions (whether tradeable cap or a carbon tax), powering cars with electricity, powering trucks with natural gas, moving goods onto railroads, building neighborhoods where people can walk or bike to stores, upgrading our homes and offices for energy efficiency, roof top solar, wind power—none of which seem beyond our capacities, and all of which mix sustainable development and a sustainable biosphere, blending economics, policy, and ethics.

Is there any hope, human or wild? Whether we have hope will depend considerably on what we think about human nature and our capacities to face an unprecedented crisis. Globalism, multi-culturalism, and group conflict must be reconceptualized from an ethical perspective if we are to appreciate and understand the extent to which people are likely to act on behalf of others in a global world. We must forge ethical ideals that provide new vocabularies for global concern (Scuzzarello, Kinnvall, and Monroe, 2009). That is the challenge of environmental ethics.

Claiming that we are biologically unable to act globally due to our genetic legacy, our inbuilt appetites, is no excuse. That commits the genetic fallacy, arguing that we are "nothing but" what we were in the Pleistocene. Humans have proved capable of advanced skills never dreamed of in our ancient past— flying jet planes, walking on the moon, building the Internet, decoding our own genome, setting aside wilderness areas, restoring endangered species, and designating world biosphere reserves. We would not allow the claim that humans cannot be monogamous because they were polygamous in the Pleistocene, nor that women ought not to have equal rights with men, nor that there are no universal human rights, because they neither believed or practiced any of these things in the Pleistocene. It would be tragic in the future if we let our left-over Pleistocene appetites become an alibi for continuing our excesses. *Homo sapiens* can and ought be wiser than that. Can we gain a global vision?

5. Sustainable Biosphere: Ultimate Survival

We began this chapter recalling the powerful impact of views of Earth from space. "Once a photograph of the Earth, taken from the outside is available,... a new idea as powerful as any in history will be let loose" (Fred Hoyle, quoted in Kelley, 1988, inside front cover). That idea is one world or none, the unity of the home planet, our global responsibility. We had to get off the planet to see it whole. Leaving home, we discover how precious a home is. Once Earth is seen from a distance, the distance lends enchantment, the distance brings us home again. The distance helps us to get real. We get put in our place.

In a stunning volume of photographs and existential reflections produced by the space explorers, a pivotal and repeated theme is the awe experienced at the first sight of the whole Earth (Kelley, 1988). Although the hundred and more astronauts who record this experience come from many countries and cultures, their virtually unanimous experience is of being grasped, shaken, and transformed by an astonishing encounter with Earth as it truly is—in the words of Edgar Mitchell, "a sparkling blue-and-white jewel ... laced with slowly swirling veils of white ... like a small pearl in a thick sea of black mystery" (quoted in Kelley, 1988, at photographs 42–45). Their perceptions are of Earth's beauty, of its fertility, of its smallness in the abyss of space, of its light and warmth under the sun in surrounding darkness—and, above all, of its vulnerability. In this sense, the most important spinoff of the space program is to leave us earthstruck. Behind the vision of one world is the shadow of none.

Indeed, Earth is awesome, the critics may concede, but that does not make Earth an object of duty. That this is "our home planet" reveals the real focus of ethical concern: humans and their sustainable future. Humans can and ought to be held responsible for what they are doing to their Earth, which is their life support system. But—so this argument goes—these are duties owed by people to other people; caring for the planet is a means to this end. Bryan G. Norton claims that fully-enlightened anthropocentrists and more naturalistic environmentalists will almost entirely agree on environmental policy, what he calls a "convergence hypothesis" (Norton, 1991; Minteer, 2009; Stenmark, 2001).

Ethics—this argument claims—ought not to confuse people and their Earth. Earth is a big rock pile like the moon, only one on which the rocks are watered and illuminated in such a way that they support life. Earth is no doubt precious as a means of life support, but it is not precious in itself. There is nobody there in a planet. There is not even the objective vitality of an organism, or the genetic transmission of a species line. Earth is not even an ecosystem, strictly speaking; it is a loose collection of myriads of ecosystems. So, any ethicist must be talking loosely, perhaps poetically, or romantically, of valuing Earth. Earth is a mere thing, a big thing, a special thing for those who happen to live on it, but still a thing, and not appropriate as an object of intrinsic or systemic valuation. We do not have duties to rocks, air, ocean, dirt, or Earth; we have duties to people, or sentient things. We must not confuse duties to the home with duties to the inhabitants. Nature, not ultimately important, is (in the literal sense) provisionally important. Any condition of nature that supplies and sustains such opportunities will be acceptable.

The radical environmental ethic finds, however, that this humanistic account fails to recognize the globally relevant survival unit: Earth and its biosphere. The bottom line, transcultural and non-negotiable, is a sustainable biosphere. That is the ultimate expanding circle: the full Earth. The us-and-our-sustainable-resources view is not a systemic analysis of what is taking place. The planet is a self-organizing biosphere, which has produced and continues to support all the Earthbound values. Maybe we can convince ourselves that we socially construct "wilderness," and have differing worldviews about "nature." True, we have earth-views: a global village, Gaia, God's creation. Still, looking at those photographs from space, it seems incredible that we socially construct the planet Earth. Earth is the source of value, and therefore value-able, able to produce value itself. This generativity is the most fundamental meaning of the term "nature," "to give birth." Do not humans sometimes value Earth's life-supporting systems because they are valuable, and not always the other way round?

Jacques Attali, then president of the European Bank for Reconstruction and Development in London, faced the new millennium with this conclusion: "Each nation will search in its own way and according to its own traditions for a new equilibrium between order and disorder, between plentitude and poverty, between dignity and humiliation. ABOVE ALL, a new sacred covenant must be struck between man and nature so that the earth endures.... The ... object that we must protect above all others in the earth itself, that precious corner of the universe where life is miraculously perched" (Attali, 1991, pp. 129–130, capitals in original). The ultimate unit of moral concern is the ultimate survival unit: that is Earth as sacred biosphere.

If that sounds almost too religious, or if the astronauts sound too romantic, then come back to the politically correct word: *sustainability*. Everybody agrees on that. But sustaining what? Originally at the Rio Conference in 1992, this was "sustainable development." For some that meant sustaining opportunity, sustaining growth, sustaining profits, sustaining capital, artificial or natural, sustaining quality of life, sustaining freedom to choose an abundant life. At this point the ecologists appear warning us that nobody yet has it pinpointed right. The ultimate goal is: "sustainable biosphere."

The Ecological Society of America advocates research and policy that will result in a "sustainable biosphere." "Achieving a sustainable biosphere is the single most important task facing humankind today" (Risser, Lubchenco, Levin, 1991, p. 627). Any sustain-economic-development ethic needs to be brought under a sustainable biosphere ethic. The fundamental concern is that any production of such goods be *ecologically* sustainable. Development concerns need to focus on natural support systems as much as they do people's needs. So, "development," which has long been a concern and at which the West has been so successful in the modern epoch, is now entwined with and constrained by "environment."

The enthusiastic developers will say: To save humanity, we must destroy nature. People have got to sacrifice nature to get food, shelter, fuel, to build their cultures. But ecologists may ask whether we might better turn that around, making it into a fearful question. If we destroy nature, can we save humanity? Those same people need soil, forests, water, air, fish, earthworms, insect pollinators, microbial decomposers, stable climates, ecosystem services, sustainable biospheric resources, without which their human societies will degrade and perish.

A recent way of bridging sustainable development and a sustainable biosphere is to think of a "safe operating space for humanity." Johan Rockström argues (using scientific data) that there are nine planetary systems on which humans depend. These can be seen by analysis of: chemical pollution; climate change; ocean acidification; stratospheric ozone depletion; biogeochemical nitrogen-phosphorus cycles; global freshwater use; changing land use; biodiversity loss; atmospheric aerosol loading. For at least ten thousand years (what geologists call Holocene times) these systems have remained stable. But since the Industrial Revolution, in three of these systems the boundaries have already been exceeded: biodiversity loss; climate change; and the nitrogen cycle (Rockström, 2009). Humans, in a mixture of ignorance and power, produce changes the results of which we only partially know and sometimes cannot predict. We anticipate some foreseen changes, but we cannot know all the unforeseen changes, and often also we find ourselves unable to deal with even those adverse foreseen changes—as evidenced by global warming.

Surely it is both rational and ethical to take intelligent precautions. This is often expressed as the precautionary principle. If some proposed activity poses environmental threats to human health and safety, precautionary measures ought to be taken, even if the causal connections are not yet fully established. This can include a moratorium pending further research, or bans on especially high-risk undertakings, or on those that may produce environmental degradation difficult to reverse, or on those of global scale. It may require shifting burdens of proof and liability to those proposing the changes (Manson, 2002). At the same time, we do need to recognize that some risks are justified; one can be overly precautious. Generally, the Europeans have been more inclined to include the precautionary principle in regulatory legislation than has the United States (Burnett, 2009).

Certainly it is in human interests to sustain not simply development but the biosphere. This may be the most we can do at global scales, even national scales, with collective human interests. Convinced of this need for safe operating space, we may prove able to work out some precautions and incentive structures. The European Union has transcended national interests with surprising consensus about environmental issues. Kofi Annan, former Secretary General of the United Nations, praised the Montreal Protocol to protect the ozone layer, with its five revisions, widely adopted (191 nations) and implemented as the most successful international agreement yet. There are over one hundred and fifty international agreements (conventions, treaties, protocols, etc.) registered with the United Nations, that deal directly with environmental problems (United Nations Environment Programme, 1997; Rummel-Bulska and Osafo, 1991). All the developed nations, except the United States and Australia, signed the Kyoto Protocol—even if Copenhagen failed to continue or replace that protocol.

The Earth story is the larger history to which we humans also belong, along with the myriads of creatures great and small. Evolutionary natural history has generated humans too, and global ecology still supports us. This is a concern about resources, but it is more than that. It is a concern about our sources past, our story continuing, our future entwined with the planet's future. Our identity is cultural, culturally specific, yes, but our identity is also flesh and blood, emplaced in the array of metabolic processes in which we are set: webworks of ecosystems, trophic pyramids, photosynthesis, plant geography, soils, weathers and climates, the perennial cycling and re-cycling of water, oxygen, carbon dioxide, the geo-solar ecology and economy. Earth is not simply the stage, but the story. In that sense we do not just want sustainable development, maximum exploitation of Earth's resources, but a sustainable biosphere, because we are incarnate in that biosphere. We are Earthlings. Our integrity is inseparable from Earth integrity.

6. Future Generations on the Planet with Promise

A generation back, the mark of an educated person could be summed up as *civitas*, the virtue of community loyalty and responsibility. Colleges and universities produced good citizens, productive in their roles in their communities, leaders in business, the professions, government, church, education. Education, of course, enables humans to be consumers, especially training in the applied sciences, industry, and business; but educated persons, adding literature, philosophy, politics, and history, wish not so much more consumption as to be better citizens. State and national citizenship have increasingly been elevated to international levels; persons may want to think of themselves as "cosmopolitan citizens" who play roles of international significance (Dower, 2007).

But to be a "cosmopolitan" (citizen of "world polis"), however desirable, is still too urban(e)-sounding. It is not enough to be a good "citizen," it is not enough even to be "international," because neither of those terms have enough "nature" or "earthiness" in them. Neither is "worldly" enough. "Citizen" is only half the truth; the other half is that we are "residents" on landscapes—as we said in Chapter 2, placing humans on their landscapes. We need to be "ecological citizens" (Dobson, 2003). Cosmopolitan though "international" may seem, is too narrow a vision; it features nations in encounter, and that is only half the truth on planet Earth. "Global" is a more holistic theme; it knows cultural systems entwined with natural systems. The wisdom we need is not just that of politicians, generals, technocrats; it is that of ecologists in the philosophical sense, those who know the logic of their home, "oikos"; or, if we may borrow a religious word, ecumenists, those whose vision is the "oikumene," the whole inhabited Earth. We need environmental ethics without borders.

Two centuries ago, a call for community was typically phrased as the brotherhood of man and the fatherhood of God. Increasingly in the last century, continuing into this one, the call has been phrased as justice and human rights. Increasingly in this century such a call must be more ecological and less paternalistic, less humanistic, and more global. At depth, such an Earth ethics asks whether the European Enlightenment is compatible with the emerging ecological movement, both theoretically and practically. Science, technology, industry, democracy, human rights, freedom, preference satisfaction, maximizing benefits over costs, consumerism—all these "management ethics" are outcomes of the Enlightenment worldview. And they are all seriously implicated as causes of the environmental crisis. Much of the enthusiastic humanism that the Enlightenment stood for has been a good thing in modern times; but today, with an environmental turn, it needs to be ecologically chastened.

Development in the West has been based on the Enlightenment paradigm/ ideal/myth of endless growth. But in the United States and Europe, whether one considers agricultural development, forests cut, rivers dammed and diverted for water, lands fenced, minerals extracted, or highways and subdivisions built, the next hundred years cannot be like the last hundred years. None of the developed nations have yet settled into a sustainable culture on their landscapes.

We seem to have reached a critical point in our human self-understanding, a threshold where we are unable to know who we are without realizing where we are, facing a future where culture must be reintegrated with nature. We worried throughout most of the last century, the first century of great world wars, that humans would destroy themselves in interhuman conflict. Ample such fears remain, and, unfortunately, are being joined by a new one. The worry for the next century is that humans may destroy their planet and themselves with it. Planetary developers are taking huge risks, not only with their own but with other people's futures. The challenge of the last millennium has been to pass from the medieval to the modern world, building modern cultures and nations, an explosion of cultural development. The challenge of the next millennium is to contain those cultures within the carrying capacity of the larger community of life on our home planet. We are natives of nations and we are Earth natives too.

Spelled in the lower case, earth is the ground under our feet; we can own it and manage it to our liking, or live in a penthouse and hardly ever touch it. Spelled in the upper case, Earth is not something we outgrow or rebuild and manage to our liking, it is the ground of our being. We humans too belong on the planet; it is our home, as much as for all the others. Humans are certainly a dominant species—what other species takes pictures of Earth from space? But the glistening pearl in space may not be something we want to possess, as much as a biosphere we ought to inhabit with love. Environmental ethics is the elevation to ultimacy of an urgent world vision. We are searching for an ethics adequate to respect life on this Earth, an Earth Ethics.

Earth is the only planet with this display of life, so far as we yet know; its natural history warrants respect, reverence, and care. Managing a landscape that has reared up such a spectacle of life becomes a moral responsibility. The ancient Hebrews had their promised land, a land flowing with milk and honey, their corner of which they envisioned, in ideal if not in reality, as a garden earth, a sacred gift, provisioned for life. We have been arguing that peoples everywhere ought to be rooted in whatever the landscapes of their residence. Landscapes around the globe, east and west, north and south, on six continents (though not seven) have proved homelands that peoples can come to cherish and on which they can flourish. The caring has gone global. Today and for the century hence, the call is to see Earth as a planet with promise, destined for abundant life.

When Earth's most complex product, *Homo sapiens*, becomes intelligent enough to reflect over this earthy wonderland, nobody has much doubt that this is a precious place, whether prophetic Hebrew sages or earthstruck astronauts, ecologists or capitalists, politicians or philosophers. Nobody has much doubt that Earth is the ultimate survival unit. There is no greater solidarity than our togetherness on planet Earth. Alas, facing the next century, this planet of promise, is a planet in peril. "A generation goes, and a generation comes, but the earth remains forever" (Ecclesiastes 1.4). That ancient certainty needs now to become an urgent future hope. At this rupture of history, environmental ethics is vital for today and tomorrow.

References

Acton, Lord (John Emerich Edward Dalberg-Acton). 1887/1949. *Essays on Freedom and Power*, ed. Gertrude Himmelfarb. Glencoe, IL: Free Press.

Aiken, William. 1980. "The 'Carrying Capacity' Equivocation," *Social Theory and Practice* 6:1–11.

Anderegg, William R. L., James W. Prall, Jacob Harold, and Stephen H. Schneider. 2010. "Expert Credibility in Climate Change," *Proceedings of the National Academy of Sciences, USA* 107:12107–12109.

Arnold, Denis G. 2011. *The Ethics of Global Climate Change*. Cambridge: Cambridge University Press.

Atkinson, A. B., and T. Piketty, 2010. *Top Incomes: A Global Perspective*. Oxford, UK: Oxford University Press.

Attali, Jacques, 1991. *Millennium: Winners and Losers In the Coming World Order*. New York: Times Books, Random House.

Attfield, Robin, 1999. *The Ethics of the Global Environment*. West Lafayette, IN: Purdue University Press.

Attfield, Robin, and Barry Wilkins, eds., 1992. *International Justice and the Third World: Essays in the Philosophy of Development*. London: Routledge.

Beck, Ulrich, 2000. *What Is Globalization?* Malden, MA: Blackwell.

Berger, William C. 2003. *Perfect Planet, Clever Species: How Unique Are We?* Amherst, NY: Prometheus Books.

Blackstock, Jason J., and Jane C. S. Long. 2010. "The Politics of Geoengineering," *Science* 327(29 January):527.

Bongaarts, John. 1994. "Population Policy Options in the Developing World," *Science* 263:771–776.

Boutros-Ghali, Boutros. 1992. Extracts from closing UNCED statement, in an UNCED summary, *Final Meeting and Round-up of Conference*. UN Document ENV/DEV/RIO/29, 14 June.

Brown, Donald A. 2010. "A Comprehensive Ethical Analysis of the Copenhagen Accord." University Park, PA: Rock Ethics Institute, Pennsylvania State University. Online at: http://rockblogs.psu.edu/climate/2010/01/a-comprehensive-ethical-analysis-of-the-copenhagen-accord.html#more

Burnett, H. Sterling. 2009. "Understanding the Precautionary Principle and Its Threat to Human Welfare," *Social Philosophy and Policy* 26(no. 2):378–410.

Cohen, Joel E. 1995. "Population Growth and Earth's Carrying Capacity," *Science* 269:341–346.

Collins, Michael. 1980. "Foreword," in Roy A. Gallant, *Our Universe*. Washington, D.C.: National Geographic Society.

Daly, Herman E. 2003. "Globalization's Major Inconsistencies," *Philosophy and Public Policy Quarterly* 23(no. 4):22–27.

Daly, Herman E., and John Cobb, Jr. 1994. *For the Common Good: Redirecting the Economy toward Community, the Environment, and a Sustainable Future*, 2nd ed. Boston: Beacon Press.

Dobson, Andrew. 2003. *Citizenship and the Environment*. New York: Oxford University Press.

Dower, Nigel. 2007. *World Ethics — The New Agenda*, 2nd ed. Edinburgh, Scotland: Edinburgh University Press.

Ehrlich, Paul R., and Anne H. Ehrlich. 1996. *Betrayal of Science and Reason: How Anti-Environmental Rhetoric Threatens Our Future*. Washington, D.C.: Island Press.

Evernden, Neil. 1993. *The Natural Alien: Humankind and Environment*. Toronto, Canada: University of Toronto Press.

Food and Agriculture Organization (FAO). 2009. *More People than Ever Are Victims of Hunger*. Press relese. Online at: http://www.fao.org/fileadmin/user_upload/newsroom/docs/Press%20release%20june-en.pdf

Friedman, Thomas I. 2005. *The World is Flat: A Brief History of the Twenty-First Century*. New York: Farrar, Straus, and Giroux.

Gardiner, Stephen M. 2004. "Ethics and Global Climate Change," *Ethics* 114:555–600.

———. 2006. "A Perfect Moral Storm: Climate Change, Intergenerational Ethics and the Problem of Moral Corruption," *Environmental Values* 15:397–413.

———. 2011. *A Perfect Moral Storm: The Ethical Tragedy of Climate Change*. New York: Oxford University Press.

Garvin, Lucius. 1953. *A Modern Introduction to Ethics*. Cambridge, MA: Houghton Mifflin.

Gasper, Des. 2004. *The Ethics of Development*. Edinburgh, Scotland: Edinburgh University Press.

Giddens, Anthony. 2009. *The Politics of Global Climate Change*. Cambridge, UK: Polity Press.

Grimes, Ralph W., and William J. Nuttall. 2010. "Generating the Option of a Two-Stage Nuclear Renaissance," *Science* 329:799–803.

Hardin, Garrett. 1968. "The Tragedy of the Commons," *Science* 162 (December 13):1243–1248.

———. "Carrying Capacity as an Ethical Concept." Pages 120–137 in George R. Lucas, Jr. and

Thomas W. Ogletree eds., *Lifeboat Ethics: The Moral Dilemmas of World Hunger*. New York: Harper and Row.

Henrich, Joseph, Jean Ensminger, and Robert McElreath. 2010. "Markets, Religion, Community Size, and the Evolution of Fairness and Punishment," *Science* 327:1480–1484.

Holden, Barry, ed. 1996. *The Ethical Dimensions of Climate Change*. Basingstoke, UK: Macmillan.

Hollander, Jack. 2003. *The Real Environmental Crisis: Why Poverty, not Affluence Is the Environment's Number One Enemy*. Berkeley: University of California Press.

Homer-Dixon, Thomas F. 1999. *Environment, Scarcity, and Violence*. Princeton, NJ: Princeton University Press.

Intergovernmental Panel on Climate Change. 2007. *Climate Change 2007: The Physical Science Basis*. Online at: http:// www.ipcc.ch

International Fertilizer Industry Association. 2011. *Statistics*. Online at: http://www.fertilizer.org/ifa/HomePage/STATISTICS/

Jamieson, Dale. 2001. "Climate Change and Global Environmental Justice." Pages 287–307 in Clark A Miller and Paul N. Edwards, eds., *Changing the Atmosphere: Expert Knowledge and Environmental Governance*. Cambridge, MA: MIT Press.

Jolly, Alison. 1980. *A World Like Our Own: Man and Nature in Madagascar*. New Haven, CT: Yale University Press.

Kelley, Kevin W., ed. 1988. *The Home Planet*. Reading, MA: Addison-Wesley.

Kerr, Richard A. 2009. "Amid Worrisome Signs of Warming, 'Climate Fatigue' Sets in," *Science* 326:926–928.

Knoll, Andrew H. 2003. *Life on a Young Planet*. Princeton, NJ: Princeton University Press.

Kristof, Nicholas D. 2010, "A Hedge Fund Republic?" *New York Times*, November 18, 2010, p. A37.

Leichenko, Robin M., and Karen L. O'Brien. 2008. *Environmental Change and Globalization: Double Exposure*. New York: Oxford University Press.

Lewis, N. Douglas, Sorcha MacLeod, and Roger Brownsword, eds. 2004–2008. *Global Governance and the Quest for Justice*, 4. vols. Oxford, UK: Hart Publishing Ltd.

Linden, Eugene, 2006. *The Winds of Change: Climate, Weather, and the Destruction of Civilizations*. New York: Simon and Schuster.

Manson, Neil A. 2002. "Formulating the Precautionary Principle," *Environmental Ethics* 24:263–274.

McCright, Aaron M., and Riley E. Dunlap, 2010. "Anti-reflexivity: The American Conservative Movement's Success in Undermining Climate Science and Policy," *Theory, Culture and Society* 27:100–133.

McKibben, Bill. 1998. *Maybe One: A Personal and Environmental Argument for Single-Child Families*. New York: Simon and Schuster.

Minteer, Ben A. ed. 2009. *Nature in Common: Environmental Ethics and the Contested Foundations of Environmental Policy*. Philadelphia: Temple University Press.

Morriss, Andrew P. 2009. "Politics and Prosperity in Natural Resources," *Social Philosophy and Policy* 26(no. 2):53–94.

Noah, Timothy. 2010. "The United States of Inequality: The Great Divergence," *Slate*, September [series of ten articles]. Online at http://www.slate.com/id/2266025/entry/2266026/

Norberg, Johan 2003. *In Defense of Global Capitalism*. Washington, D.C.: Cato Institute.

Nordhaus, William D., 1977. "Do Real Wage and Output Series Capture Reality? The History of Lighting Suggests Not." Pages 29–66 in Timothy F. Bresnahan and Robert J. Gordon, eds., *The Economics of New Goods*. Chicago: University of Chicago Press.

Northcott, Michael S. 2007. *A Moral Climate: The Ethics of Global Warming*. London: Darton, Longmans and Todd.

Norton, Bryan G. 1991. *Toward Unity Among Environmentalists*. New York: Oxford University Press.

Oreskes, Naomi, and Erik M. Conway. 2010. *Merchants of Doubt: How a Handful of Scientists Obscured the Truth on Issues from Tobacco Smoke to Global Warming*. New York: Bloomsbury.

Piketty, Thomas, and Emmanuel Saez. 2007. "Income Inequality in the United States, 1913–2002." Pages 141–225 in A. B. Atkinson and T. Piketty, eds., *Top Incomes over the Twentieth Century: A Contrast betweem European and English Speaking Countries*. Oxford, UK: Oxford University Press.

Pogge, Thomas W. 2002. *World Poverty and Human Rights: Cosmopolitan Responsibilities and Reforms*. Cambridge, UK: Polity Press.

Pojman, Louis P. 2000. *Global Environmental Ethics*. Mountain View, CA: Mayfield Publishing.

Posner, Eric A., and David Weisbach. 2010. *Climate Change Justice*. Princeton, NJ: Princeton University Press.

Rasmussen, Larry L. 1996. *Earth Community Earth Ethics*. Maryknoll, NY: Orbis Books.

Rees, Martin. 2001. *Our Cosmic Habitat*. Princeton, NJ: Princeton University Press.

Risser, Paul G., Jane Lubchenco, and Samuel A. Levin. 1991. "Biological Research Priorities—A Sustainable Biosphere," *BioScience* 41:625–627.

Roberts, David. 2009. "Is the 'Climate Debt' Discussion Helpful?, *Grist*, December 17. Online at: http://www.grist.org/article/2009-12-17-is-the-climate-debt-discussion-helpful/

Rock Ethics Institute. n.d. *White Paper on the Ethical Dimensions of Global Climate Change*. Online at: http://rockethics.psu.edu/climate/whitepaper/edcc-whitepaper.pdf

Rockström, Johan. 2009. "A Safe Operating Space for Humanity," *Nature*, 461(24, Sept):472–475.

Rolston, Holmes, III. 1995. "Global Environmental Ethics: A Valuable Earth." Pages 349–366 in Richard L. Knight, and Sarah F. Bates, eds., *A New Century for Natural Resource Management*. Washington, D.C.: Island Press.

Rummel-Bulska, Iwona, and Seth Osafo, eds. 1991. *Selected Multilateral Treaties in the Field of the Environment, II*. Cambridge, UK: Grotius Publications.

Sachs, Jeffrey 2008. *Common Wealth: Economics for a Crowded Planet*. New York: Penguin.

Schlosberg, David. 2007. *Defining Environmental Justice: Theories, Movements, and Nature*. New York: Oxford University Press.

Scuzzarello, Sarah, Catarina Kinnvall, and Kristen R. Monroe. 2009. *On Behalf of Others: The Psychology of Care in a Global World*. Oxford, UK: Oxford University Press.

Scott, Bruce R. 2001, "The Great Divide in the Global Village," *Foreign Affairs* 80:160–177.

Sen, Amartya. 1999. *Development as Freedom*. New York: Oxford University Press.

———. 2004. "Why We Should Preserve the Spotted Owl," *London Review of Books* 28(no. 3):10–11.

Simon, Julian L. 1981. *The Ultimate Resource*. Princeton, NJ: Princeton University Press.

Singer, Peter. 2002. *One World: The Ethics of Globalization*. New Haven, CT: Yale University Press.

Speth, James Gustave. 2008. *The Bridge at the Edge of the Word: Capitalism, the Environment, and Crossing from Crisis to Sustainability*. New Haven, CT: Yale University Press.

Stanley, Steven M. 2007. "An Analysis of the History of Marine Animal Diversity," *Paleobiology* 33(no. 4, supplement):1–55.

Steffen, Will, et al., 2004. *Global Change and the Earth System: A Planet under Pressure*. Berlin: Springer.

Stenmark, Mikael. 2001. *Environmental Ethics and Policy Making*. Aldershot, UK: Ashgate.

Stiglitz, Joseph E. 2000. "The Insider: What I Learned at the World Economic Crisis," *The New Republic* 222(no. 16/17, April 17 and 24):56–60.

———. 2002. *Globalization and Its Discontents*. New York: Norton.

———. 2006. *Making Globalization Work*. New York: Norton.

Stiglitz, Joseph E., Amartya Sen, and Jean-Paul Fitoussi, 2009. *Report by the Commission on the Measurement of Economic Performance and Social Progress* [report commissioned by the French government] Online at: http://www.stiglitz-sen-fitoussi.fr

Thoreau, Henry David. 1860/1906. *The Writings of Henry David Thoreau, VI, Familiar Letters*, ed. F. B. Sanborn. Boston: Houghton Mifflin.

United Nations Department of Economic and Social Affairs/Population Division. 2008. *World Urbanization Prospects: The 2007 Revision*. New York: United Nations.

United Nations Development Programme (UNDP). 2000. *Human Development Report 2000.* Oxford, UK: Oxford University Press.

United Nations Development Programme (UNDP). 2005. *Human Development Report 2005.* New York: United Nations Development Programme.

United Nations Environment Programme (UNEP). 1997. *Register of International Treaties and Other Agreements in the Field of the Environment.* Nairobi, Kenya: United Nations Environment Programme.

United Nations Environment Programme (UNEP). 1999. *Global Environmental Outlook 2000.* London: Earthscan.

United Nations Framework Convention on Climate Change, 1992. Introduction. Online at: http://unfccc.int/resource/docs/convkp/conveng.pdf

United Nations World Commission on Environment and Development, 1987. *Our Common Future.* New York: Oxford University Press.

U.S. Census Burea, 2010. *Resident Population Data.* Online at: http://2010.census.gov/2010census/data/apportionment-pop-text.php

Vaughan, Diane. 1996. *The Challenger Launch Decision: Risky Technology, Culture, and Deviance at NASA.* Chicago: University of Chicago Press.

Ward, Peter D., and Donald Brownlee. 2000. *Rare Earth: Why Complex Life Is Uncommon in the Universe.* New York: Copernicus; Springer-Verlag.

Wenz, Peter S. 1988. *Environmental Justice.* Albany: State University of New York Press.

Wilson, Edward O. 1984. *Biophilia.* Cambridge: MA: Harvard University Press.

———. 1992. *The Diversity of Life.* Cambridge, MA: Harvard University Press.

World Bank, 2008. *2008 Development Indicators: Poverty Data.* Online at: http://siteresources.worldbank.org/DATASTATISTICS/Resources/ WDI08supplement1216.pdf

World Bank. 2010. *World Development Report: Development and Climate Change, 2010.* Online at: www.worldbank.org/wdr2010.

World Commission on Dams. 2000. *Dams and Development: A New Framework for Decision-Making. The Report of the World Commission on Dams.* London: Earthscan.

INDEX